American Gamelan and the Ethnomusicological Imagination

AMERICAN GAMELAN
and the Ethnomusicological Imagination

ELIZABETH A. CLENDINNING

UNIVERSITY OF ILLINOIS PRESS
Urbana, Chicago, and Springfield

1 2 3 4 5 C P 5 4 3 2 1

♾ This book is printed on acid-free paper.

Publication supported by grants from the Bruno Nettl Endowment for Ethnomusicology and from the AMS 75 Publication Awards for Younger Scholars Fund of the American Musicological Society, supported in part by the National Endowment for the Humanities and the Andrew W. Mellon Foundation.

Library of Congress Cataloging-in-Publication Data
Names: Clendinning, Elizabeth A., 1987– author.
Title: American gamelan and the ethnomusicological imagination / Elizabeth A. Clendinning.
Description: Urbana : University of Illinois Press, 2020. | Includes bibliographical references and index.
Identifiers: LCCN 2020011741 (print) | LCCN 2020011742 (ebook) | ISBN 9780252043383 (cloth) | ISBN 9780252085291 (paperback) | ISBN 9780252052262 (ebook)
Subjects: LCSH: Gamelan—United States. | Ethnomusicology—United States. | Gamelan—Instruction and study—United States—History. | Music—United States—Indonesian influences.
Classification: LCC ML1211.9 .C54 2020 (print) | LCC ML1211.9 (ebook) | DDC 784.6/80973—dc23
LC record available at https://lccn.loc.gov/2020011741
LC ebook record available at https://lccn.loc.gov/2020011742

To teachers and students—may we always be both.

Contents

Acknowledgments

Though this book is credited to a single author, its journey from conception to fruition has been guided by a community of scholars, artists, and friends. In particular, I am grateful to Michael Bakan, who patiently nurtured these ideas over the course of many years, and to I Gusti Ayu Candra Dewi, whose friendship inspired me to first ask many of the questions investigated here. Denise Von Glahn, Frank Gunderson, and Kathleen Erndl were instrumental in launching this project and encouraging me to see it through. My work with the members of the Florida State University gamelan and world music communities has also been particularly influential; their kindness and humor have shaped me as a teacher, scholar, and musician ever since.

This research would have been impossible without the generosity of the leaders and members of the nearly two dozen gamelan ensembles in North America and in Bali who have welcomed me into their rehearsals and their lives. I am profoundly grateful to I Made Lasmawan, Ni Ketut Marni, Putu Hiranmayena, Ade Wijaya, and Aji Guyasa for welcoming me into their gamelan communities and their homes for the past eight years. I also thank Elizabeth Macy, the "first Liz" in Bangah, and Ni Nyoman Pinti, I Ketut Argita, I Ketut Bujana, I Made Daya, and Kadek Santika Yasa for patiently welcoming *bulé* into their community for many years. I am grateful to Ian Rowen for first introducing me to these communities. I extend thanks to the members and organizers of Gamelan Çudamai—especially Emiko Saraswati Susilo, Dewa Berata, and Judy Mitoma—for making my first trip to Bali a special one. I am also thankful for the patience and generosity of the founders, directors, and members of Sanggar Manik Galih, Gamelan Tunas Mekar, and other gamelans in the Rocky Mountain region who welcomed me into their communities and spoke with me at length about this work, including Victoria Levine, Michael Fitts, Jill Frederickson, Aleanna Collins, Robert Ledbetter, Jeremy Grimshaw, and Dorothy Morrison. Across the United States and around the world, I owe particular debts of gratitude to Dewa Ketut Alit Adnyana, Sonja Downing, Ellen Koskoff, Megan Arns, I Ketut Gede Asnawa, I Nyoman Suadin, I Nyoman Wenten, I Dewa Ketut Alit, I Made Bandem, Ni Suasthi Bandem, and I Gde Made Indra Sadguna, whose conversations and assistance deeply influenced this work. I am additionally grateful to members of the Emory Gamelan, the members of Gamelan Giri Murti, and my colleagues at Wake Forest University for their support and encouragement.

Both within and outside the gamelan community, my scholarly colleagues have exerted a profound influence on this work. The mentorship of Andy McGraw as a musician and a scholar has lit the way for me since my first trip to Bali. I am deeply grateful for the ongoing support of Damascus Kafumbe, Rebecca Dirksen, I Wayan Sudirana, and Eric Hung, who not only discussed this project with me for several years but also gave their attention to large portions of this text.

I also extend thanks to Meghan Hynson, David Harnish, Michael Tenzer, Henry Spiller, Lisa Gold, Bethany Collier, Deborah Wong, Anne Rasmussen, Jeremy Wallach, Leslie Gay, and Gavin Douglas; I am grateful for our conversations, which, whether plentiful or few, always came at the right time.

Initial stages of this project were supported by the U.S. Department of State Critical Language Scholarship and by the International Dissertation Semester Research Fellowship and the Dissertation Research Grant at Florida State University. Later stages of the project, including continuing travel to Indonesia and writing support, were funded by the Friends of Music grant at Emory University and by the Faculty Development Award, Archie Fund for the Arts and Humanities Grant, Paul S. Banks Family Fund, Humanities Institute Summer Writing Grant, Dean's Office Publication Fund, and the Scott Family Fellowship at Wake Forest University. Funding from many sources, but particularly the Wake Forest University Department of Music, the Global Affairs Fund for International Scholars, and the Interdisciplinary Performance and Liberal Arts Center at Wake Forest University, has allowed me to continue my own development as a teacher and collaborator with Gamelan Giri Murti. In addition, I am grateful for the efforts of the University of Illinois Press and especially editor Laurie Matheson, acquisitions assistant Julianne R. Laut, mapmaker Bill

Nelson, copyeditor Jane Zanichkowsky, indexer Sheila Hill, and the anonymous manuscript reviewers for helping transform this work from manuscript to book. The AMS 75 Publication Awards for Younger Scholars Fund of the American Musicological Society, supported in part by the National Endowment for the Humanities and the Andrew W. Mellon Foundation, helped bring this book to fruition.

This text would not exist without the help of my family, who support me unfailingly wherever I am in the world and who have been active participants in the creation of this work. I am grateful to David Clendinning for his encouragement and commentary on portions of this text; to Jane Clendinning, with whom I have spent many happy hours discussing and playing gamelan; and to David Stifler, whose undying support has been fundamental to all things.

Finally, I thank my past and future students, whose energy convinces me that time spent as a teacher, scholar, and musician will always be worthwhile.

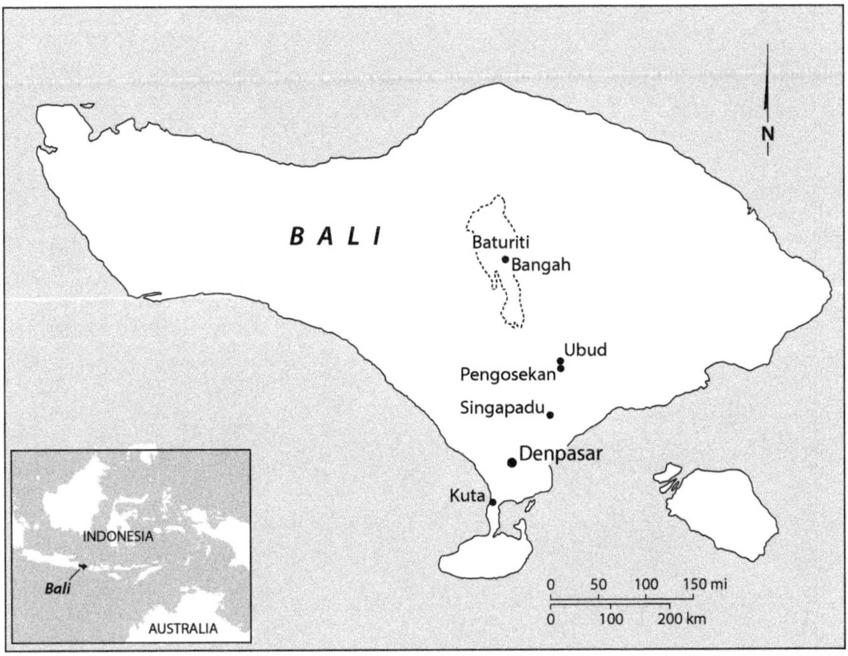

Bali, Indonesia. Cartography by Bill Nelson.

American Gamelan and the Ethnomusicological Imagination

CHAPTER 1

Interlocking Sounds, Interlocking Communities

The first note shimmered and shone like molten sonic gold. The notes of the *gangsas*, small keyed metallophones, flowed like rivulets over the melody played by their lower-pitched cousins, the *calung* and the *jegogan*, which repeated cyclically over the great booming tones of the gongs. The drummer initiated a new musical sequence on his loud, double-headed *kendang*, and the *Barong*—a large, lion-like creature embodied by two dancers—toed its way onto the stage. Its shaggy beard waggled as it clacked its teeth, its furry torso bristling as it danced in battle against the demon queen Rangda, the music of the Balinese gamelan ensemble mirroring its every move. Above the fanged visages of the *bhuta-kala* (protector spirits), scenes from the Hindu epic the *Ramayana*, and depictions of animal fables that were carved into the wooden bodies of the instruments, the hands of the musicians flew at seemingly superhuman speeds. Finally, both the Barong and Rangda departed the stage. The musicians' hands went still. No one moved until the final gong faded into silence. Then the crowd burst into applause.

As the audience members collected their belongings, the artists began to remove costumes and pack up instruments and supplies backstage. By the time of this performance in 2013, Packard Recital Hall at Colorado College had hosted concerts of the college's gamelan (Indonesian percussion orchestra) consistently for two decades. However, this concert—the capstone of a weekend-long celebration of the ensemble's twentieth anniversary—felt special to performers and audience members, Indonesian and American alike. "It almost felt like being in Bali," I heard an audience member gush as I pushed the keyed gangsa that I had been playing to the back of the stage. Putu Hiranmayena, who had danced as one half of the Barong in the final number, also recalled feeling a special energy in the air; unusually for a performance in America, he had felt seized by the spirit of the Barong as he danced. His father, the co-founder of this gamelan, I Made Lasmawan, had even felt this spirit bounce off his back as he drummed out the conclusion of the performance.[1] The air had felt electrified, alive. Had we just collectively experienced *taksu* (divine inspiration) in our performance, a relatively rare occurrence for non-Balinese musicians?

For an American audience member experiencing a live gamelan performance for the first time, it might seem as if such a distinctive ensemble must be rare outside Indonesian contexts. The United States, for example, is home to an Indonesian expatriate community representing a fraction of 1 percent of the nation's overall population, and gamelan music has never topped the commercial music sales charts. At most, gamelan in America can be considered what Slobin (1992) called a micromusic: a musical practice with limited but passionate adherents. First-time audiences might be surprised to learn, however, that approximately five hundred gamelans have sprouted roots in communities outside Indonesia, of which about 150 reside in the United States. It is striking that half of these are primarily supported by institutions of higher education. Though rich musical relationships have been formed between Indonesia and many areas of the world—including Australia, Japan, and Great Britain, all of which are deserving of extended study—this book focuses on the particular and in some ways peculiar academic ties forged through gamelan between Indonesia and North America, specifically between Bali and the United States.

The association between gamelan and American academic institutions is neither coincidental nor inconsequential. The first gamelan established in North America, the central Javanese gamelan Khjai Mendung (The Venerable Dark Cloud), began as a faculty-student study group at the University of California, Los Angeles in 1958; the initial Balinese gamelan at the same institution, Gamelan Sekar Anyar (New Flower), began rehearsals in 1959.[2] Since that time, more than a thousand other "new flowers"—new academic ensembles representing musical genres from around the world—have been planted across the continent. In aggregate, such ensembles are frequently referred to as "world music ensembles" to distinguish them from the orchestras, choirs, and wind bands that constitute more standardized Western classical music offerings at the same institutions. As the European-American artistic canons taught across the Western world were fractured and reassembled in more globally inclusive forms in the decades following World War II, it was gamelan—a versatile evocation of the world's "other orchestra"—that found itself at the heart of this self-consciously diversified new order.

Diversification in music education has proved to be a complicated and fraught process, sparking practical and ethical debates about what musical genres and skills are crucial for students to learn in order to prepare for careers in music or to be musically literate citizens, which professional qualifications and types of lived experience teachers need in order to educate students, and how and to what extent college music programs should engage with local, national, and international music communities. This rise in diversification efforts has developed alongside the academic discipline of ethnomusicology, a field that, despite developing vast topical, theoretical, and methodological breadth in the past seven decades, has most centrally concerned itself with researching and teaching about the world's musics from an anthropological perspective. World music ensembles, which are often taught by or in collaboration with ethnomusicologists, have at many educational institutions been treated as add-ons to a more Western-focused musical education with the intent of increasing the diversity of music course offerings and music faculty, and to connect with local communities. Yet the burdens that individual instructors and ensembles bear as beacons of diversity are large because they must navigate practical challenges in creating compelling learning experiences, produce artistically satisfying products at appropriate levels, and use musical practice and their own lived experiences to provide students with insight into different ways of being musicians. Because of its longstanding and widespread nature, the American academic gamelan community provides a compelling case study for examining these issues as they affect systems of education and performance, as well as the lives of the teachers and students involved.

This book examines how gamelans came to be a cornerstone of American world music education and the academic discipline of ethnomusicology and how the creation of college gamelans has impacted the lives of participants. I approach these issues by examining the career and community of one performer-teacher, I Made Lasmawan of Bali and Colorado, as a key case study among others to show how teaching gamelan in the United States fosters local and global musical communities, creates transnational musical lineages, and affects teachers and students in the United States and in Indonesia. I argue that participation in gamelan and world music ensembles more broadly is a powerful means for students to increase musical and cultural competence, engage in critical modes of self-discovery, and make rich interpersonal connections that can transcend age, race, gender, ethnicity, and national origin. Ensembles such as collegiate gamelan can also substantially impact local and transnational musical ecosystems, providing new opportunities and challenges for musicians, teachers, and scholars in American and global educational institutions and broader artistic communities.

Such global communities can be fragile, however, because their continuity, growth, and fruitfulness often are contingent on the continued work of a handful of dedicated supporters. I therefore highlight issues concerning educational and artistic sustainability that have emerged in tandem with introducing world music ensemble education to American curricula, and I demonstrate how individual artists and educators continue to address these issues in order to create stable and rewarding artistic communities. Finally, I consider the impact on individuals of living a life devoted to gamelan and why—in a cultural climate in which many people around the world express more enthusiasm for building walls to keep others out than for building bridges to let them in—cross-cultural ensemble education is worth pursuing, both for those who are taught and those who teach.

An American in Bali and a Voice for Transnational Communities

How did you first encounter gamelan? Was it from a record or a CD that you had bought or a YouTube video that a friend had shared? Was it from investigating the instruments after learning about Western compositions purportedly inspired by them, such as piano works by Claude Debussy? Was it from seeing this foreign word *gamelan* in print and then seeking out the instruments' sounds? Was it from watching a live performance of a local or touring ensemble? Was it in a class in school? Or were the sounds of gamelan an integral part of the fabric of your childhood, the aural backdrop to hours spent watching your relatives in rehearsals and performances until you, too, were old enough to hold a mallet and begin to play?

In Indonesia and in twenty-first-century North America, all those routes are common entry points to discovering gamelan. For myself, it took several encounters with gamelan—in my formal education and in casual listening—before it became a part of my musical idiolect (Nettl 2015, 66). I had my first encounter with Balinese gamelan through participant-observation as a middle school student: I chose the gamelan class as my daily one-hour elective during one session of summer band camp at Florida State University (FSU). Half a decade later, before I became a music major at the University of Chicago, I chose a world music survey course to fulfill my undergraduate arts credit requirement. One of our first assignments was to visit the neighborhood Javanese gamelan,

Friends of the Gamelan, during their Sunday evening rehearsal. Although the ensemble captured my interest, the rehearsal time did not fit in my schedule; I focused my music making on the Middle Eastern Music Ensemble and early music groups instead.

Several years later, as an ethnomusicology graduate student at FSU, I began to play Balinese gamelan under the direction of Michael Bakan in Florida's only such ensemble, Sekaa Gong Hanuman Agung (the Gamelan Club of the Great Monkey-God Hanuman). It was only when I began additional study of Balinese dance with I Gusti Ayu Candra Dewi, a nonprofessional dancer who had accompanied her husband to Tallahassee while he pursued a doctoral degree in education, that my interest in Balinese performing arts and culture began to crystallize. I soon found myself spending ten hours per week with the strikingly blended group of ensemble members—undergraduates and graduate students, pre-professional musicians and those with limited musical experience, English and bilingual Spanish speakers—all of whom had chosen to learn to play and dance together.

At the same time, I noticed that the assigned readings in my history and theory of ethnomusicology courses were generously peppered with works by authors who had lived in Indonesia. Central among them was Mantle Hood, who advocated for bimusicality—the idea that scholars in the West could and should learn to play the non-Western musics that they were studying. Gamelan served as a fundamental example in Hood's argument, which provoked spirited debates about the nature and aims of American ethnomusicology during the first decade of its existence (Hood 1960; Merriam 1964). Such debates have long since fallen out of fashion alongside the now-archaic presuppositions that certain types of music making were only approachable for individuals of certain racial or ethnic backgrounds and that people in a specific location grew up as natives or insiders in only one type of musical culture. The concept that globalized musical study should be built on a globalized experience of music making, however, remains a core principle of many ethnomusicology programs, including that of which I was a part at FSU. Gamelan was frequently among such ensemble offerings. It seemed that gamelans had not only captured the ethnomusicological imagination but also played a significant role in imagining what ethnomusicology could be.

As the Indonesian performing arts increasingly worked their way into academic, artistic, and personal aspects of my life, I began to question how and why such a coalescence of information was possible. What types of scholarly and artistic exchanges had brought literally tons of carved wood and bronze Indonesian percussion instruments not only to northern Florida but to more than a hundred academic institutions across the United States? How had the adoption of gamelan as a seemingly canonic world music genre shaped and embodied the theory and practice of academic world music pedagogy? What were the individual, institutional, and systematic impacts of supporting academic and cultural exchange between Indonesia and the United States? Perhaps most crucial, what did it mean for my teacher Candra to be teaching Balinese dance in this country? And likewise, what did it mean for other Indonesian teachers—such as two of Bakan's gamelan mentors, I Nyoman Wenten and I Ketut Gede Asnawa, both of whom held gamelan teaching appointments at American universities at that time—to be essentially devoting their lives to teaching Indonesian performing arts to American students? I also wondered about the meaning of all of this for North American musicians and academics whose work I had encountered—including musician-teacher-scholars such as Michael Bakan, Michael Tenzer, David Harnish, Jody Diamond, Evan Ziporyn, Henry Spiller, Andrew McGraw, Sonja Downing, Lisa Gold, Benjamin Brinner, and increasingly, scholars of my own generation—whose professional and personal lives were deeply intertwined with the Indonesian performing arts.

Early in this period of questioning, I knew that my investigation would need to take me beyond the bounds of my own schooling to a variety of gamelan-hosting institutions across North America and back to the music's source: Bali and Java. I still remember my initial nighttime arrival in 2010 in Ubud—advertised to tourists as the "artistic heart" of Bali. The warm night air was only punctuated by the sounds of frogs, the music of distant gamelan practices, and the occasional hum of a passing motor scooter—a blissful quiet impossible to experience only a few years later as the streets increasingly thrum with tourist activity until late at night. I traveled a short distance down the road to Pengosekan for intensive study at Gamelan Çudamani's annual summer institute. The artistic instruction and cultural excursions provided by this internationally renowned performance group inspired me to continue my studies.

The following summer, when I visited Bali for a brief four days while on vacation from Indonesian language studies in East Java, I went with a friend from the program to see I Made Lasmawan, director of the Denver-based community group Gamelan Tunas Mekar. It turned out that Lasmawan—or Pak Made, as he liked to be called—was primarily employed as a gamelan teacher at a number of institutions in the Rocky Mountains, and he had built an entirely new performing arts *sanggar* (club) within his *banjar* (village ward) of Bangah in a remote mountainous region of the Tabanan Regency to host his American students. As I began to learn more about his work, I was intrigued by the academic connections that Lasmawan had fostered, in particular how they presented a vision of intercultural exchange that bridged short-term academic study, longtime community gamelan practices in North America, and non-professional Balinese village arts practice. The musicians, teachers, and students from all over North America who made summer pilgrimages to Bangah became the living heart of my own transnational gamelan community.

Conducting ethnographic research, participating in artistic practice, and building interpersonal relationships became inseparable tasks in the seven trips I took to Indonesia; the more than a dozen site visits that I conducted across North America; and countless conversations that I conducted via email, on the phone, and through social media and messaging applications. As I continued to learn, I also began to teach and collaborate, first as a visiting director for the gamelan at Florida State while I was completing my doctorate, and then at Emory University, as a visiting instructor and director of world music. At my current institution, Wake Forest University, I now lead the Balinese gamelan, Gamelan Giri Murti (Gamelan of the Enchanted Forest), whose membership consists of students, faculty, staff, and alumni from Wake Forest and the North Carolina School of the Arts, as well as members of the local community. Though I am sometimes concerned that my continued attraction to gamelan is simply a method of self-exoticization (Spiller 2015), I find myself more deeply involved in the world of gamelan than I could have imagined only a decade ago. I play, study, and teach gamelan not only because I am fortunate enough to have had it become an integral part of my job but also because it has inspired me, challenged me, and led me to become colleagues and friends with an outstanding collection of artists. The issues of transnational exchange that I examine in this work are not only ones that I have observed from a distance and encountered in the stories of others that I tell, but also have been illuminated in the stories that I have lived.

Gamelan: The Indonesian Icon and Its Sound World

In order to understand the roles that gamelans have played outside Indonesia and how gamelan culture has been adapted to new circumstances, it is important to consider the roles that the ensembles have played in their location of origin. Gamelan music and its associated performing arts, primarily dance and shadow puppetry, are central to the unique social structures and Islamic and Hindu religious practices that define traditional cultural life in parts of Java and in Bali, respectively. Although there is evidence that instrument types such as bamboo flutes and gongs used in gamelan music have been present in the region for more than a thousand years, the earliest forms of gamelan that are still practiced today are at least as old as the period of the Majapahit Empire (the late thirteenth through the early sixteenth century; Bandem 2013; Dibia and Ballinger 2004; Spiller 2008). Ensemble types and playing styles distinctive to different royal courts and their surrounding geographic regions in West, Central, and East Java as well as Bali began to crystallize from the sixteenth through the eighteenth century, with continued development during the Dutch colonial period from the nineteenth to the mid-twentieth century.

The period immediately leading up to and following the declaration of Indonesian independence in 1945 vastly reshaped the political, religious, and cultural structures that had been in place—and artistic practices with them. As Bali's and Java's royal courts transitioned from being explicitly political ruling entities to maintaining primarily symbolic power, court ensembles and dance troupes were restructured and classicized (for example, in Central Java; see Sumarsam 1995; Hughes-Freeland 2008) or supplanted by musical production at the village level (in Bali; see Vickers 2012). After independence, the founding of governmental arts conservatories and the dissemination of officially approved arts performances on nationally owned television and radio networks professionalized formal artistic training and codified certain types of artistic practice (Fraser 2015; Hough 1999; Weintraub 2004).

Today, musicians, dancers, and puppeteers regularly decry the decline in quality of performances and the perceived lack of interest in traditional arts among younger generations. Although it is not necessarily popular music in most places, however, gamelan is regularly supported on the institutional level; traditional arts are taught in primary and secondary school settings, as well as in the high school and college-level conservatories in Bali and Java. Private clubs, moreover, offer opportunities for children and adults to play gamelan in social settings. Though all-night events such as shadow puppetry performances are on the decline, public performances of the arts in civic settings still occur regularly. Owing to differences in religious practices and historic political structures, gamelan culture in Bali remains particularly vibrant. The centrality of gamelan to Balinese Hindu ritual practice means that nearly every banjar is host to at least one ensemble. In addition, because gamelan and the performing arts more broadly have become a major part of cultural tourism, thousands of Balinese artists perform at least semiprofessionally for tourist audiences. The overarching prevalence of the performing arts has caused events like the Bali Arts Festival (Pesta Kesenian Bali), a month-long festival held in Denpasar, to regularly draw more than a thousand visitors per night. Smaller venues host gatherings devoted to more niche artistic practices. Not limited to live performances, gamelan musicians now also share their videos and sell their music online, which reinforces their popularity with interested listeners and fellow gamelan musicians around the globe. Gamelan has become a metonym for Indonesian culture, one that is also recognized as having significant adherents outside Indonesia. In the governmental bid to have gamelan recognized on the UNESCO Intangible Cultural Heritage list in 2019, Indonesian education and culture minister Muhadjir Effendy specifically included foreign participants among the gamelan community that he hoped would support the bid (Zamani 2018).

Since the mid-twentieth century, the availability of written information about gamelan and related performing arts has proliferated, much like the music itself. Overviews that include the music, the history, and the cultural context of Javanese or Balinese gamelan or both as comprehensive practices (including the English-language sources Brinner 2005; Dibia and Ballinger 2004; Gold 2005; Spiller 2008; and Tenzer 2011, among many others in various languages) are complemented by numerous books, articles, and essays that explicate specific genres, theoretical approaches, and social issues pertinent to the practice of gamelan music and the often inseparable practices of song, dance, theater, and shadow puppetry. Here, I provide a basic overview of gamelan sound and structure to orient the reader and to suggest which elements of gamelan practice have been perceived as compelling by Western listeners; further detail is provided in the subsequent chapters and in the book's glossary.

The word *gamelan* is thought to derive from the Javanese word *gamel*, meaning "to handle"; it can also refer to a type of hammer or mallet (Sumarsam 1995, 319–320; Spiller 2008, 48). Often referred to as "percussion orchestras" in English, gamelans, though largely percussive, consist of a number of different groups of instruments that often play together in instrument families, including groups of hanging and mounted gongs; keyed instruments made of metal, wood, or bamboo; wooden drums with skin heads; spiked fiddles; bamboo flutes; and other small idiophones. The ensembles may be accompanied by singers. Though only a few ensemble types are commonly known outside Indonesia, there are dozens of different types of gamelan, which can consist of as few as two or four players (in the case of Balinese gamelan *gender wayang*, which accompanies shadow puppetry) or as many as fifty (in the historic Balinese *gong gede*). Functionally speaking, each family of instruments plays a specific role in the construction of the overall sound. The form of individual sections in a piece is outlined by a cyclical, repeating core melody that frequently moves more or less at the beat level and is punctuated at regular points in the cycle by gongs.[3] Other instruments, generally higher in pitch than those playing the core melody, elaborate on it while lower-pitched instruments play a less rhythmically dense abstraction of the melody. Finally, other instruments control ensemble timing and transitions as well as coordination with art forms that the ensembles accompany. This cyclical, stratified form is referred to as *colotomic structure*.

Properties of pitch and melody inherent to gamelan ensembles are similarly distinctive. In earlier eras gamelans in different locations likely used a wider variety of tuning systems and scales than they do today; these systems have been codified into two general tonal frameworks: the *slendro* (or *salendro*) scale, consisting of five tones, and the *pelog* scale, consisting of seven tones. Specific instruments (in Central Javanese gamelan) or entire ensembles (for example, in Bali) are generally only able to play in either slendro or pelog; some are tuned to specific modes in which only a subset of the slendro or pelog pitches are available. Though most modern gamelans have tunings that could be categorized as slendro, pelog, or incorporating both, there is no absolute pitch reference for the scales; each gamelan is tuned precisely to itself, with particularly wide variations in tuning found between different villages in Bali. Variations in timbre and tuning across the ensembles provide additional layers of aural interest—for example, the twangy sound of the Central Javanese *celempung* (plucked zither), which plays fast elaborating parts, or the paired tunings in Balinese gamelan genres in which instruments of the same family are often tuned in pairs conceived of as being male (*lanang*, higher) and female (*wadon*, lower) that reflect cultural conceptions of male-female dualities and division of labor.

For individuals encountering gamelan for the first time, the visual aspects of performance can be just as entrancing as the aural aspects. Each of the several dozen types of gamelan showcase a visual feast of instrument types, each played with their own distinctive mallets and techniques. The ensembles most common in the United States—Central Javanese gamelan, Sundanese gamelan *degung*, and Balinese gamelan *gong kebyar* and gamelan *angklung*—are quite distinctive from each other but may appear similar to people seeing them for the first time. Large bossed gongs hang toward the back or the side of the ensemble. In front of them, smaller gongs perch horizontally in sets on carved wooden racks alongside rows of keyed metallophones in different sizes. Kendang (drums) that serve as the leading instruments are generally located in the center. Stage lighting causes keys made of bronze to gleam, and instrument cases are often fancifully carved and stained or painted, particularly in the Balinese tradition, in which elaborate scenes from Balinese folktales and the Hindu epics grace the cases. When joined by elegantly costumed dancers with their intricate, precise movements or elaborate shadow puppet plays, the effect of a performance is stunning. Whether experienced as an accompaniment to dance or shadow puppetry or on its own, the visibly and aurally complex musical structures presented by gamelans create a spectacle, one that has entranced audiences around the world.

In addition to these sonic and visual aspects of the ensembles, certain technical and cultural features of learning to play gamelan have historically made it appealing to teach in academic settings. If given a simple musical arrangement—for example, a section of a piece with a short gong cycle, a simple core melody, and little elaboration, played at a consistent and moderate tempo—novice musicians can produce a decent, satisfying group sound on the struck percussion instruments in the space of less than an hour. However, full mastery of instrumental technique and ensemble interaction, implicit understanding of musical structure, and the ability to produce a satisfying *rasa* (flavor or feeling) in playing take years if not decades to achieve. Because different instruments require different types of physical skill, coordination, and musical understanding to play at a beginning level, learners with a wide variety of musical and technical abilities can play together in the same ensemble and still feel challenged. Finally, musical and cultural features of gamelan music, such as the adherence to largely cyclical structures and the need for group cooperation, provide straightforward ways for learners to feel a sense of musical and cultural difference in playing gamelan as opposed to hearing or playing more familiar types of music.

Considering Gamelan Outside Indonesia

Indonesians and non-Indonesians alike have questioned the nature of the cultural and musical relationship between gamelan as practiced in Indonesia and as practiced elsewhere in the world. Part of the issue in North America lies in the curiously avid interest in gamelan as compared to other Indonesian musical forms and even other gong-chime traditions—an interest that is rooted not only in aesthetic preferences but also historical circumstances (discussed in chapter 2). For example, in introducing the genre of *talempong* from the Minangkabau Highlands of West Sumatra, a genre seemingly similar to gamelan, at least from an outsider's viewpoint, Jennifer Fraser laments, "In the United States, Australia, and Canada, musicians and scholars, myself included, often first encounter musics of Indonesia through Central Javanese or Balinese gamelan. After they fall in love with it, they rarely make it farther afield into the incredibly diverse wealth of practices in other parts of the archipelago" (2016, n.p.).[4] The complex relation between North American musicians and aficionados of the music can be illustrated in the sheer variety of contexts in which gamelan music appears: on college and community stages, at farmer's markets and weddings, as spectacles at large outdoor festivals such as Burning Man, as enrichment programs in prisons, and as sound color within the works of a variety of classical and film composers, all of which require substantive adaptation to the artistic and social approaches used in gamelan performance.

Without the cultural standard of courtly, religiously oriented, or neighborhood club groups such as those found in Indonesia, community gamelans outside that nation have been identified as having social and cultural characteristics distinct from those of their Indonesian relatives. Initial in-depth scholarship modeling these differences turned to the term *affinity* as employed by Slobin (1992) to highlight non-Indonesians' element of choice in affiliating with a music with no specific relation to their ethnicity, familial identity, national identity, or religious beliefs; *affinity* instead captured the idea of individual interest in the music or the spirit of *communitas* (intense feeling of togetherness as a group) created by non-Indonesian gamelan practitioners in pursuing this distinctive art form. In contrast, Strohschein (2018, 115) argues that though such individual interests may originally bring together members of gamelans outside Indonesia, it is important to emphasize that this communitas forges community, undergirding a process through which long-term gamelan musicians and ensembles "establish a shared and evolving identity based on internally created coherence principles." The process of individual musicians' making choices, coupled with group negotiations of ensemble identity both as a discrete entity and in relation to other gamelans, creates new cultural terrains with artistic and social practices and traditions that are constantly being established and renegotiated—much as in Indonesian ensembles themselves.

The adaptations of tradition and innovations associated with affinity groups, however, have long been subject to questions of whether they present a problematic distortion of Indonesian culture. Is the sense of communitas artificially cultivated by obscuring hierarchical elements of Indonesian gamelan practice, thereby allowing non-Indonesian musicians to live out their fantasies of "an idealized humanity, a harmonious, non-conflictual form valuing group over individual" (McGraw 2013b, n.p.)? Does performing only a limited set of traditional compositions threaten to calcify certain musical traditions (ibid.)? Are American groups who don traditional costumes for their performances dressing respectfully, or are they guilty of exoticizing Indonesian musical culture by performing in "ethnodrag" (Harnish 2004)? Does the imperfect performance of an amateur group degrade the art form as a whole? Does playing gamelan as a foreigner inherently mean appropriating a foreign culture to exoticize one's sense of self? And, how does one negotiate representing and creating culture within educational settings, where every social and artistic choice serves as a model of the essence of not only "gamelan" but "Indonesian culture" for students?

The answers, as long-time gamelan musicians on both sides of the Pacific acknowledge, are complex; the aesthetics and ethics of gamelan practice can be interpreted in many ways, and notions of respect and creativity with regard to tradition and its transformation are highly personal. It is surprising, however, that other than highlighting specific collaborations (J. Diamond 1990; Tenzer 2000) or debating certain aspects of musical or pedagogical authenticity (for example, in the five essays on gamelan in Solís 2004), relatively little has been written about the complex negotiations of these issues within academic and community gamelan ensembles outside Indonesia. Not until the turn of the twenty-first century did a flurry of scholarly activity appear that might well be considered a small reflection of the intellectual zeitgeist. In addition to documenting the culture of contemporary Western community-based gamelans (Mendonça 2002; Lueck 2012; Strohschein 2018), scholars more closely examined historical artistic dialogues and borrowings (Spiller 2015; Sumarsam 2013), suggested and illuminated systematic ways in which the Indonesian and non-Indonesian gamelan scenes were connected (Brinner 2016; Clendinning 2016; Steele 2013), positioned foreign gamelan tourism to Indonesia as a part of community development (Clendinning 2017; Dunbar-Hall 2016; Macy 2010), and expanded the previously limited literature by Indonesian authors about cross-cultural gamelan learning and instruction (Sudirana 2018; Sumarsam 2016), as well as exploring other transnational topics concerning the gamelan.

The combination of narrative, perspective, and scope variously differentiates this book from these antecedents. Histories, life stories, community stories, and analysis: All of these are positioned as integral parts of a lived whole, seamless and inseparable ways of interpreting the habitus (Bourdieu 1977) of gamelan practitioners. The core approach used here, selective comparative biography, stems from the desire to recognize the importance of individual teachers whose work has long been underrecognized by scholars and cultural organizations in both Indonesia and the United States. In examining such work, I expand on prior ethical discussions that have focused primarily on world music ensembles as a curricular method of cultural representation in order to approach issues relating to instructors and ensemble participants, including imbalances of economic and cultural influence in ensemble teaching, and issues of academic labor, including educational and economic support for teachers. Although community-based ensembles are a part of this discussion, I focus on academic settings because of the ways in which gamelan has been used as a means of cultural and musical diversification, and because it is the means through which most gamelan teachers in North America make a living by practicing their art. Most of all, I am interested in documenting specific types of collaboration and exchange that have occurred with gamelan ensembles in the past to promote more impactful, equitable, and enjoyable forms of teaching, learning, and music making in the future.

The first step to creating more equal and equitable gamelan practices is to firmly establish that despite their differences, American and Indonesian gamelan communities are integrally related. From my work, conducted primarily in Bali and the United States, I have come to consider transnational gamelan communities as interlocking like *kotekan*, a technique of melodic elaboration used in Balinese gamelan.[5] Also referred to as the *bunga* (flowers) of a composition, the kotekan is said to embellish the slower-moving *pokok* (core melody) like flowers ornamenting the branches of a tree, growing to fill out the beat in subdivisions that generally are four or eight times shorter than the rhythm of the lower-pitched melody. Kotekan is divided into two interlocking parts played by different musicians. These parts, *polos* and *sangsih*, are often referred to as being more on-beat or off-beat, respectively, but, more accurately, they trade off articulating different portions of the elaborative line, creating an ever-shifting rhythmic emphasis within the part. Polos and sangsih parts are utterly dependent on each other (and reliant on the pokok) and are conceived of by musicians as comprising the same part (Vitale 1990, 3–5). Even when the tempo is slow enough that a single musician could play the whole line of kotekan, the feeling is different than when it is played by two musicians (Tenzer 2011, 55–56). Although sometimes the rendition of kotekan by a single person is favored, the emphasis on cooperation and reciprocity on all levels of Balinese society means that the two-person version is often preferred because of the way it seamlessly joins a greater number of individuals together in communal activity.

As Tenzer (2011, 55) points out, new types of kotekan are being invented all the time; "they provide endless beguilement for gamelan musicians and are a showcase for the talents of their composers." Similarly, the pedagogical and performative expansion of gamelan outside its region of origin can be viewed as a new type of embellishment; a "new flower" nourished by cross-cultural collaboration that flourishes on the branches of a tradition that is still strongly rooted in its native soil. These transnational gamelan communities sometimes showcase the talents of composers but, more important, rely on the talents of Indonesian and American teacher-artists and supporters whose creativity, collaborative spirit, and hard work have been key to these communities' flourishing. Gamelan communities outside Indonesia have attracted new artists and audiences, thereby creating more widespread interest and a larger stake in the welfare of the art form within a global artistic ecosystem.

Although the model of the musical ecosystem is not new, it was only recently applied to academic gamelan by Brinner (2016), who modified Piekut's (2014) adaptation of the ecological exemplar of ecosystems to musical contexts in order to model the international exchanges of Indonesian teachers and American students. Brinner hews closely to biological views of ecological processes, framing different elements of the dynamics of gamelan groups in terms of selection, adaptation, competition, and reciprocity. This book addresses these core issues in depth, including asking: What is required for individual musicians and academic ensembles to thrive, and what conditions might instead cause their demise? I consider gamelan's role in two interrelated musical and pedagogical ecosystems: first, the narrow space of college music and its immediate communities, and second, the transnational communities within which collegiate world music ensembles by necessity exist. Schippers and Grant's (2016) sustainability index speaks to the latter, including support by official institutions such as colleges and universities as a measure of artistic health; Dunbar-Hall (2016), writing specifically about Bali, is one of the first to acknowledge that interest in Balinese performing arts from outside Indonesia has played an influential role in the health of the island's arts.

In addition to the historic importance of transnational influences on gamelan culture (Sumarsam 2013), one model for understanding this exchange that has been introduced by Indonesian teachers is seeing transnational pedagogy as forming "a bridge to Java" (Hardja Susilo, quoted in Harnish, Solís, and Witzleben 2004). This "bridging" of gamelan cultures through teaching, performance, composition, and other activities can be modeled in several ways. One way to consider these relationships is by examining musical lineages. Diverging from Brinner, I pinpoint much of the communal value in the maintenance of artistic lineages and kinships that cut across generations and geographic locations.

The lineage model is particularly interesting in approaching gamelan from Bali, a place where familial relationships form a major part of the structural framework of society; relationships based on biological and matrimonial lineages, caste, and one's position within the family structure in large part determine an individual's social obligations to others (Geertz and Geertz 1975; Eiseman 1990). Identifying an individual's family members, in tandem with identifying his or her geographic origin (region and village), contextualizes that person within Balinese society. Early training for performing arts professionals often begins in the context of the family and home village, in which a new learner is exposed to local and widely known repertoires that are rendered in accordance with regionally specific aesthetic preferences. Performers' studies then continue with specific lineages of teachers inside and outside the formal conservatory systems, all of whom also impart their own ways of interpreting music. When these musicians teach abroad, they transmit portions of knowledge accumulated from a lifetime of study and performance. Seeing Indonesian American teachers and their American students—some of whom who have become gamelan teachers in their own right—as direct participants in Indonesian traditions is crucial to mapping the structures of artistic transmission.

A focus on individual lives and individual stories becomes a vivid way to illustrate how transnational musical lineages that transmit a teacher's distinctive influences are constructed and maintained. Although authorial reflexivity is relatively common in writings in anthropology, ethnomusicology, and related disciplines from the late twentieth century, biography has traditionally been more heavily favored as a theoretical approach in historical rather than ethnographic studies of music (Nettl 2015, 188–198). However, biography is an essential tool for interpreting how significant social and cultural phenomena shape an individual life. Moreover, biography emphasizes the importance of the work of individuals whose stories might otherwise be marginalized or forgotten. In presenting Lasmawan's work as the central narrative among other case studies, I use a biographical focus to examine the world of Balinese traditional gamelan and its interrelated systems of individuals and institutions, teachers and students, performers and audiences, which interpret certain repertoires of musical and cultural concepts for different geographical and temporal situations. I also provide ethnographic perspectives on the way these interrelated musical and cultural systems shape the lives of individuals, bringing them personal and professional opportunities, challenges, and a sense of achievement. Building on previous works that use biography to examine individual foreigners' engagements with Indonesian performing arts (L. Miller and Lieberman 2006; Oja 1990; Spiller 2015), influential Indonesian musicians working in transnational contexts (Bakan 1999; Harnish 1997; Tenzer 2000, 2011), and pioneering teachers and scholars of world music and ethnomusicology (Morelli 2019; Sarkissian and Solís 2019), I present stories that are meant simultaneously to be normative and exceptional and to encourage further documentation of the lives and works of teachers, specifically, who have until recently played a underacknowledged role in shaping transnational musical communities.

Pedagogy as Living Ethnomusicology

The ethnomusicology of academic music, or "fieldwork at home," has by this point a long if inconsistent history as a research practice. Seven years before Nettl (1995) queried how an ethnomusicologist from Mars would view the cultural and musical traditions embodied by a prototypical school of music in the

American Midwest, Kingsbury (1988) had leveraged much the same approach in building a cultural critique of East Coast conservatories. As participant-observers who are both insiders and outsiders in the worlds that they investigated, Nettl and Kingsbury presented structural observations and critiques that illuminated musical, academic, and social hierarchies that they recognized as governing academic music practices. Kingsbury found world music to be nearly a non-presence in the conservatory; Nettl saw it reserved for the "exotic corner" in colleges of music.

There have been profound transformations in collegiate music education in recent years—in particular, increased attention to reshaping curricula to include more non-Western classical musical experiences for students, including ensembles. New programs that bring in popular and vernacular music ensembles (as well as more world music ensembles), new pedagogic approaches to oral history, reconsiderations of the value of teaching local musics, a renewed emphasis on embodied and experiential models of education, and more flexible undergraduate curricula that encourage exploration (including cross-cultural exploration) are emerging practices for solving perceived disconnects between formal music studies and students' musical lives (Moore 2017). These trends have emerged alongside broader movements in academia such as questioning the increased reliance of colleges and universities on contingent faculty, debating whether undergraduate education should be narrowly pre-professional or more broadly focused, and investigating issues of accessibility and privilege in obtaining a college education.

Yet pedagogy as an important facet of what ethnomusicologists do has largely been written out of Nettl's and others' historiographies of the field. As Nettl (2010) notes, the history and legacy of ethnomusicology have been defined primarily as a succession of theoretical paradigms presented in reference to the way they have shaped fieldwork (Barz and Cooley 2008). Several competing narratives of the development of the field based on fieldwork have emerged. The first posits a Euro-American origin story built on two events: first, the historical transformation of comparative musicology into ethnomusicology and second, the bifurcation of the anthropologically based and musically based approaches to research in ethnomusicology articulated by Alan Merriam and Mantle Hood, respectively, in the early 1960s. An alternative model with more diverse disciplinary roots suggested by McLean (2006) envisions a field consisting of a greater geographical, historical, and cultural variety of music workers who may or may not have called themselves ethno/musicologists at all.

In contrast, Titon (2015, 14) critiques such narratives for primarily (if not exclusively) tracing the discipline's identity and development through scholarly research and publication, as opposed to other activities that have been integral to the work of ethnomusicologists, folklorists, and others who work with culture and sound. He attributes this tendency to a postwar focus on research on the scientific model and a general wariness of being associated with the ways in which ethnomusicological knowledge could and was being used to serve political, religious, or other ideological ends (18–19). The specific goal of his analysis was to introduce applied ethnomusicology—"an ethnomusicology based in social responsibility where knowledge is intended for beneficial use in communities outside the academic world" (5)—into the history and self-conception of the discipline. Again, the importance of academic teaching is largely omitted from this model, though academic instruction can be activist, and ensemble instruction is perhaps one of the key areas in which applied and academic ethnomusicology overlap.

Inquiries into the specific nature and impact of world music ensemble pedagogy crystallized surprisingly late in the writings of ethnomusicologists. A watershed moment came with the publication of *Performing Ethnomusicology: Teaching and Representation in World Music Ensembles*, which contains more than a dozen essays concerning logistical, theoretical, and ethical issues in "trying to make a place for world music performance and its evaluation" (Solís 2004, 1). In doing so, it addresses matters that ensemble teachers regularly face, including navigating intercultural and intergenerational relationships, cultural representation, aesthetic value, and methods of transmission and translation. All these factors shape not only how the target music and culture are perceived by students but also how they are valued in local communities and what types of connections can be made via music with immigrant or transnational artistic communities. For the first time, collegiate world ensemble pedagogy—an activity integral to the jobs of one-quarter of the members of the Society for Ethnomusicology, according to a 2014 survey, as well as countless full-time and part-time professionals in other music-related subfields—had become a subject of concentrated critical-reflexive discourse (B. Diamond 2014, 9). Aside from Dor's *West African Drumming and Dance in North American Universities: An Ethnomusicological Perspective* (2014), however, there have been few efforts to expand the consideration of world music ensembles to examine current and historical societal and musical systems that they embody, reflect, and shape.

This book revisits these issues within a twenty-first-century context. In doing so, it encourages renewed discussion of our definitions of the field and our responsibilities to our colleagues in research and performance. Given that these extended communities are populated not only by gamelan musicians and ethnomusicologists but also by broader communities within which they work and play—communities of educators, academic administrators, performing artists, and culture workers of varying disciplines—this book is intended for them as well. Finally, although it provides a narrative and structural analysis, this work also constitutes a personal reflection on what it means to live one's work among colleagues, informants, teachers, students, and ultimately friends.

Structure of this Book

One of my most vivid memories from my first visit to Bali was of seeing Batuan-style paintings for the first time. The Batuan style, first developed in the village of the same name in the 1930s, is a type of Balinese art in which minute details of daily life are captured in tiny brushstrokes that juxtapose frenetic interactions of the sacred and the secular, the everyday and the magical, the traditional and the modern. In such an artwork, the viewer's eyes might begin at the top of the frame, where, in front of mountains rising in the distance, a forest scene unfolds with birds and monkeys playing among the palm fronds. Under the treetops, cars and motorcycles drive by the walls of family compounds where women are processing to the temple carrying offering baskets. By the temple walls, a gamelan is playing to accompany a sacred Barong performance. Finally, at the corner, a figure with glaringly white skin, shorts, and a camera—a Western tourist—is being documented in his documentation of the event. In Western art criticism, the relentless busyness might be described using the Latin phrase *horror vacui*, a fear of empty spaces. In Bali, this *rame* (crowded, busy) aesthetic is instead viewed as a positive aspect of social life.

Even as every figure in every scene of a Batuan-style painting can be interpreted individually, the true nature of the artwork can only be conceptualized by literally stepping back to examine its overall structure and metaphorically stepping back to understand its historical and cultural context. I conceive of this book as taking a narrative approach that is similar to the way a viewer might approach a painting in the Batuan style: by examining individual scenes that, when taken together, illuminate broader interpretations of more globalized contexts.

The initial portion of this book represents a first glance, as if one is first spotting a monumental painting from across the room. This chapter, "Interlocking Sounds, Interlocking Communities," has introduced the subject and scope of this study, as well as highlighting some of the various ways one might look at these scenes and why such examination might be fruitful and rewarding. The second chapter, "Early Encounters in Bimusicality," presents the historical landscape within which gamelans were first introduced to North America as well as the conditions under which the ensembles assumed a major role in the philosophy and practice of American collegiate world music education. I juxtapose a handful of influential events from the 1890s to the 1980s that helped establish gamelan music within public and academic educational discourses about music and cultural diversity. I demonstrate how exhibitions at world's fairs, the dispersion of early recordings, transnational performance tours, and the work of Western composers and pedagogues led to the importation of instruments and founding of early academic gamelans. The ensemble programs embodied a new and important paradigm in ethnomusicology and bimusicality, as well as sparking the collegiate world music ensemble movement. Zooming out once more to the larger picture, the chapter concludes with a brief overview of the current gamelan scene in the United States, thereby reconnecting the early development of academic gamelan ensembles to contemporary practices.

The next three chapters invite the reader to take a metaphorical step closer to the canvas to examine the formation and sustenance of specific gamelan communities in America. The focus narrows to the Balinese performing arts to provide a more musically and culturally detailed portrait of one subset of the transnational gamelan scene. I explore the life and musical community of one Balinese gamelan teacher, I Made Lasmawan, as a narrative starting point for investigating how transnational gamelan pedagogy alters and forms transnational community and shapes the lives of teachers involved in this work. Lasmawan is first introduced as the central figure of chapter 3, "From Bali to America: Teachers and Transitions," which examines different models of how the earliest generation of Balinese American teachers (born in the period from the 1940s to the 1960s) were educated and how their work eventually brought them to North America for the long term. This chapter uses individual narratives to connect the adoption of gamelans in the American context to contemporaneous cultural, political, and educational developments in Bali, thereby positing a type of parallel development between contemporary American gamelan education and modern performing arts education in Bali. Chapter 4, "Creating and Conceptualizing a Balinese American Gamelan Community," moves from examining teacher-musicians as individual figures to examining how these figures may forge connections between different ensembles. The unusually extensive set of gamelans that Lasmawan teaches along the Front Range of the Rocky Mountains again serves as a key case study against which gamelan communities in other parts of the country are compared. In chapter 5, "Teaching, Learning, Representing," I discuss logistical and ethical challenges and approaches to teaching musical and cultural competency in academic ensemble settings.

Following a close consideration of these individuals and scenes, the second half of the book invites the reader to step back once more and consider different ways of approaching transnational gamelan connections as an interconnected artistic and educational ecosystem. Chapter 6, "Americans Learning Gamelan in Bali," and chapter 7, "*Kembali*: To Return or Change," focus on the movement of individuals between North America and Bali and the impacts of such movement on social structures and on people. The former chapter brings American gamelan practices back into a Balinese context by examining the rise of short-term artistic study programs for foreigners and their effects on the island's cultural, economic, and artistic profile; the latter examines how working and living in two countries has affected the lives of long-term Balinese teachers and musicians, including shaping the educational, artistic, and career opportunities of younger generations of gamelan musicians.

The final three chapters examine how academic gamelan ensembles can grow beyond the context of teaching within ethnomusicology and the potentials and challenges facing American academic gamelans in the future. Chapter 8, "Bimusicality and Beyond," discusses the way gamelan also intersects with three other fields in music outside the world music context—percussion, composition, and music education—and the distinctive contributions that study of gamelan can make to these areas. Serving as a capstone to the previous structural considerations of community, chapter 9 addresses the sustainability of this transnational, pedagogically oriented community. Together, the two chapters re-interrogate the concept of the world music ensemble in general and gamelan's specific role in academic settings as well as nonacademic ones. The final chapter, "Cultivating New Flowers," returns to a single compact narrative to reconsider elements of artistic collaboration, power, status, and personal relationships, thus providing concluding thoughts about current directions of gamelan outside Indonesia and academic world music ensemble pedagogy.

My own work in this area began and remains rooted in my series of initial questions about transnational gamelan communities. As my practice and connection with the gamelan community deepened, I realized that much of this community's artistic and social work remained unrepresented and unacknowledged, both in North America and Indonesia. The experiences of novice or hobbyist musicians were routinely discounted as tangential to an understanding of the international importance of gamelan practice; the life work of teachers was routinely ignored or reduced to straight biography or pedagogical analysis. I was surrounded by musicians from multiple continents who *lived in gamelan*—whose artistic lives were predicated on its practice, whose friendships and even marriages were built on the structure of rehearsals and performances, who spent years developing a craft to a high level, if only to use it to teach the rawest of beginners, and who envisioned exposing new people to gamelan as a major part of their life's work. Although no single book could represent all these voices, it is my hope that this work will encourage fuller considerations of gamelan in an international context and provide frameworks for more stories to be shared.

As I have become more and more fully a person who "lives in gamelan," I see the growth in writings about transnational gamelan culture as a way for enthusiasts and professionals to fill in those gaps in history and contextualization in the field, as well as to draw attention and encourage representation of their own practices. The importance of such work is not only to document the past or recognize those whose contributions have widely been underacknowledged but also to evaluate these past relationships to build a more productive future. Where can transnational applied arts education go in the twenty-first century, within and beyond the Indonesian arts? Has the time of the academic world music ensemble drawn to a close? What can we learn from the present and the past to build more sustainable and fulfilling cultural and artistic partnerships in the future? This book provides one perspective on these questions.

CHAPTER 2

Early Encounters in Bimusicality

At the end of August 2018 I received an email. The fall academic semester was just about to begin, and having returned from Bali only ten days earlier, I was struggling to finish preparations for returning students while reacclimating to my home time zone. As a result, I nearly missed seeing the short missive that was simply titled "Gamelan." It was from someone who had seen my Facebook posts publicizing the gamelan at Wake Forest University, Gamelan Giri Murti; he was writing to inquire if the group was open to community members. I receive community inquiries about the group a few times per year, but this one caught my eye because of its final sentence: "It would be a dream come true if I could play Balinese gamelan." As it turned out, this person—now a committed member of the group—had first experienced gamelan not by hearing groups live in the United States or encountering them in college, as a significant portion of younger Americans do today. Instead, he had first heard gamelan decades earlier on the record *Bali: Music from the Morning of the World* (released by Nonesuch Records in 1966; Lewiston 2003) and had been acquiring new recordings ever since. After many years of listening, he had traveled to Bali with his wife, now deceased. Finally, several years later as a retiree, he began to play gamelan for the first time.

The option for a community member and novice musician to join a gamelan ensemble like that at Wake Forest would have been unthinkable only a few decades ago; the foundation of the initial world music study groups at UCLA rightly presents a turning point in the way Americans are able to experience Indonesian music and culture. Yet the development of such groups would have been improbable without the other facets of musical and cultural dissemination that support live gamelan culture today: the development of museum exhibits and cultural displays, live performance tours by Indonesian musicians, recordings, and other types of formal or informal public education. To understand how and why gamelans came to flourish in educational settings and beyond, it is important to understand how these forms of often one-sided cultural engagement set the stage for a more substantive adoption of gamelan into American life. Embedded in the politics of race, ethnicity, and education, the logistical and ethical challenges that arise from early historical engagements in gamelan decisively prefigure complex social and artistic relationships that animate the transnational gamelan scene today.

This chapter examines a series of early encounters between Indonesian performing arts and American culture that have deeply influenced the subsequent positioning of Indonesian gamelan music abroad. Stretching from the 1890s through the early 1980s, these examples are intended to serve not only as a general backdrop for this book's examination of contemporary academic gamelan culture but, more important, to illuminate the influential roles of public and institutional education, composition, recording, and performance in building academic and public interest in the Indonesian performing arts. Finally, I draw attention to important practices and ethical issues contemporary to each period whose echoes continue to inform gamelan and academic music practice today.[1]

"Weird, Wonderful" Sounds in the White City

Gamelan made its debut appearance in the United States at one of the most prestigious public events of the nineteenth century, the World's Columbian Exposition (or World's Fair). It was 1893, and in Chicago, the substantial metropolitan area that had been destroyed by the Great Chicago Fire only two decades earlier was being replaced with brick-and-mortar buildings designed to be permanent and elegant in design, to rival the cities of Europe. On the south side of town, however, two other "cities" were being erected for the fair, ones that only had to last for its six-month duration. One, called the White City for its gleaming white spray-painted walls, was constructed from artificial stone and built in neoclassical style, once again with the aim of rivaling the unparalleled sophistication and glamour of European construction. Inside the buildings of this city were collected representatives of the latest agronomic, scientific, and cultural achievements of the West. Outside the White City's orderly thoroughfare, however, a different sort of city also rose. Instead of broad thoroughfares and white walls, it consisted of a warren of traditional buildings and peoples that had been imported from across the world, including the display of entire "villages" from the Americas, Africa, East Asia, and Southeast Asia. This area, the Midway Plaisance—now contained within the University of Chicago campus—became a temporary home to hundreds of individuals from around the world who had been convinced or coerced to put their traditional lifestyles, cultures, and arts on display in a living museum exhibit. Together, the two cities within a city formed the core of this event that exposed twenty-seven million attendees—approximately one quarter of the nation's population—to new ways of thinking and being.

The scholar of music education Terese Volk identifies the Exposition as a key event in the early development of multicultural music education in the United States, writing, "It was a way for thousands of people to see how other thousands lived . . . this was probably the first time that many people paid attention to other cultures in the world" (1998, 23). With participants from more than fifty countries as well as dozens of colonized areas, it was certainly the largest such display in the country's history—and a means by which Exposition organizers also sought to rival their European peers in a display of economic and cultural capital (Bourdieu 1984). Visitors flocked to the Midway to consume, taking in the performative, culinary, and material products of re-created villages from Germany, Turkey, Japan, Australia, Mexico, Egypt, and eight Southeast Asian and Pacific islands, as well as other far-flung locales. A star among these villages was West Java (Sunda), which represented the culture of this specific area of the Dutch East Indies (now modern Indonesia). Sponsored by the Java Chicago Exhibition Syndicate, the village's presence was an unabashedly commercial attempt to introduce Javanese coffee and tea to new markets. Yet visitors could hardly escape without exposure to Javanese culture, including Islamic prayer, textile production, and music making.

Music played no small role in the exhibit's overall character and popularity. At the entry of the exhibit stood the mosque, where the *bedug* (large drum) preannounced the call to prayer. Beyond that, the music of bamboo angklung intermittently permeated the soundscape of the village grounds. Interested visitors could also pay twenty-five cents to hear the performances of *kacapi suling* (a small zither-based ensemble) or see *wayang golek* (rod puppet) and *wayang topeng* (masked dance) performances accompanied by the exposition's gamelan; eighty-two thousand of the village's six hundred seventy thousand visitors did so (De Vale 1977; "Java Village"). Visitors found the sights and sounds intriguing, if not entirely in accordance with their aesthetic preferences. One visitor to the fair, William H. Crane, reported,

> Of all the music I ever heard that manufactured in this place is the most wild, weird, and wonderful. The idea of a fellow getting melody out of a row of kettles which he beats with a hammer was funny enough until the ear detected that there was a certain rhythm to the music. Then it became astonishing. Like the Chinese the Javanese make one scene do for everything and place the orchestra on the rear of the stage. Here were seventeen fellows, crowned with hats that were shaped like the dishpan you find in farmhouses, each possessed of two hammers and squatting before some instrument of torture. When the orchestra got going you could easily imagine you were in a boiler shop. If you could close your ears to the music you could suppose yourself looking at a lot of cobblers driving pegs into shoes. (1893, 35)

Wax cylinder recordings of these performances taken by Benjamin Ives Gilman constitute the earliest known recordings of Indonesian music in existence.[2]

In his extensive analysis of music at Java Village, Spiller identifies the event as the root of the American fascination with Java, and by proxy, the islands of the future Indonesian nation-state.[3] Like other exhibits at the Exposition, however, this limited exposure did as much to feed the imaginative fantasies of American audiences as it did to induce cultural understanding. Spiller argues that "the performances of music and dance in the Java Village contributed to and became emblematic of a particular brand of exoticism associated with Java—an idyllic image of gentle, childlike creatures who spent their time crafting objects of exquisite beauty and mounting spectacular dramatic productions" (2015, 27). He also characterizes the American experience of the village as "voyeuristic" and "one-sided," noting that—despite the wealth of information available about the performers in the official fair pamphlets—most popular writings about the village performances continued to portray the Javanese performers as primitive.

Educators, historians, anthropologists, and political scientists throughout the past century have cited the Exposition as a turning point in American cultural history, in large part for its role in public education. Historian Henry Adams described the event as "the first expression of American thought as a unity" (1946, 343). Though he refers most directly to the explosive, ambitious, half-guided, raw ingenuity that he found showcased in the displays of mechanical engineering, the concept can be applied more broadly to the cultural orientation of the event. According to official print media campaigns of the time, the organizing objectives of the fair were to elevate America's international standing with an event that would rival the Exposition Universelle held in Paris in 1889, as well as foster and feed a desire for American self-improvement. Paradoxically, the primary method by which both goals were attempted was high-level re-creation of European cultural practices, including the performances of bands, orchestras, and choruses whose renditions of light classical music standards rang through the performance spaces of the White City (K. Miller 2003). The relegation of "ethnic" artistic practices to the Midway seemingly reaffirmed this aspirational hierarchy, putting the Americans—like their European peers—in the role of colonizers, able to command and exploit supposedly lesser cultures for their own entertainment.

After the Exposition concluded, most traces of the Midway, including that of Java Village, were dismantled. The exotic sounds of the gamelan, though variously transcribed and reproduced, never found a home in prominent compositions or recordings—unlike Claude Debussy's "Pagodes" (1903), whose composition was supposedly inspired by hearing gamelan at the Paris Exposition Universelle. The Javanese musicians returned home, and their gamelan, a set unusual for its large size, anthropomorphic carvings, and vividly colored painting, was incorporated into the collection of the new Field Museum of Natural History and not played again until the 1970s. It would be decades before American musicians and educators would create formal opportunities for in-depth study of this music. It is difficult to tell how the hundreds of thousands of individuals who encountered the Village and its artistic performances conceived of the Javanese or their music in the decades that followed. Yet the case of the Columbian Exposition presents an important starting point for understanding gamelans and the academic world music ensemble because it highlights ways in which academic education shared its roots with its public educational counterparts. World's Fairs—in Paris in 1889, Chicago in 1893, New York in 1939 and again in 1964, Montreal in 1967, and Vancouver in 1986—became not only points of public education about Indonesian performing arts but also catalysts for performers to meet and exchange ideas and instruments.

The Java Village model, however, also bears a striking resemblance to the Dutch colonial rhetoric guiding the development of tourism to Bali just three decades later. *Puputan* (mass ritual suicides) had rocked the island in 1906 and again in 1908 as kings of Badung and Klungkung led their households to public ceremonial death rather than be outmatched and defeated in battle by Dutch forces.[4] Ashamed of the negative international press that followed, Dutch government agencies partnered with commercial entities to rebrand Bali as a tourist destination beginning in the 1920s (Vickers 2012). The island was cast as a paradise, and efforts were made to preserve a local culture believed to be a direct heir to the storied Javanese Hindu Majapahit kingdoms. Cultural tourism policies operated under the rhetoric of creating a "living museum" in which exotic, supposedly ancient and static ways of life could be displayed in situ for Western visitors (Picard 1996). Among the many changes to Bali that the living museum model did not account for was the ways in which the Balinese themselves would adapt this model after Indonesian independence—not only through official policy but also via the entrepreneurship of individuals who opened their family compounds to paying guests with the promise that they would experience an authentic Balinese lifestyle.

The Midway Plaisance in 1893 and its incorporation of diverse cultures, though not yet specifically prefiguring cultural diversity initiatives of the late twentieth century, also evokes an ambiguous relationship between hegemonic American culture and other cultures that continues to this day: an appearance of inclusion couched in the structural language of cultural dominance that continues to be echoed in classification of recordings for sale ("world" music) and the peripheral incorporation of non-Western or nonclassical musics into college curricula and elsewhere. The figurative and sometimes literal museumification of instruments and peoples in educational and touristic spheres, though generally undertaken with clearer consent than in the past, remains a relevant point of consideration today.

Indonesia and the West at the Turn of the Twentieth Century

Although the Javanese village at the 1893 Columbian Exposition served as the first large-scale introduction of Indonesian music to audiences in North America, Indonesian-Western artistic exchanges had flourished since at least the seventeenth century, albeit, once again, not in explicitly educational settings. *Keroncong*—a genre of music that originated in and around Batavia (present-day Jakarta) from Portuguese string band traditions and that later fused with Javanese traditional musics—is one of the earliest examples of such artistic hybridity and exchange (Yampolsky 2010). Centuries later, at the Javanese courts that hosted government representatives of the Dutch East Indies, discourses between native and Dutch observers contributed to the development of early Javanese musical notation (Sumarsam 1995, 2013). Despite early interest in these types of music on the part of nonnative listeners, both local and colonial social practice in the nineteenth century made the idea of Westerners learning to perform Javanese music unthinkable, just as it had been for visitors at the Columbian Exposition. The first Indonesian artists to perform in Europe—a troupe of thirteen musicians and two dancers from the Solonese court of Mangkunegaran who performed *ronggeng* dance in the Netherlands in 1879—were received with curiosity, but their art forms were not categorized as on a par with those of Western ensembles that made similar European tours. As Cohen writes, "Touring Javanese performers were regarded in Europe more as ethnological curiosities than artists"; their dancing took place within cultural exhibitions rather than in performance series (2010, 10). Regardless of classification, the dancers and Indonesian arts more generally proved to be popular with European audiences. Based on the success of this initial tour, by 1900, Javanese musicians, dancers, and shadow puppeteers had played in many of the capitals of Western Europe. By the first decade of the twentieth century, scholarly and artistic events populated primarily by Indonesian students and professionals but sometimes also by European intellectuals could be found in the major cities of the Netherlands, which served as venues for promoting European-Indonesian relations as a more equal (rather than colonial) relationship built on cultural exchange (109–113).

These Indonesian performances coincided with a wider Oriental craze that swept Western Europe and North America from the end of the nineteenth century through World War II. Appetites for exotic material goods were matched by those for performing arts, for example, the "Hawaiian" and "Chinese" themes that found their way into early films and Tin Pan Alley songs in the United States (Garrett 2008). Embracing an *Indische* (Indies) lifestyle, including dressing in *sarong* and eating spicy *sambal*, was primarily an affectation of the Dutch, reflecting a certain fascination with their colonial holdings. Yet interpretations of Indonesian culture were popular across the Western world. The widespread European and American adaptations of songs and dances from the Dutch East Indies often were presented with a veneer of supposed authenticity. Internationally renowned performers of the early twentieth century such as Mata Hari, Eva Gauthier, and Stella Bloch interpreted Javanese dance styles for their audiences in concerts and lecture recitals with greater or lesser degrees of experience and attention to performative and sartorial detail (Cohen 2010; Spiller 2015).

It is curious that, while embodied adaptations of non-Western dance genres were encouraged by the institutions and audiences of modern dance and advertised as authentic, music rarely entered the same sphere until the mid-twentieth century, unless it was vastly altered from its original form. Why? Was it that the body served as a more neutral canvas than did an instrument, which would have to be imported and learned with some skill to replicate the sound of the original? Was it a matter of gender—that feminine bodies were permitted or encouraged to emulate the Other, even as such an act would remain too transgressive for predominantly male instrumentalists learning male-dominated

Indonesian musical practices? Were ethnic dance and singing, both subjects taught to American school children at the time (Volk 1998), deemed to be more democratic, participatory, and approachable than instrumental traditions? Whatever the reasons, the initial representations of Indonesian performing arts in the public sphere in North America frequently focused on dance and embodiment, even as interest in gamelan music began to take root within the more cerebral realm of composition and music scholarship.

Whether performed accurately by Indonesian artists, interpreted through American and European eyes and bodies, or embraced as symbolic affectation of worldliness, elements of Asian cultures encountered in the West highlighted the complexity of perceptions of Asian cultures and identities at the time. On one hand, the permanent immigration of individuals from Asia was largely viewed with displeasure by citizens of the United States. By the 1920s, immigration from the entire spectrum of Asian nations (as well as eastern and southern Europe) to the United States was at its lowest point in decades thanks to legislation such as the Immigration Act of 1924, which set firm quotas on the number of immigrants from each nation allowed to enter during any given year. On the other, the incorporation of forms of ethnic dance and song into American public education systems provided one way of addressing the discomfort that some school districts faced in incorporating immigrant children into their classrooms. Participatory dance lessons demonstrated tokenistic respect for students' native cultures while firmly positioning their practice in proscribed settings outside the American mainstream cultural milieu. Among the more socially elite, however, semi-knowledgeable consumption of exotic art forms served as a mark of cosmopolitan cachet in a way that is not dissimilar to contemporary travel selfie culture. This mixed attitude toward immigration, foreign culture, and the adaptation and safe adoption of performing arts is one that would not only carry through to the establishment of the first gamelan ensembles but that continues in discourses about world music education to this day.

Recordings, Composers, and Teachers

Although early exhibitions and dance performances caught the attention of thousands of viewers, ultimately their impermanence limited the degree to which the performances could be transformed from one-time experiences into regular elements of individuals' lives. Even when recordings of early touring ensembles were made, their circulation was limited. Without access to or popular interest in such recordings outside the context of live performance, such prominent events as the Sundanese exhibition at the 1893 World's Fair faded quickly from public memory. Recording, however, was growing as a catalyst for the preservation and study of foreign musics (Nettl 2010). Record labels devoted to making recordings of folk and ethnic musics in North America, Europe, and beyond flourished in the first three decades of the twentieth century, closely followed by popular interest in recordings of vernacular musics in the 1920s and 1930s—the "race" and "hillbilly" music crazes. During this new era of sonic exchange, regional musical genres suddenly found new general audiences, composers were exposed to new sounds and source material, scholars had static sources that they could analyze, and instructors in music and dance suddenly could have the world at their fingertips, forever reshaping humanity's relation to global sound.

By the 1920s, increased affordability of travel and relative political stability in the Dutch East Indies made the region a target for ethnological recording projects. One of these occurred in 1928 when representatives of the German recording company Odeon and Beka embarked for Bali, tasked with expanding their offerings to the area. Their efforts yielded more than one hundred tracks of Balinese vocal and instrumental music performed by some of the most prestigious individual artists and music clubs in Bali. Considered to be an invaluable resource by the Balinese and non-Balinese alike following their restoration and re-release between 2010 and 2016 as a part of a CD series titled *Bali 1928*, these recordings were a spectacular commercial failure in their own time. Why would the Balinese choose to buy expensive technology to play back recordings limited to only three minutes in length when they could hear the full versions of the performances live and for free? The record dealer charged with selling the completed discs reportedly only sold a few individual records and one copy of the complete set before smashing the remainder in a fit of rage (McPhee 2000, 72).

The recordings that survived ended up in influential places, however—not in Bali or Java but in North America. Their most influential buyer was the Canadian composer Colin McPhee, who was so inspired by the sound of the music that he traveled to Bali twice, living on the island for six years (1931–1933 and 1936–1939) with the stated goal of "hear[ing] every gamelan in the countryside" (McPhee 2000, 111). While in Bali, he transcribed hundreds of works of gamelan music in addition to documenting his impressions of island life. Most notable among his Balinese teachers were I Nyoman Kalér (1892–1969), with whom he worked in resurrecting a gamelan club in the coastal town of Kuta, and I Made Lebah (1905?–1996), who served not only as McPhee's chauffeur but also as his guide to Balinese music. McPhee, who did not play any of the gamelan instruments himself, would check his transcriptions with his Balinese teachers by playing them back on a piano that he kept in his home (Oja 1990).

It was a time of transnational collaboration and counter-influence in the arts in Bali. Just as local groups of artists reacted to the materials and styles of the foreign artists who had flocked to Bali in the early 1930s and begun to develop new styles to sell to visitors (Vickers 2012), local transnational performers created genres that would be internationally influential for the following century. One example of such cross-cultural influence can be found in the development of modern *kecak*, also glossed outside Indonesia as the Balinese "monkey dance." Kecak is a form of *gamelan suara*, or vocal gamelan, in which a traditionally all-male chorus chants accompaniment for dancers performing a story from the Hindu epics, most commonly today "The Abduction of Sita" from the *Ramayana*. Whereas the *cak* (vocal chanting) part of the performances is derived from historic *sanghyang dedari* (trance-dance) performances, its use to accompany scenes from the Hindu epic was an innovation of the early 1930s, the result of a collaboration between the expatriate German painter Walter Spies and the dancer Wayan Limbak (Dibia 1996). The genre would become a staple of tourist performances on Bali, a source of inspiration of avant-garde performance pieces such as Keith Terry and Wayan Dibia's "Body Tjak," a source of sonic exoticism in Western film (Bakan 2013), and perhaps the genre of Balinese performing arts most commonly adapted in Western educational settings, pre-collegiate and collegiate alike.

McPhee's legacy in this transitional period of the Balinese performing arts is manifold and includes supporting children's gamelan groups in Bali (Downing 2019) and writing *Music in Bali* (1966), which remains one of the most comprehensive single texts on Balinese music in the English language. The publication of McPhee's *A House in Bali* in 1947 introduced a new classic into the growing international literature on Bali. It has been reprinted and is still sold widely in English-language bookshops on the island today. Moreover, in addition to Jaap Kunst—whose brief working honeymoon in Bali resulted in the first extensive written account of Balinese music (Kunst and Kunst–van Wely 1925), which stands among other substantive contributions to international gamelan culture, discussed below—McPhee was a pioneer in the study of foreign music, initiating a learning process similar to those used by foreign students studying in Bali today that involved both written and applied musical translation. McPhee recalled:

> For a small sum I could engage the musicians to go through and repeat their traditional repertories of music. Exclamations of pleased surprise would be heard from the men when, after noting some nuclear melody the first time it

> was played, I sat down at an instrument [the piano] to play it along with them on the repeat. Work was always a pleasure. Even in the most isolated villages information was given willingly, and rare musical manuscripts of palm leaf were generously offered for my inspection and sometimes even copied at my request. (1966, xvi)

McPhee's role in bringing back the music of Bali to North America was also influential. In addition to his compositional work, he hosted nights of Balinese music and culture in which his transcriptions of Balinese music for Western instruments accompanied silent film footage he took in Bali, accompanied by lectures about his experiences. As the partnership between McPhee and like-minded contemporaries expanded into the foundation of the Pan-American Association of Composers, McPhee traveled to Mexico City at the end of 1935 to work on a "rhapsody" on Balinese themes. He was inspired in this effort by his Mexican colleague in composition, Carlos Chávez (1899–1978), whose works were based on Mexican themes. The resulting piece, *Tabuh-Tabuhan* (A group of percussion instruments; it was also subtitled "Toccata for Orchestra and 2 Pianos"), combined Balinese and Western melodic, harmonic, and rhythmic idioms (Oja 1990). It has become his most often-performed work.

With regard to the early development of gamelan in American pedagogical contexts, the most important part of McPhee's legacy was, perhaps, the introduction of these recorded materials and his own anecdotes to the "ultra-modernists," a loosely defined group of New York–based composers and musicians whose experimental interests involved non-Western and nonclassical musics. One of its members, the composer, impresario, and educator Henry Cowell (1897–1965), was one of the first to use technology to teach about the Indonesian performing arts. As a young, self-taught composer who grew up in southern California, Cowell had absorbed not only the Irish music of his father but also the sounds of nearby Asian American communities. Following studies with Charles Seeger that exposed him both to American folk traditions and to radical concepts of modernist composition, Cowell toured the country extensively as a pianist and became the de facto leader of the ultramodernists. Cowell's early exposure to non-Western musics led him farther beyond the American sphere than many of his compatriots in his educational pursuits. He studied comparative musicology with Erich von Hornbostel, who had previously worked for several decades with recordings from around the world as director of the Berliner Phonogramm-Archiv. A Guggenheim Fellowship awarded in 1931 allowed Cowell to travel to Europe to study Carnatic music theory with Pichu Sambamoorthy and Central Javanese gamelan and Balinese gamelan angklung with Raden Mas Jodjana and Roemahlaiselan (also spelled Ramaleislan), respectively (Sachs 2012, 190). Though perhaps not the most reliable bearers of Indonesian tradition—the degree of Jodjana's formal Javanese performing arts training is unknown and his fame as a performer largely rested on his interpretive fusions in dance, whereas Roemahlaiselan was born in Ambon and only lived briefly in Bali as a youth (Cohen 2010, 106–139)—Cowell's teachers impressed upon him fundamental principles of gamelan music that substantially furthered his knowledge of and interest in the art form.

Cowell translated these experiences into his work as a pedagogue. Starting in the 1930s he began teaching at the New School for Social Science Research in New York, as well as at other institutions in the city. According to sources in the Henry Cowell Papers archive at the New York Public Library, in addition to more traditional courses in music theory, composition, and orchestration, Cowell taught "Music of the World's Peoples," offered for the first time in 1930 and repeated regularly throughout his appointment. It was the first college-level course in the United States to place a global focus on studying the performing arts, and it was followed in 1936 by a course titled "History of the Music for Dance." Cowell drew extensively on a personal collection of recordings to represent as many musics as possible, perhaps including eight of the *Bali 1928* sides that were released by von Hornbostel on the 1934 recording *Music of the Orient*, to populate his radio program and course listening lists; these recordings from all over the world would eventually constitute the core of the set of recordings that he produced for the Smithsonian in the 1950s.[5]

By the mid-1930s Cowell wished to move back to the West Coast. He found teaching work in the summers at Mills College, Stanford (in the psychology department), and at the University of California, Berkeley, where he brought his pedagogical approaches to world music with him. These included a draft order to purchase a large selection of instruments from many cultures for students to study in what would have been the first world music ensembles. Additionally, in 1933 Cowell expressed his frustrations about the current state of music education in a treatise that advocated for, among other things, an introductory course in Western and non-Western music for majors as well as non-majors, approaching the study from perspectives of theory, anthropology, psychology, and physiology. The course and overall curriculum were never implemented (Sachs 2012, 208). His insistence on living within "a whole world of music" resonated with several of his students, however, including the composers John Cage and Lou Harrison, whose adoption of Indonesian idioms into their compositions was likely rooted in this interaction (L. Miller and Lieberman 2006). Though he did not compose in a substantially Indonesian idiom himself, Cowell used a model of pedagogy that prefigured the hands-on experimental classes that would become the hallmark of world music at UCLA, as well as grounding gamelan firmly within the canonical repertoire of world music examples through which it found favor with influential composers.

The World Was Watching: International Tours and Artistic Development

While recordings and lectures whetted the appetites of academics and professional musicians for the distinctive sounds of Indonesia, a series of public performance tours instilled an appreciation of gamelan in a broader subset of the international public. The reception of such groups in these initial postwar tours exemplifies a transition in the treatment of Indonesian artists away from being mere ethnological curiosities. They also reveal entrenched power structures in the music industry—in particular, the dominance of white men as managers who regularly controlled the performing schedules, presentational aesthetics, and compensation of nonwhite performing artists. This disparity in artistic control was hardly a phenomenon reserved to non-Western musicians; the early histories of jazz, blues, rhythm and blues, and rock 'n' roll in the United States reveal similar patterns. Just as tours to America by Indonesian performing arts groups or guest artist residencies remain a key way in which audiences experience Indonesian culture, however, artistic control and representation remain important and heated issues in both public and academic contexts. The mid-twentieth-century performance history of one group, Gamelan Gunung Sari (Essence of the Sacred Mountain), highlights these ethical issues and demonstrates in concrete ways how such tours set the stage for the flourishing of gamelan ensembles based in North America.

Gunung Sari, from Peliatan, Gianyar, was the first gamelan in Bali to be founded independent of either royal courts or the banjar (village ward). Membership in the ensemble was a coveted privilege because musicians in the gamelan were allowed a respite from Dutch-organized corvée labor—forced labor, mostly manual, that fell disproportionately to Bali's *sudra* (commoner) caste.[6] The group specialized in gamelan gong kebyar, a genre developed in reaction to the conquest of Bali by the Dutch in the first decade of the twentieth century and the political dissolution of the Balinese royal courts. Like its namesake "flash" or "spark," the explosive and virtuosic gamelan gong kebyar spread like wildfire across the island in the course of the next two decades. Beginning in northern Bali near Singaraja, the music had been developed in Karangasem and Tabanan before being picked up in the Denpasar area and then in Peliatan.

After Gamelan Gunung Sari won a gong kebyar competition, Dutch government officials recommended that they perform at the Universal Exposition in Paris in 1931. This initial performance of Balinese music in Europe was met with rave reviews, and Gunung Sari was established as an influential name in Indonesia and abroad.

Following two decades of high-profile performances in Indonesia—including that for the first president of Indonesia, Sukarno—Gunung Sari became the first Balinese gamelan group to tour the United States, doing so from 1952 to 1956. It was the nation's first major encounter with live Indonesian music since the Columbian Exposition in Chicago. Organized by the British journalist and author-turned-performing arts impresario John Coast and artistic director Anak Agung Gde Mandera, the gamelan's tour thrilled viewers and listeners not only in the tour's hub, New York, but also in Boston, Philadelphia, Washington DC, Las Vegas, Los Angeles, and Miami, as well as dozens of stops in between. They continued on to perform in Brussels, Bonn, Paris, and Rome. More than thirty million additional viewers tuned in to watch the group's performance on the *Ed Sullivan Show*. Back in Bali, the Peliatan group became famous for its interpretations of pieces already considered to be classics in Bali that, at Coast's request, had generally been shortened and simplified for non-Balinese audiences. Though Indonesian critiques of the lack of agency that the musicians and dancers had on the tour began to emerge in the 1960s, their work largely remains a historical point of pride for Balinese arts communities. A commemorative plaque still located at Puri Kaleran Pusaka in Peliatan, Bali, characterizes the tour in one word: triumphant.

Gamelan Gunung Sari continues to perform programs for tourists to this day. However renowned, the group has been criticized by musicians and scholars because the musical alterations that they popularized may have lessened the diversity of the development of the kebyar style and because of a subsequent lack of artistic innovation (Tenzer 2005; Ziporyn 1997). Yet it is certain that Gunung Sari's tour provided a level of artistic familiarity and direct connection that was necessary for establishing gamelans in the United States in the following decade. Musicians and administrators who had witnessed the program—including the future founding supporter of the first degree-granting program in ethnomusicology, Richard Winslow at Wesleyan University—reportedly were inspired by what they witnessed in the tour to include non-Western ensembles in general and gamelan specifically at the heart of their programs (Lueck 2012). It was because of this tour that McPhee first spotted the talent of Wayan Gandera, whom he later recommended to help start the gamelan program at UCLA. The tour is remembered as being so historically important for international Balinese performing arts that beginning in 2017, a series of video clips of the tour from the *Ed Sullivan Show* began to circulate on Facebook; by early 2019 the main video of the "bumblebee dance," or Oleg Tambulilingan, had garnered more than fifty-five thousand views. One person who reposted the video tied the tour directly to the subsequent development of academic gamelans, stating, "Anak Agung Gde Mandera must be proud to see this music and dance are now taught in many major universities in the US" (Mount Agung, Facebook post, September 21, 2017). The unparalleled visibility of this performance continued to bring the Indonesian performing arts further into the awareness of the American public.

The Dutch Connection

Though the educational ideal of the world music ensemble would be assumed much more strongly in the United States than in Europe, its model, in fact, was in the Netherlands. During World War II, the first-ever gamelan ensemble in Europe, Gamelan Babar Layar (Setting Sail), was created by non-Indonesian instrumentalists. The new gamelan was indirectly based on the work of Jaap Kunst, who toured the Dutch East Indies as a young violinist in 1919. Fascinated with Javanese music, he decided to remain on the island and obtained a government post in Batavia. Besides performing his duties, Kunst collected recordings and musical instruments, in part on behalf of von Hornbostel at the Berliner Phonogramm-Archiv. After returning to the Netherlands in 1936 he became curator of the Tropenmuseum (Royal Tropical Institute) in Amsterdam and, in 1958, a faculty member at the University of Amsterdam, where he gave lectures and worked with students.

Even more than McPhee's, Kunst's fieldwork in Indonesia had remained firmly grounded in colonial notions of appropriate social practice. Despite having maintained a correspondence with the Javanese prince Mangkunegoro VII (1885–1944) of Solo (Surakarta) for two decades (Djajadiningrat and Brinkgreve 2014), it was in Dutch, and he noted that only "some knowledge" of a native language is necessary in order to undertake fieldwork (Kunst 195, 15). Also the majority of Kunst's informants, drawn from the Dutch-speaking Javanese nobility, arguably were substantially detached from quotidian musical practices. One of the principles that emerged from Kunst's scholarly lineage—bimusicality—was beyond his reach, as well. As his student Ernst Heins described it,

> As a result of the colonial situation it was unthinkable for a European, someone from the colonizing elite, to learn, for example, to play the gamelan. The mutual social barriers between Javanese musicians and colonial researchers were too high for that. Musicological research in the Dutch East-Indies was carried out

> within the context of the colonial reality: alongside of, but completely detached from, the indigenous world, no matter how much genuine appreciation and love Kunst had for Indonesian culture. (quoted in Kunst 1994, 20–21)

As a mentor, however, Kunst was active in guiding those interested in researching exotic music using a more hands-on approach. Notably, it was Kunst who, on his return to the Netherlands, provided recordings, notation, and expert advice to the first groups of Dutch instrumentalists in Gamelan Babar Layar. Kunst's initial group consisted of students from Indonesia and seamen who were stranded in the Netherlands during World War II who practiced at the Tropenmuseum. It inspired a more permanent group that at first consisted entirely of Dutch teenagers. On a trip to Amsterdam from Haarlem, a young man named Bernard Ijzerdraat heard the gamelan and was so impressed that he and his friends eventually decided to build their own gamelan and learn to play it. Although metal was difficult to come by in the occupied Netherlands, they cast their own bronze instruments. The group learned some pieces by observing the Amsterdam musicians, but primarily Ijzerdraat learned them from gramophone recordings and written Yogyanese *kraton* musical notation provided by Kunst and then taught to the remainder of the group (Mendonça 2011, 62).

These developments directly influenced a young doctoral student who had been studying with Kunst, Mantle Hood (1918–2005). Following early careers as a wartime engineer, fiction writer, and performing musician, Hood had enrolled at UCLA in 1945 to study composition with Ernst Toch. He migrated into non-Western musical studies after completing his bachelor's and master's degrees in 1951 and pursued the study of Indonesian music with Kunst at the University of Amsterdam, and he witnessed the gamelans there and in Haarlem in action. After completing his doctoral work in 1954, he studied in Indonesia for two years on a fellowship from the Ford Foundation. His work there with local communities convinced him of the value of cultural context and hands-on performing experience. He was hired at UCLA in 1958 in part to work with the nascent Institute of Ethnomusicology. Founding the UCLA gamelan ensembles was one of his first tasks.

The ensemble model that Hood chose to adopt, though based on that of Gamelan Babar Layar, also had significant differences. Mendonça contextualizes Babar Layar as an affinity group: one formed outside the framework of heritage affiliations or original contexts and based instead on a profound individual connection with the music and the cultural context created by the formation of the new group. Affinity and a sense of individual self-identification have been central to current understandings of gamelan as it is practiced in the United States (Spiller 2015). Yet though this affinity is in large part what continues to animate community groups, bringing gamelan to educational settings added an extra burden of musical and cultural representation not necessarily inherent in the work of early community-based gamelans. The tension brought about by awareness of educational norms to groups that are also held together by affinity informed the earliest developments of Hood's concept of bimusicality, manifested in the ensembles he founded at UCLA.

The Origins of the UCLA Gamelan Program

The transnational studies and collaborations pursued by McPhee, Cowell, Kunst, and others of their generation represented a pedagogically based bridge to Indonesia; the formation of Gamelan Babar Layar demonstrated that Western musicians were both interested in and capable of sustaining study of non-Western musical genres generally and Indonesian music specifically. The ensemble's initial successes in drawing on the recorded resources at the Tropenmuseum underscore the importance of recorded sound in spreading this music beyond its initial boundaries. Yet some exposure to native musicians and Indonesian-made instruments—unavailable only a few decades earlier—was critical to the establishment and maintenance of Babar Layar and the groups that followed. Though still few in number in 1955, when the Society for Ethnomusicology was founded and began documenting available resources for its new members, academic programs that offered coursework in non-Western music were increasing. The foundation of the Institute of Ethnomusicology at UCLA presented the first systematic approach to building world music ensembles as a form of music pedagogical technique.

As an institution, UCLA was ripe for the development of such a program as the institute. During World War II the campus had devoted itself almost entirely to supporting pre-military training, and its enrollment dropped as young men delayed attending college owing to the war. A postwar building boom brought new construction and new programs to the campus. In music, department chair Laurence Armstrong Petran introduced course programming in the psychology of music, systematic musicology, and ethnomusicology. When Hood was hired in 1958, the stage had already been set for the development of innovative world music programming. In a relatively new model for music in higher education, he purchased new instruments and supported foreign performing artists who would teach in exchange for a scholarship to study at the university.

Hood entered a vastly different academic environment than that initially encountered by Petran. The postwar boom and the corresponding preference for supporting graduate programs and scientific research had transformed the university from its origins as a liberal arts institution into a research university. Gone, too, were its militaristic associations; instead, along with the rest of the University of California system, faculty members were under suspicion of being Communist agitators. Conveniently, the artistic exchange model supported by Hood was seen to foster cultural exchange between the United States and non-aligned powers such as Indonesia during the Cold War, even as it also spoke to more general desires to increase the global artistic presence on campus and more closely adhere to the dictates of the new institutional focus on research.

The UCLA Javanese gamelan, Khjai Mendung, was purchased in 1958 and found its first Indonesian leader in Hardja Susilo; the Balinese gamelan gong kebyar, Sekar Anyar, was purchased from an unknown man in Kesiman with the help of the Balinese musician Cokorda Agung Mas in 1959. Mas and Wayan Gandera, who had been recommended to Hood by McPhee (who was now also at UCLA), were the first to teach the Balinese ensemble, which at first was called a study group to emphasize its group learning aesthetic. In choosing the instruments, Hood understood that although they were purchased to aid students in ethnomusicology in their practical study, the gamelan would also serve as a visual and aural representative of the university's commitment to diversity. Contemporaries of Hood recall that,

> In addition to its sound, Hood was delighted with the carving on the gamelan in which the main designs were larger in size than in many other gamelan he had seen; i.e., in his concern that the visual beauty of the gamelan be as accessible to the audience as its aural beauty, Hood knew from experience that the larger designs would read better on stage than a gamelan with intricate carving which can become unreadable at a distance. (DeVale and Dibia 1991, 6)

As the gamelan and other study groups gained an increased presence on campus and beyond in the 1960s by performances with guest teachers and the release of recordings, they were gradually converted into official ensembles and allocated pedagogical and financial resources. Students who graduated carried what they had learned from playing with them, and some began to form ensembles of their own. The first pedagogical gamelan lineages in North America were beginning to take root.

Gamelan, Bimusicality, and Multiculturalism

On its own, the gamelan at UCLA might have become only a niche enterprise in American musical history. Yet Hood's insistence that Western music students have hands-on musical training in the non-Western musics that they were studying became a cornerstone, if a contentious one, of ethnomusicological theory in the early 1960s. The central concepts of Hood's theory are most concisely explained in "The Challenge of 'Bi-Musicality'" (1960), a short paper in which he explained why he thought bimusicality was important and offered suggestions for how it can be achieved. Hood recommended learning by rote, even when notation is available, in order to be able to capture distinct musical playing techniques such as striking keys correctly and paying special attention to listening in order to be able to overcome biases favoring Western systems of pitch and rhythm. The crowning achievement in learning a musical style, according to Hood, is being able to improvise appropriately within the given genre. He emphasized that initial advantages in this style of learning may fall to students who are musical but who have no prior musical training; musicians trained in Western classical styles may have difficulty overcoming their learning biases. It is crucial to note that Hood's argument about the merits of bimusicality was largely drawn from the process of studying gamelan; consequently, his descriptions of best practices in approaching tonality, rhythm, rote learning, and instrumental playing techniques resemble gamelan rehearsals more than anything else. Though it begins with the assumption that readers would be "natives" of the language of Western classical music and proceeds from that standpoint, the basic principles of the article can be and have been applied to cultivating broader musical competency for individuals of all backgrounds.

Use of the word *bimusicality* to describe an individual's musicality gradually fell out of fashion even as it lived on pedagogical requirements, because of both the growing awareness that one's "native music" was not geographically determined and the increase in access of musicians from around the world to different types of musical materials. Even so, Hood's work stood as a challenge to the Western classical music world. He argued against the previously common stance that non-Western musics were either inferior in quality or incomprehensible to Western musicians. He maintained that since musicians around the world—from the Middle East to Japan—had not only incorporated Western musical materials into hybrid forms of their own local traditions and could also play perfectly well in Western classical styles, Western musicians should be able to do likewise. He concluded that music students can progress in learning a new genre as far as they have time and energy to devote to the enterprise. By the end of the twentieth century, formally trained and self-taught musicians from around the world had chosen to learn multiple musical systems and genres, gradually eroding many of the social and logistical boundaries that had precluded such activity in earlier decades.

Since Hood's time, whether musical performance is integral to the ethnomusicological endeavor has been a subject of debate. It has no cognate concepts in related scholarly disciplines such as anthropology and folklore, in which artistic participation of any kind on the part of observers is accepted but not specifically expected. In historical musicology, familiarity with Western musical systems is assumed, but maintaining an active performance profile in specific repertoires is not. Subsequent scholars engaged in this debate, such as Titon (1995), have pointed out other important reasons why bimusicality is an important practice—that playing previously unfamiliar musics allows for a displacement of a musician's sense of self and perspective and that it may create a cultural unity between musicians that cannot be found by observation alone. *The Anthropology of Music* (1964), by Hood's contemporary Alan Merriam, served as a strong theoretical counterbalance to Hood. A proponent of viewing ethnomusicology as a hard science, Merriam argued that the real work for scholars was accomplished by theorizing about culture, not musical practice.

Concerns about the musical and cultural appropriateness of non-Indonesian student learners' serving as representatives of Indonesian culture began almost immediately on the establishment of the study group ensembles. Early reviews of professional recordings released by the UCLA Balinese and Javanese gamelans highlight their paradoxical nature as learning and aesthetic experiences (Heins 1969). As Heins noted, "Playing the music of another culture proved initially to be an excellent study tool, but before long it became an end in itself . . . it is one thing to play Balinese music within the framework of an academic education, but to make the results of collective classwork commercially available is something quite different" (393). He highlighted, too, the changes in attitude expressed by Indonesian professional musicians when they learned that the recordings were made by Americans. At first they were critical of artistic flaws, but upon learning that the musicians were American students, the expert listeners instead began to praise "the experience and skill of these foreign gamelan musicians. They [thought] the foreign performers [were] amazingly clever. [One listener saw] it as proof that Javanese gamelan music is not only meant for Javanese but for everybody. He [thought] that by continued study under first class guidance the group [would] eventually meet Javanese standards" (394). Though the opportunities for foreign musicians to study gamelan have expanded substantially, many of the same types of critiques and praise are common today.

Ethnomusicologists continue to debate the necessity for students to have hands-on musical study in previously unfamiliar musics as a part of their research and graduate training; there is a nearly even split between American graduate programs in ethnomusicology that do and do not require world music ensemble experience as a part of the degree. Non-Western ensembles have proliferated in American colleges and universities nonetheless. In a handful of places such as the California Institute of the Arts (CalArts), students approach playing gamelan or other types of music from a pre-professional perspective. More frequently, world music ensembles have become models of experiential, liberal arts–style educations in which the ensemble is meant to provide nonspecialists with a type of hands-on musical and cultural enrichment that cannot be found elsewhere. Bolstered by trends toward hands-on pedagogy and multiculturalism (later, cultural diversity) in education, the world music ensemble became a standard way of exposing college students to an array of global musics.

These distinct ways in which gamelans are situated within academic contexts, though sometimes mutually reinforcing, speak to different educational agendas that can be envisioned on a spectrum from focusing on pre-professionalism (the conservatory model, based on demonstrated musical and sometimes cultural competency) to experientialism and creating a well-rounded graduate (the liberal arts model). In a conservatory-like setting, the presence of an ensemble can be directly paired with the educational goal of proficiency in specific musical styles; for example, CalArts offers BFA and MFA programs in a variety of world performance styles with the central stated goal of musical proficiency at a high level. In contrast, liberal arts–style programming at many of the institutions that are home to gamelans focus on their potential for cultural and artistic enrichment for students planning to pursue a wide range of professions after graduation, rarely positioning them as pathways for future career development. Undergraduate and graduate programs in ethnomusicology that embrace world music ensembles combine both models, cultivating a baseline musical competency for students pursuing deep study of the art form at the same time as they provide recreational or exploratory musical opportunities for other students. This trifecta of pedagogical models and agendas, which is found in a relatively small number of countries, has helped gamelans develop their own niches within the American branch of the transnational gamelan ecosystem.

The Transnational Gamelan Ecosystem Develops

Tracing the specific path of the development of gamelan ensembles in the United States from the earliest to the most recently established would be a Sisyphean task; however, understanding the symbiotic structures that connect them is important for understanding the broader gamelan community and its lives within and outside academia. Early academic ensembles were founded starting in the 1960s at Wesleyan University, the University of Michigan, Oberlin College, the California Institute of the Arts, Cornell University, and the University of Hawaii at Manoa, among other places. These first ensembles were almost entirely procured, advised, or directed by Hood's former students or native Indonesians who studied and taught as part of these early programs—including Susilo, the first Indonesian gamelan instructor to conduct most of his career in the United States. The realignment of the political relationship between Indonesia and the United States in the 1960s (see chapter 3) allowed for simpler international exchanges of musicians and dancers, including formal academic study and professional nonacademic teaching.

Throughout the 1960s and 1970s, exposure to gamelan music through popular recordings released by Smithsonian Folkways and Nonesuch Records, its inclusion in world music survey courses, and contact with other gamelan aficionados also inspired responses by American artists. One of these was the creation of "American gamelan," which was Javanese-inspired but locally designed and built by musicians such as Dennis Murphy, Barbara Benary, Lou Harrison, William Colvig, and Daniel Schmidt beginning in the early 1960s. Found in educational and community settings, American gamelans can be used to perform traditional Indonesian repertoire but are largely devoted to performing new and avant-garde compositions.

Only in the 1970s did Indonesian performing arts programming that made use of Indonesian-made instruments become established in the United States, beginning first as summer workshops held primarily at universities on the West Coast. Some early examples included programming at the American Society for Eastern Arts (founded by Sam and Luise Scripps in 1963; this later became the Center for World Music, directed by Bob Brown) and the Asian Performing Arts Summer Institute (coordinated by Judy Mitoma). The first long-term community-based gamelan groups, the Balinese Gamelan Sekar Jaya (Victorious Flower) in California and the Javanese Gamelan Laras Tentrem (originally the Boston Village Gamelan) in Massachusetts, gave more permanent opportunities for artistic study; both were founded in 1979.

Gamelan Laras Tentrem was founded by Sam Quigley, at the time a graduate student at Wesleyan University, and Alan Robinson. The gamelan, which has been under the direction of Barry Drummond since 1992, is also taught as a course at its home institution, Tufts University. The gamelan performs primarily in the style of the courts of Surakarta (Solonese style) and has had as guest director eminent Javanese musicians including K. R. M. T. Bojrodiningrat (also known as R. M. Soekanto Soedarsono), I. M. Harjito, Sumarsam, Wakidi Hardjo Martoyo, and Djoko Walujo.

On the opposite coast, Gamelan Sekar Jaya began in collaboration between the Canadian composer and scholar Michael Tenzer, the American performing arts presenter Rachel Cooper, and the Balinese musician I Wayan Suweca. The three met for the first time in Peliatan, Bali, in 1979. Tenzer had gone to study in Bali after encountering the Nonesuch gamelan recordings while an undergraduate at Yale University; Cooper had studied in and worked as assistant director at the Summer Institute and was traveling with her teacher, Suweca, who had been teaching in California (Gillitt 2017; Tenzer 2011, 10). Using a small gamelan gong kebyar that Tenzer had purchased, the three cultivated the new ensemble in Cooper's and Suweca's living room in Oakland while Tenzer pursued a PhD in composition at the University of California, Berkeley. The ensemble has toured Bali five times, and the governor of Bali awarded Gamelan Sekar Jaya the *Dharma Kusuma*—Bali's highest award for artistic achievement—in 2000. Berkeley-educated composers who have played with the ensemble such as Tenzer, Wayne Vitale, and Evan Ziporyn have released compositions that have been influential in Bali as well as in American gamelan circles; Tenzer and Ziporyn have founded artistically renowned programs for students and community members at the University of British Columbia and MIT, respectively.

The interconnectivity of people, physical resources, and creative ideas in the gamelan world—what Brinner (2016) describes as a gamelan ecosystem—can be contemplated through the connections of the cultural institutions that serve as focal points for artistic and social activity. Gamelans based in academic institutions generally serve pedagogical functions and are populated mostly or entirely by students. The demographics, practice and performance structure, and aims of community gamelan groups vary on a spectrum from truly amateur ensembles to semi-official groups hosted by Indonesian embassies (such as those in Washington, DC, and Los Angeles) and semiprofessional performing groups such as Gamelan Sekar Jaya. Hybrid groups that contain both enrolled students and non-enrolled community members may share aspects of both sets of groups. Although some form more tight-knit connections that do others, all are arguably more closely interlinked in the early twenty-first century than they were decades ago. Once gamelans in North America relied on the direct and often slow transfer of people and physical materials traveling thousands of miles; the past few decades have sped up the process through in situ and online exchanges of ideas about pedagogy and performance.

This historical outline of key points in the history of academic gamelans highlights issues that are still inherent in gamelan practice today. Though the exhibition of the Java Village at the Chicago World's Fair was masterminded by the fair's organizers, the subsequent dissemination of gamelan recordings and instruments and their use as pedagogical materials was initiated by individuals or pairs of musicians and teachers whose names and legacies are known; similarly, the contemporary gamelan programs that have become a staple element in American education in many cases were founded and subsequently supported by the unflagging efforts of a small number of individuals. Further, much as the initial dissemination of gamelan in North America via recordings, courses, and live performances, interest in gamelan in America today is predicated on live performance by Indonesians and Americans, support in academic institutions and in community settings, and dissemination of audio and audiovisual recordings, both in tangible copies and online. The showcasing of teachers' lives that is common in musical and cultural immersion programs potentially echoes the display of ethnicity highlighted in historic living museums. Transnational partnerships have also flourished, allowing for an exchange of goods, people, and ideas undreamed of a few decades earlier. The founding generations of Balinese performing artists who built careers in North America have been central to the growth and sustenance of such exchanges.

CHAPTER 3

From Bali to America: Teachers and Transitions

The banjar of Bangah is located in the central mountainous region of Tabanan Regency, south of the village of Baturiti and east of the city of Tabanan, surrounded by the banjar of Apuan, Pacung, Uma Poh, and Abian Luang. Bangah is a relatively recent settlement by Balinese standards; according to oral history passed down by local priests, the area was forested and uninhabited until the nineteenth century. Families from other areas of Bali including Klungkung, Karangasem, and Gianyar subsequently settled there, leaving their ancestral lands to forge a new community. This same oral tradition emphasizes that one of the banjar's foundational principles is equality: in consultation with the king of Tabanan, the first *mekel* (head) of Bangah abolished caste within the new banjar. The area is also celebrated by its residents for the strong spiritual power of the land—in large part imbued by the outflow of water from nearby Lake Beratan—as well as for having a population that was untouched by the violent Communist purges of 1965 in which up to a million Indonesians were killed.

Although it is located in a mountainous part of the island with climatic conditions to match, Bangah is at a much lower altitude than Pura Besakih, the island's largest and most sacred temple, which is located near the top of Mount Agung, the island's highest and most sacred peak. Still, the land around Bangah is hilly; the winding roads have steep grades in some places, and the houses and buildings perch on the hilltops, their attached lands sloping down steeply toward the rivers or into the verdant terraced rice paddies. Today, the main road leading past Bangah and into Baturiti is always clogged with traffic. Locals on scooters whiz past the small houses, *warung* (snack shops), the shell of a now-defunct Internet café, small chain convenience stores, and the giant tour buses that transport mostly Javanese and Japanese visitors on lumbering voyages along the narrow main roads toward the beaches at Lovina in the north. While local farmers can still skirt the main road by foot or motorbike to arrive at their daily destinations, increasingly, residents travel the main road to neighboring villages or to areas of tourist development in the south and near the coast to pursue paid work.

Each banjar in Bali must have at least three different temples in order to fulfill the dictates of the Balinese Hindu faith—Pura Puseh (the origin temple, devoted to Vishnu and the village founders), Pura Desa (the village temple, devoted to Brahma and to spirits who protect villagers in their daily lives), and Pura Dalem (devoted to Shiva, Durga, and other deities and associated with death rituals)—but many also have other temples for other purposes. It is Pura Arak Api that one passes first on the way from Baturiti, through Bangah, on the way to locally popular hot springs. Pura Arak Api is dedicated to taksu, the transcendent feeling of divine inspiration that enables the individual to surpass the self, that Balinese Hindu artists pray for before their performances begin, whether they are performing for the temple or merely for tourist entertainment.

Less than half a kilometer down the road in a transnational arts school and practice space called Sanggar Manik Galih, dozens of burgeoning artists pursue study and hope to one day attain such taksu. Groups of Balinese boys, girls, men, and women play gamelan in their own regular and separate rehearsals; some of these groups are of long standing, while others have cycled in and out of activity since their founding in the first decades of the twenty-first century. For a few months per year, rooms near the stages that house the instruments are flooded with foreign visitors, college students studying abroad and other musicians who have come to study independently. Founded in 2011, the sanggar (private club) serves to formalize and increase the types of artistic activity that had begun in this small hamlet two decades earlier. The foundation and maintenance of this artistic space is a deeply collaborative process. Yet the impetus for planting this seed of a community—for Manik Galih means "grain of rice," a food that plays a sacred role of sustenance in Balinese Hinduism and implies the potential for new growth—originated in the work of the musician-teacher I Made Lasmawan, who built the main part of his career not in Bali but, rather, in the United States.[1]

Lasmawan (family name: Tangkas; called Pak Made or Pak De by his students) was born in Bangah in 1958, the year the first participatory gamelan ensemble was founded in the United States. In 1990 Lasmawan made the long overseas journey from Indonesia to the United States to work as a director of gamelan, extending the nascent network of academic gamelans that had been growing on the two coasts to the Front Range of the Rocky Mountains. Working first in California and then in Colorado, Lasmawan has founded, revived, or assisted in the foundation of approximately two dozen gamelan ensembles, almost a third of which he continues to teach or guest direct regularly.

American musicians and administrators play substantial roles in the maintenance of world music ensemble programs, but their current academic and community gamelan programs could not exist in their current form without the expertise and partnership of such Indonesian teachers, many of whom, like Lasmawan, have maintained their original citizenship despite decades of work in the United States. Their own academic and community ensembles often serve as models to which others look for inspiration. In addition, their presence as pedagogues is felt across the nation because they frequently also direct ensembles in partnership with a local teacher or as guest artists. Essential for coordinating the arrival of new instruments and dance costumes, training new American teachers, providing guidance for new cultural experiences within the United States and abroad, and generally promoting the ensembles and Indonesian culture, the teachers' contributions can be felt not only in the lives of their students but also in the shape and systematic maintenance of the entire transnational artistic network.

Every American gamelan program has its origins in a different time, place, and situation, and so each ensemble has its own specific identity and story. Similarly, Indonesian teachers' individual paths differ from each other on the basis of specific opportunities that they were offered and those that they pursued. A visiting teacher will have a very different American experience than will one who has lived for decades in the United States, just as a teacher who is an Indonesian governmental attaché first and ensemble instructor second will have different experiences than will those who are employed primarily by academic institutions. Yet for teachers of the same generation, certain commonalities emerge in the life events that brought them to the United States, the performing and pedagogical experiences that shaped their teaching, and the successes and setbacks that ultimately shaped their personal and professional lives.

This chapter uses biography, discussions of musical lineages, and the concept of artistic ecosystems to illuminate some of the "hidden" factors—the social, educational, and economic conditions—that have shaped the lives and careers of the oldest current generations of Balinese gamelan teachers. Following a discussion of the circumstances that brought the first Balinese American teachers to the United States, I focus on Lasmawan's early life and training to examine the life paths of teachers who are approximately the same age as American baby boomers born from the 1940s to the 1960s. I suggest that just as certain political and educational conditions were necessary for the first academic gamelan ensembles to form at UCLA, so, too, were critical structural changes to Indonesian educational patterns and Indonesian American political relations necessary to form the type of exchanges that have spanned from the late twentieth century to today.

Artistic Opportunities and Politics

The eldest of the gamelan teachers who arrived in the United States in the late 1950s and early 1960s were born during the Dutch colonial period, and they witnessed the profound transformation of Indonesia from Dutch colony to Japanese-occupied territory to independent nation-state. These transitions of government not only affected the political and economic systems of Java and Bali but also shifted local perspectives on religion, language, and artistic patronage and transmission. Writing in 2010, the first Javanese gamelan teacher in the United States, Hardja Susilo (1934–2015), recalled three major transformations in musical life that occurred during his childhood: the association of musicianship with both professionalism and poverty when he was very young, the suppression of traditional arts under the Japanese during the 1940s, and the reclamation of pride in traditional Javanese performing arts traditions after Indonesian independence in 1945. The post-independence establishment of the governmental conservatory system and Radio Republik Indonesia (RRI) diversified the artistic patronage system, which previously had been centered at the Javanese royal courts. It was only at this time that Susilo, who had been fascinated with the music since his youth, was able to pursue musical studies within the new, democratized system of learning gamelan (H. Susilo 2010).

Although in Bali the historic royal families still held cultural and economic sway, systems of political and economic development and musical patronage continued to be diversified as they were in Java. The backgrounds of the first two Balinese music instructors in the United States, Wayan Gandera (1933–2002) and Cokorda Agung Mas (1920–1988), reflect the competing types of capital that could be obtained during this period. Both were from the Gianyar region of Bali, but they could hardly have had more different social backgrounds. Agung Mas, a hereditary prince, had access to both local and cosmopolitan forms of cultural capital via the formal elements of his upbringing. He hailed from an illustrious Sukawati family, could speak English, and knew some Western music theory, in addition to serving as the lead drummer of the Ubud gamelan. He applied to the Rockefeller Foundation to study Western music in the United States but was brought over by the new Ethnomusicology Institute at UCLA to teach Balinese music as part of an American arts diplomacy program. He was influential in helping Hood locate and procure the UCLA Balinese gamelan. Gandera, the son of I Made Lebah, was born in the neighboring town of Peliatan. Lebah, a member of the sudra caste, had learned English and established international contacts by serving as McPhee's driver and guide; his son had first come to McPhee's attention during the tour of Gamelan Gunung Sari to the United States in the 1950s. Although a commoner, Gandera had connections within his eminent musical family, so he, too, had extensive musical experience within his own banjar and had performed with the Peliatan court ensembles during their waning years. Both musicians were given permission to pursue study at the university in exchange for lending their expertise as teachers of the traditional performing arts.

Ruby Ornstein, who studied with Gandera, Agung Mas, and Hood at UCLA in the early 1960s, recalled the pair of Balinese instructors as being foils to each other in character: Agung Mas was a man of "poise and dignity," Gandera, "full of charm and mischief" (2006, 143). A video recording from the online UCLA video archive that shows them demonstrating the opening lines of "Legong Kraton" bears out her impressions. They are dressed the same, in collared white shirts with matching striped skinny ties. Both sit at the gangsas, keyed metallophone instruments that play an elaborated melody. Agung Mas, performing the part of the leader, plays the leading *ugal* part with a workmanlike expression; Gandera plays the follower, grinning to himself as he strikes the keys. Like the duality between polos and sangsih, the magnetic duality of their personas and their contrasting claims to expertise and social capital shaped the program.

The lines of funding that brought Agung Mas and Gandera to California were explicitly envisioned as a method of exercising American political soft power (McGraw 2013a, 31–38). The consolidation of the Indonesian nation after the declaration of independence in 1945 occurred at the same time as the beginnings of the Cold War. The new Indonesian state was already facing internal pressure to unite a vast archipelago of approximately six thousand inhabited islands, each with its own linguistic and cultural heritage, and to help the nation recover from the more immediate effects of Japanese occupation and the more long-term effects of colonization by the Netherlands. The first president of Indonesia, Sukarno, positioned Indonesia firmly within the global Non-Aligned Movement and as a result was able to secure aid from both the Sino-Soviet and Western Bloc countries. However, following the adoption of Demokrasi

Terpimpin (Guided Democracy) in 1957—a system that blended principles of traditional village government, common across many of the islands' ethnic groups, with Chinese-style communism—Western powers felt that Indonesia was slipping away from them. Artistic exchanges and the funding and establishment of new radio networks were among the cultural tools that the United States used to curry influence in the early 1960s.

After their fellowships ended by the mid-1960s, Agung Mas and Gandera returned to Bali—but major political changes were under way that would open the door to more long-lived Indonesian American artistic partnerships. The pivotal year in this transition was 1965. After the adoption of the Demokrasi Terpimpin model, political tensions had been building for several years between the three most powerful factions in the country: the Indonesian army, Islamic groups, and the nation's multiple distinct communist parties, the last of which had increasingly been supported by Sukarno and which had begun to undertake rural looting campaigns (Ricklefs 2008; Robinson 1998). After an intermilitary coup killed six Indonesian generals in the 30 September Movement (Gerakan 30 September), General Suharto took control of the army in order to put down the coup. Members of the Indonesian Communist Party (Partai Komunis Indonesia, or PKI) were blamed, and in retaliation, in the fall of 1965, members and suspected associates of the party were massacred in a wave of killings that spread across the islands for several months, resulting in the deaths of more than half a million Indonesians. The perpetrators of the killings, though Indonesian, were clandestinely supported by the United States government in an attempt to counteract Chinese communist influence in Indonesia. Bali, home to Sukarno's mother's family and one of his main bases, which was built above the holy spring Tampaksiring, had been hit particularly hard by the massacre. His supporters in Bali killed approximately eighty thousand Balinese (about 5 percent of the island's population) who were suspected of being affiliated with the PKI. As a community, the performing artists whose very bodies had been portrayed as symbols of Sukarno's power were disproportionately affected by the Communist purge.

In the aftermath of this turbulent power struggle, Suharto seized the nation's highest office in 1968. He consolidated power through a series of five-year plans that applied top-down pressure on the population, including those in the performing arts. Local social and cultural practices with their unruly and potentially contentious variations were suppressed in favor of codified versions of the same practices (a not uncommon practice at the time in Asian countries in political transition; see Howard 2014). So revised, regional Indonesian culture was presented for consumption both by Indonesians and by foreign visitors (for example, see Pemberton 1994; Vickers 2012). With their close associations with ethnicity and religion and their ability to compellingly showcase diversity, the performing arts became a potent site for such policy making during the Suharto era, particularly as public expression became increasingly governed by the establishment of conservatories, state-run arts bureaus, and media outlets (Fraser 2015; Harnish 2005; Weintraub 2004).

During this political transition into the Orde Baru (New Order) government (1966–1998) led by Suharto, Indonesia became more closely allied (if not formally aligned) with the West, and the Indonesian and American governments fostered more elaborate political and cultural exchange systems. In artistic terms, this shift was represented mainly by the presentation of codified versions of Indonesian culture for foreign audiences. At the same time as the volatile political situation in Indonesia shifted toward a stronger alliance with the United States, the introduction of the Immigration and Nationality Act of 1965 (enacted in 1968) vastly restructured the way visas were granted, in general loosening restrictions on immigration from Asian counties. Though Indonesian immigration to the United States was never as prevalent as that to other locales, particularly Australia, the enactment of such a new social policy allowed the Indonesian population in the United States to grow and flourish.

The challenges of being an Indonesian teacher during this period are revealed in Susilo's experience of pedagogical challenge (Harnish, Solís, and Witzleben 2004) and of personal challenge. In comments published in 2010, a half century after he became the first permanent Javanese gamelan teacher at UCLA, Susilo recalled the following about his initial experiences working in the United States:

> I entered UCLA in the fall of 1958. Indonesia was a very young country, so that, understandably not too many educated people at UCLA knew where Indonesia was. Some thought I was from Indochina, a.k.a. Vietnam, some asked if Indonesia was part of Bali, and several times the immigration officers mistook me for an illegal alien from Mexico. Many Mexicans themselves were sure that I was Mexican—in fact, one of them disliked me so much because he thought that I was a Mexican who had turned my back on my heritage by pretending not to speak Spanish, and "by putting on a phony accent." To make things worse, my close friends called me by my nickname, "Sus." When they called to me from a distance they would yell, "Hey Sus!," which in Southern California suggested the Spanish name "Jesus." I mused, "I am a Moslem. How could they think my name was Jesus?!"
>
> But in retrospect, the culture shock I experienced in 1958 was mild compared to the shock that Americans experienced in the following decades. Anyone who was more socially aware than I was would have known that America was about to

> undergo a cultural revolution. Even an outsider like myself could see the beginning of change in the social and moral outlook of UCLA students when they elected Rafer Johnson, a Negro (as they referred to African-Americans at that time), to be the president of their student body. By 1958 the House Un-American Activities Committee (HUAC) had lost its fearsome power. The study of folk music of America and of any other parts of the world was no longer associated with a clandestine leftist movement. (2010, 48)

Susilo's comments, given to preface the explanation of specific pedagogical techniques he adapted at the time, describe his presence in Los Angeles not only at the juncture of individual cross-cultural experiences but also within a greater framework of cultural negotiation that resonated throughout the arts and, indeed, throughout the United States. Once the province of "clandestine leftists," teaching and learning world music gradually became a more acceptable site of individual enrichment, cultural exchange, and contested representation.

The next generation of Indonesian gamelan teachers would be the ones to solidify the patterns of Indonesian American artistic and pedagogical exchange that continue largely to this day. They arrived after the return of Gandera and Agung Mas to Indonesia. Among the first of this generation was I Made Bandem (b. 1945). After completing undergraduate studies in Bali and with several years of teaching under his belt, Bandem arrived at the East-West Center at the University of Hawaii in 1968 on a scholarship from the Rockefeller Fund to study dance. He continued his studies with Mantle Hood at UCLA (BA 1970, MA 1972) and Fredrik Eugene deBoer at Wesleyan (PhD 1980). Bandem's continued influence as a teacher, administrator, and politician in Bali and then as a teacher in the United States played a significant role in shaping transnational artistic communities (Goodlander 2013). The artists I Nyoman Wenten and his wife Nanik Wenten—who at the time of writing are continuing in longstanding permanent teaching residencies at UCLA, CalArts, and other institutions in California—were first invited for workshops in 1972 (Denny 2009), in part owing to the influence of the Javanese teacher K. P. H. Notoprojo (best known in the United States as Pak Cokro), one of the earliest Javanese music teachers in the Americas. These teachers paved the route for others whose specific generational training and careers embody substantial shifts in both Balinese and American artistic and pedagogical systems.

Lasmawan: Education and Opportunities in the New Order

Though born during the Sukarno presidency, Lasmawan was just young enough that much of his education and artistic experience took place in the context of the New Order government. During his childhood it was expected that any performance training and career be locally based, not necessarily extending to Java, much less to another continent. When Lasmawan was young, Bangah's only public ensembles were the sacred *gamelan semar pegulingan/pelegongan* and later the village gong kebyar. Ensemble membership was not open; instead, the members (all male, as is traditional) were chosen by the community to present music as a form of *ngayah*, devotional service, within religious contexts. Yet Lasmawan's family was already playing a key role in forging more secular artistic connections that reached beyond the banjar. His father, I Wayan Rinjin, was a drummer who led members of his own sanggar in performing genres that were popular at the time, including *janger*, *joged bumbung*, and *drama gong*. Rinjin had also studied *gender wayang batel* in Apuan, and Lasmawan's uncle I Nyoman Kembang had studied northern-style gamelan gong kebyar in Munduk, thereby bringing a more diverse set of musical styles to the village. Because of these familial connections, Lasmawan was permitted to join both the sanggar and the banjar gamelan at a young age, learning a wide array of repertoire from the beginning.

Lasmawan's formal primary and secondary education brought a more regionalized and institutionalized approach to his musical study. The music teachers were all young graduates of the high school–level conservatory of the performing arts who brought with them musical styles such as kecak that had not been performed in the area before then. Lasmawan remembers several of the teachers as hailing "from far away, almost twenty miles" to the west or the south of Baturiti. One of these teachers convinced Lasmawan, in spite of his early passion for mathematics, to enroll at KOKAR, the high school arts conservatory, and move to Denpasar. He was the first student from Bangah—and, indeed, the Baturiti region—to attend the school.[2]

Diversity in performing arts genres was a hallmark of education at KOKAR at the time. Although they were pursuing a single specialty, music students learned a broad program of gamelan gong kebyar, gamelan semar pegulingan, gamelan pelegongan, *gamelan gambuh*, Javanese gamelan, and Western music and had to demonstrate a basic proficiency in Balinese dance. The school's profile represented a mix of traditional Balinese, pan-Indonesian, and Western pedagogical values and experiences. By the early 1970s, conservatory founders and *seniman alam* ("natural artists," those without formal degrees) I Wayan Beratha and I Nyoman Rembang, luminaries in composition and performance in gong kebyar and pelegongan, taught alongside younger colleagues such as I Wayan Sinti, who had been one of the first of Bali's conservatory graduates in the early 1960s. Though the musical experiences offered at the conservatory were diverse, they were not comprehensive, nor did they represent the variations in interpretation found in the different regional styles or specialized repertoires that had developed across Bali. In addition to working with this wide array of faculty during class time, Lasmawan traveled to other areas of the island to learn from great teachers in the villages, including I Gede Manik of Singaraja, I Wayan Tembres of Gianyar, I Gusti Ketut Sedahan of Karangasem, and I Nyoman Sumandhi of Tabanan, each known for his expertise in specific repertoires.

Given his previous playing experience and access to learning opportunities outside the conservatory, Lasmawan remembers initially doubting his choice to pursue higher education in the arts because he could not see the benefit of the formal degree. He recalls:

> The second year at conservatory, I was confused, because my brain was a mathematical brain. I was good at mathematics from elementary school until middle school. And after that, I switched to "culture brain, history brain," you know? And I was confused at second year at the conservatory, so I quit. I quit the school and came to Bangah thinking, "Why am I going to the conservatory? I already know how to play gamelan. I'm good at playing gamelan, so why do I study there? I can study by myself at home." I had a little bit of a big head, you know, because I had performed when I was eight years old, I had already performed for the public.
>
> So, for one month I stayed home when suddenly I was surprised by a lot of motorcycles that came to the village. I think it was eight motorcycles with fifteen of my classmates—one seat was empty. My classmates said, "Made, you have to go to Denpasar." I was a drummer at the conservatory, you know. "We need a drummer, we need you, please come back." And after that, I asked my mom, I got rice, you know, and brought three kilograms of rice on the front of the motorcycle; and I brought garlic, onion, the other vegetables, because at that time when you went to Denpasar, usually you brought that for your food, you know.
>
> When I got to Denpasar, my teacher said[,] "Made, whatever you do in this world, if you do it correctly with your full dedication and with all of your time—and if you do not forget to ask for blessing and direction from the gods—you're going to be able to take care of your future life." I always remembered that. I still believe that whatever your choice—if you want to become a business person, or to be a doctor, or a police officer, or to be an athlete—if you do it with your full feeling and your full knowledge, then you're going to be successful. So after that, I went back to school and I forgot about mathematics. (2012b)

For a little while, mathematics still seemed to be on the horizon for Lasmawan; he applied to Udayana University in Denpasar after his graduation from KOKAR and planned to attend college there. Before he finalized his enrollment, however, he received a letter from Akademi Seni Karawitan Indonesia (ASKI) in Surakarta (Solo), Java, offering an opportunity to study Central Javanese gamelan while teaching Balinese gamelan.[3] It was a relatively rare opportunity; very few Balinese students had previously pursued formal study in Java. Lasmawan accepted the offer and went to Java, where he studied Javanese court gamelan in the Surakarta (Solonese) style with teachers inside and outside the conservatory. With each of these teachers he worked on instrumental technique, ensemble technique, and theory. The music and its traditions subsequently became deeply ingrained in him. Although he has had fewer opportunities for Javanese musical performance than for Balinese music during his life in the United States, Lasmawan still has a lot of fondness for his years spent in Java and for the styles of music he studied there, which he still sees as containing "the roots of Balinese gamelan," particularly in relation to music theory.

The opportunity to teach Balinese gamelan in Java provided Lasmawan with his first chance to teach in a formal educational setting and to teach non-Balinese students. Although Lasmawan's Javanese students had never before attempted to play Balinese gamelan, he was able to teach much as he had taught in Bali; the students learned quickly by rote, already having the basic coordination in their hands and the fundamental sounds in their ears. In talking about that time, he notes, laughing, that "for most of the Javanese, the technique carried over to Balinese [gamelan] . . . they just had to learn how to play fast" (Lasmawan 2012b). He was given a strict syllabus to follow, including what was deemed to be essential repertoire for the types of gamelan the institution possessed—gong kebyar, pelegongan, angklung, and joged bumbung.

In addition to teaching, Lasmawan also performed with the arts collectives Yayasan Kesenian Surakarta and Seniman Muda Surakarta and with groups from other universities including Universitas Sebelas Maret, and played for RRI. Just as he had immersed himself in classic genres, Lasmawan also became involved in the early *musik kontemporer* (contemporary or avant-garde music) scene in Surakarta, working with other students and young composers to create works that modified the playing techniques of Javanese and Balinese gamelans, as well as mixing elements of both styles together.

He graduated from Institut Seni Indonesia Surakarta with a *sarjana satu* degree (S1, the equivalent of an American bachelor's degree) in 1981 and a *sarjana dua* (S2, the equivalent of an American master's degree) in 1983. Thereafter, he continued to lecture at ASKI and then ISI in Surakarta throughout the late 1980s, performing with his local groups and touring throughout the country in government-sponsored programs. He also joined others from ASKI (later STSI) to tour in Singapore, Malaysia, Japan, and Europe via governmental cultural diplomacy programs.

The late 1980s were a productive time for Lasmawan, both personally and professionally. He married Siti Maryuni in Java, and in 1989 she gave birth to the first of Lasmawan's three sons, Putu Hiranmayena. (In the mid-1990s, he was divorced and married his current wife Ni Ketut Marni, a well-known dancer from an established Singapadu arts family who was educated at SKMI, formerly called KOKAR. She was deemed a good match for teaching the Balinese arts; she is also the mother of his two younger sons, Ade and Aji.) Lasmawan was also busy teaching and touring. During one of these tours he met the American ethnomusicologist Robert Brown. This chance encounter would set Lasmawan on an entirely new path. Brown had long since moved on from Wesleyan, where he had established the world music area in the 1960s and had been teaching at San Diego State University for more than ten years. When he met Lasmawan, he was looking for an instructor to work with the university's Balinese and Javanese ensembles. He invited Lasmawan to become the guest teacher for the ensembles. After much consideration, Lasmawan decided to take the job, and he asked for the time off from teaching at the conservatory in Surakarta. It was one of several international job offers that he had received in recent years. But the response he had received from his employers at ISI-Surakarta had not been positive. He recalls,

> In 1986, I almost got a job in the UK—but the head of my school in Java, they wouldn't let me take it. And also, this American opportunity, they don't let me go because you know, they hoped I'd stay in Java. San Diego State already sent the contract three times . . . but they sent it to the office [at ISI], you know, and they don't let me—ahhh! You know—[the San Diego State people said,] "I send the contract three times, why do you not come?" And so I'm [saying,] "I did not get any contract! Send it to my house!" And after that, they send it to my house, and I just go to America, and I get a visa, and go by myself. Same with Tokyo, Tokyo University, and London—which one is it in London? Southampton. Yeah, I almost got the job there. But finally I landed in America. (Lasmawan 2012a)

He moved his family and began teaching in California in January 1990, moving to Colorado less than three years later. It was the beginning of a three-decade journey as one of the most pedagogically prolific Indonesian musicians in the United States. Lasmawan views his path of teaching and performance as a fulfillment of his own specific *dharma*, a calling based on his personal and family history, his skills, and his temperament that helps maintain the stability and harmony of the universe. While he would be the first to recognize and honor the teaching accomplishments of his peers across the country, since he believes that no one group is better than another, and no one teacher; they all grow from a different time, place, and situation (*desa, kala, patra*)—his long-standing musical presence throughout the Rocky Mountain region makes his career unique.

Lasmawan's Education: Normative and Exceptional

Relatively few Balinese musicians, either seniman alam or those trained in a conservatory, become professional music teachers. Lasmawan recalls,

> Not many became a music teacher like me. I would say, from sixty that graduated with me—maybe ten percent got a faculty position in music, the rest of them got some other job—a banker, a police officer, a congressman, because at the time, you know, there was a lot of open work that you were able to do in Bali. . . . About the professor/faculty, it's not many, but of course when you are faculty, you can be teaching at ISI-Denpasar, or ISI-Solo, or Udayana University, but that's only a small amount of the situations [that are available]. (2012b)

Teaching the performing arts in the United States and beyond had opened a set of new career opportunities previously unavailable to Indonesian musicians, but certain types of artistic training and personal proclivities were needed to take advantage of such opportunities. Given the distinctiveness of Lasmawan's calling, it is striking that other Balinese musicians of that generation who have had long careers in the United States followed paths containing key similarities.

Lasmawan's musical education demonstrates the transition of educational norms in Bali during the mid-twentieth century from being village-based to centering more on conservatory culture, a pattern largely shared by his contemporaries. From his teachers, all preservers of and innovators in Balinese musical and pedagogical styles, Lasmawan received training in a musical lineage outside that of his family and village, with influences stretching back to some of the great artists of the early twentieth century: I Wayan Lotring, I Wayan Regog, I Nyoman Kaler, I Wayan Gurindam, and others. Although KOKAR had been founded more than ten years before Lasmawan's enrollment, and it was already common for aspiring young musicians to study there, the fact that he was still the only student from his home region indicates that his presence was a bit of an anomaly. The additional study that Lasmawan pursued outside KOKAR, while not unusual, was purposeful and extensive. And although it is more common for students to learn a musical style primarily under one teacher and Lasmawan himself encourages his students to master the lessons of one teacher before moving on to the next, he consistently sought out other perspectives on his playing.

Studying at Bali's conservatories at the high school or collegiate level presented a new educational pathway that differed substantially from the method of continuous apprenticeship under different seniman alam. The foundation of the conservatories shifted the overall structure of the Balinese arts educational system. Initially modeled more closely on the Dutch educational system than on the American one, early components of the system represented substantive shifts toward contemporaneous Western practices, including teaching from standardized repertoires, creating written notation for Balinese gamelan music, accepting women to study gamelan, and teaching dance in mirrored studios (Umeda 2007). Further pedagogical effects included the ways in which students expected to interact with their instructors; for example, in examining the difference between village-based and conservatory-based methods for teaching *wayang kulit*, Brita Heimarck noticed a difference in teaching style. Students at the conservatory receive more formalized courses and are expected to ask more questions of their teachers (2003, 147–184).

In part, the difference involved exposure to a broad and consistent set of ensemble types. I Wayan Sinti, one of the conservatory's first graduates, who became an instructor there and a longtime guest composer and instructor in the United States, recalled that at KOKAR in the early 1960s, core instrumental genres included *gong gede*, gong kebyar, angklung, semar pegulingan, and gender wayang. Dance students all practiced a range of styles from ancient to modern including *legong kebyar, legong kraton, arja, sendratari, topeng, baris, jauk, Barong, gambuh,* and *janger* (J. Diamond 1985). This widespread development of genre, coupled with unification of musical styles and standardization of curricula, presented an integrated sense of Balinese musical language as well as largely avoiding regional conflicts over artistic style. Though Balinese artists teaching abroad are not regularly called on to teach advanced students, they may be asked or feel creatively inspired to teach or perform many genres of music and dance alike, often without substantive support from other expert artists; for this reason training as a generalist is essential to meeting such demands. For Lasmawan, that has meant teaching not only different varieties of Balinese gamelan but also the basics of male dance and shadow puppetry.

For members of Lasmawan's generation and beyond, training and teaching within the conservatories also proved to be important for making professional contacts and documenting a level of credentials that would be transferable, at least to some degree, outside Indonesia. Since the 1970s, nearly every Balinese musician who has taught regularly in North America had obtained at least a high school level degree from an arts conservatory, which is notable considering that since about 2010, the average high school completion rate in Indonesia has consistently been less than 60 percent. As Bakan (1999) has noted in writing about two of his *beleganjur* (marching gamelan) teachers in Bali in the 1990s, this point of differentiation had substantial impact on the types of opportunities offered to conservatory musicians as compared to seniman alam.

Lasmawan's transition to studying in Java was, as suggested above, a bit unusual at the time in comparison to his peers. Although Balinese had studied there before, Lasmawan's educational background—an almost equal mix of Balinese and Javanese arts—is still an anomaly. Yet his experience there allowed him to benefit from the musical and social capital transmitted both within and outside the conservatory. Many of his teachers (for example, Martopangrawit) came from lineages of musicians who could trace the history of their service to the royal courts back for over a hundred years. Lasmawan's decade-long practice of Javanese music further enhanced his ability to teach flexibly.

Continued study with Indonesian or American musicians or scholars has become a common thread for Balinese teachers in North America, as well. Although he has taken graduate courses, Lasmawan has not yet completed a graduate degree in the United States, as many of his peers have done; he jokes, "I already have a job, why do I need a doctorate?" On moving to California, however, he continued to study Javanese gamelan with Pak Cokro. One of Yogyakarta's most famous Javanese gamelan musicians, Cokro served as a longtime instructor of Javanese gamelan at UCLA and CalArts; he himself had spread a vast network of gamelans across the western half of the United States (Wenten 1996).

International experiences such as touring abroad before settling in the United States were no less central to the careers of the later Balinese teachers than to their predecessors in acclimatizing to the prospect of living abroad. Such tours were largely goodwill projects sponsored by the Indonesian government. Wenten recalls that when he was touring (1964–1967), the group consisted of musicians and dancers from Bali, Java, and Sumatra, and they performed for Mao Tse-tung and Kim Jong Il; the concerts were clearly intended to bolster communist political relationships (Denny 2009). Lasmawan's later six-month residency in Japan demonstrated a continued focus on strengthening relationships within Asia.

The career paths of teachers, whether individuals or, more frequently, couples, follow different routes and structural patterns. For example, Asnawa, who has taught regularly at the University of Illinois at Urbana-Champaign since 2006, was a few years ahead of Lasmawan's class at the conservatory but then spent two and a half decades as a teacher and composer in Bali (Bakan 1999, 192–206) before moving more permanently to the United States. Still, the consistency of types of education, professional experience, and general exposure to foreign connections creates some common elements in the making of an international gamelan teacher.

"Remember your roots": Musical Lineages

In August 2018, Sanggar Manik Galih, the international sanggar run by the Tangkas family with members from Bangah, Colorado, and Lasmawan's other communities, performed at the International Gamelan Festival in Solo, Java. It was the first time in several years that Lasmawan was able to return to the city where he had spent a decade of his life as a learner, teacher, and performer. As the hybrid group of more than twenty Balinese and American musicians ate a late breakfast and prepared to get dressed for our performance at Fort Vastenburg, Lasmawan drove out to visit the gravesite of a beloved teacher of his from college who had passed away. "Remember your roots," Lasmawan had often told his students, both directly and in the many ways in which he would acknowledge and honor those who had helped him long ago. Lasmawan's memories, particularly those of his unforgettable teachers from the 1980s, traveled with us as we joined him in making new ones.

How and to what extent do Indonesian teachers transmit the contents of their formal education and life experience when they teach? How well connected are American students to these lineages of teaching and learning as a result? One way of understanding these types of relationships is via the concept of musical lineage. In Bali, familial relationships form a key part of the structural framework of society. Identifying an individual's family members and place of origin contextualizes that person within the complex interrelated sets of Balinese social signifiers. Although there are many ways in which Balinese society subdivides itself and its lineages, biological kinship—re-creating the standing generational social order—is of prime importance (Geertz and Geertz 1975). For musicians and dancers, the region where they studied is crucial to inflecting their performances with certain types of styles; musical lineages ensure that these styles and genres are passed down to the next generation. Because the different geographic regions in Bali have distinctive musics and specific teachers are renowned for certain repertoires, maintaining and establishing a musical lineage is important (Dibia and Ballinger 2004).

The importance of establishing student-teacher relationships, in a musical-social sense as well as in the types of material transmitted, is understood in musical cultures throughout the world, especially those where musical training has a hereditary element, such as the Wolof griot tradition of Senegal (Tang

2007). Another well-known example of this type of musical lineage tracing can be found in the North Indian classical music traditions, in which *khandan* (family or clan) refers to the bloodlines (from descent or marriage) within musical families. Related to this is the *gharana* system, in which the *guru* (teacher), a descendant of a specific musical lineage, teaches its *raga* (melodic systems) and their associated cultural meanings to his or her students (Ruckert 2004, 36). Individuals perpetuate these lineages by teaching new students; they put their own "stamp" on them through their own musical development (Deshpande 1973, 15). The gharana system was historically associated with royal courts and thus implies certain geographic associations as well (Ruckert 2004, 36).

In Balinese gamelan, characteristic playing styles are handed down from teachers to students, regional stylistic differences are audible in individuals' playing styles, and musicians and spectators alike note the differences in ornamentation or sound of musicians from different regions. Distinctive playing styles, though palpable in performance, are less formally codified in Balinese gamelan lineages than in gharana, and Balinese musicians do not as strictly acknowledge a single distinct lineage as their primary influence. Lasmawan does, however, use the phrase *air mengalir*, which he borrowed from his teacher Martopangrawit, to describe the process of transmission between teachers and students. Literally meaning "running water," the concept can be visualized more as water running over, running through—information passed down that has the same stylistic lineage but also carries the traces of change from each generation of teachers and learners.

Just as the existence of gamelan ensembles in American academic settings was predicated upon a broader change to educational norms, the production of teachers who were skilled and interested in filling these positions was dependent on changes in Indonesian educational structures. Musical connections between Indonesia and the West had been predicated on the dubiously consensual arrangement of international tours by foreign impresarios (such as the case of Java Village), contact based on privileged individual connections with influential outsiders (such as the case of Gandera and Hood), or both, as in the case of the tour arranged by John Coast in the 1950s. While it displaced artistic power structures that had developed over the course of the past half century, the post-independence implementation of formalized arts policies in Indonesia provided both broader access to performing arts training and international performance opportunities for conservatory graduates—even as they also restricted nonformalized opportunities.

Lasmawan's educational background represents an introduction to that era, in which learning in both formal and informal contexts remained key in the education of artists who hoped to have international careers. The possession of personal connections such as Lasmawan's connection with Brown and of university degrees was crucial for obtaining employment outside Indonesia. Being able to learn and teach within different contexts in Bali, Java, and Japan also proved critical for a successful transition to the United States, where—according to the Balinese principle of desa, kala, and patra, that correct action depends on the time, place, and situation—Lasmawan and his peers would find themselves at the center of a network of gamelans with vastly different needs from each other and from those in Indonesia. It was through building on this background and aid from his wife Marni as well as his new American partners that Lasmawan would bring the lessons of his first decades in Indonesia to animate new Balinese gamelan communities abroad.

CHAPTER 4

Creating and Conceptualizing a Balinese American Gamelan Community

"Where are we going, again?" I asked. Lasmawan and I were sitting in my rental car, about to depart for an afternoon and evening's worth of rehearsals. I had used the excuse of attending the 2017 Society for Ethnomusicology conference in Denver, Colorado, to travel there a week early to study new music and shadow Lasmawan as he made his weekly visits to gamelan groups across the state, for which I volunteered to drive. Despite having an expert navigator in my car, I entered the locations in my phone navigation app just in case: We'd leave Colorado Springs after noon, go up to Denver and fight rush-hour traffic to Boulder for two collegiate rehearsals, grab dinner to eat in the car on our way back to the community gamelan rehearsal in Denver, and then return home. Lasmawan had long emphasized to me the importance of having a durable car in teaching gamelan. "Honda is good, they last a long time," he'd said. "Also, did you know you can fit an entire angklung in the back of a Honda CRV?" After only one day making that commute, I understood this preference. As I turned off the highway into the darkened streets of Lasmawan's neighborhood ten hours after we had departed, I recalled that he had once told me that his first kecak teacher had lived near the monkey forest in Tabanan, a distance he described as "far away, almost twenty miles." That distance had felt impossibly far away in the 1960s, but now we had just driven more than two hundred miles in one day.

Performance of gamelan music in North America provides a publicly audible and tangible display of cultural difference by directly evoking Indonesian musical and cultural contexts. Yet much of the true cultural negotiation and adaptation that supports such ensemble education is invisible to the public, the result of years of labor that are not routinely and fully acknowledged. The apparent effortlessness of a high-quality performance in any artistic genre hides the training and work required to produce it. It is a different type of masking, however, that obscures the mechanics of intercultural negotiation—in this case, a veneer of Americanness that makes Indonesian artistic activity seem normative on the surface and thus able to be overlooked unless it is purposefully revealed. For example, a driver heading along a stretch of I-25 would never guess that the Honda in the next lane was carrying more than one ton of Indonesian percussion instruments. Similarly, one would never guess that the beige walls of a suburban duplex in Colorado Springs had contained a small microcosm of Balinese American cultural exchange for more than twenty years.

Inside the home that belonged to I Made Lasmawan and Ni Ketut Marni until 2018, the effect of lives cultivated as transnational teachers and performers was palpable in details both large and small. Walking in the front door, one might have been met with the sound of gamelan music, the latest news from CNN, or a soccer game being broadcast on ESPN. Dance costumes occupied the entire kitchen pantry, leaving no room there for food or cooking implements. It nonetheless was perpetually a place of delicious smells, as the aroma of Marni's preparations of rice, chicken, jackfruit, tempeh, and vegetables competed only with the distinctive sweetness of Balinese incense. A *plangkiran* (a type of shrine) hung in the corner of the living room. Below, on a small table, sat the offerings: fruit and flowers and the remnants of a stick of incense. In addition to these items, daily household offerings in Bali usually contain either a small amount of Indonesian *rupiah* or old Chinese coins. On top of this offering often perched a single American dollar. The framed degrees and certificates that hung on the walls of the house, though many in number, provided little idea of the true expertise of the home's inhabitants, who had spent decades refining their craft of performance and teaching—in particular, teaching students who often begin their studies knowing next to nothing about either Bali or its music and dance.

Colorado might seem an unlikely place to center a network of gamelans. It is far from the Indonesian consulates and their associated cultural attachés in New York, Washington, DC, Chicago, and Los Angeles and far from the academic institutions and community groups that first adopted Balinese gamelans on the

East and West Coasts of North America. The geography of the land, too, makes the region somewhat isolated. Urban areas are far apart. Wide open spaces are interrupted by towering mountain ranges. The weather can make driving difficult because the entire area can receive regular snowfall from September through May. Yet since the arrival of Lasmawan and his family to the area in the early 1990s, the number of gamelan ensembles within a day's drive has expanded from one to more than half a dozen, all interrelated in some way. But what does it mean, in terms of pedagogy and performance, to teach gamelan in this place so far away from Bali? How did so many gamelans arise, and how are they sustained? What are the implications of this network for academic and non-academic communities as well as the musicians within them?

Far from being secluded within an ivory tower, world music programs that have been established in academic institutions have the potential to make a substantial impact in their institutions and in local music communities. This chapter uses the ensembles that Lasmawan and his wife Ni Ketut Marni teach to examine the symbiotic relations between individuals and institutions—academic, community-based, and governmental—that create and sustain extensive gamelan networks. Following a close look at the interactions between these Front Range groups, I compare their structures with those of gamelans in other areas of the country. Continuing with the use of the ecological metaphor, I suggest that gamelan networks are sustained by a complex web of personal and professional relationships that rely not only on present connections but also on past generations of American students and teachers. By specifically examining the way musical and pedagogical partnerships emerge, the chapter expands on prior discussions of gamelan, pedagogy, and representation (Brinner 2016; Solís 2004) to demonstrate how pedagogical reverberations are felt far outside the classroom.

The First Colorado Gamelans

The history of the gamelans in Colorado reveals the degree to which academic, community, and official diplomatic artistic relationships create and reinforce symbiotic systems. By the early 1990s, more than thirty years since the first gamelans had arrived in the United States, new academic and community groups had been established across North America, primarily in urban areas on the coasts. Whereas many had continuously flourished for several decades, others had already fallen into disuse. Such was the case with the instruments that comprised the Denver Gamelan (now Gamelan Tunas Mekar), which first brought Lasmawan to Colorado.

Commissioned in 1974, the Denver Gamelan consisted of instruments for gamelan angklung, a genre that is associated with ritual funeral music in Bali but whose small four-tone instruments are relatively inexpensive, easy to store, and straightforward to play, making it a popular choice for ensembles based outside Bali. The instruments had first been brought to Colorado to be used by the Colorado Women's College (CWC), a private institution whose mission was to provide a western alternative to the prestige and academic prowess of similar women's institutions in the urban Northeast. The gamelan, imported with the assistance of I Made Bandem and Gertrude Rivers Robinson (a student of Hood's), was envisioned as a site for modeling intra-student cooperation such that students of different social and artistic backgrounds could learn to work together toward a unified goal. The instruments contained an older set of keys (considered to be preferable because they are thought to have a better tone quality), which were placed within newly carved wooden bodies. According to the oral history of the group, this gamelan angklung was supposedly the last village gamelan to be sold and exported intact after changes to Indonesian cultural export policy were enacted in the late 1970s to prohibit the exodus of important pieces of Balinese cultural, religious, and artistic heritage. The instruments arrived in 1976 but were not used for long. Owing to financial insolvency, the CWC was merged into the University of Denver in 1982. Like other property previously owned by CWC, the instruments were placed into storage.

Six years later, in 1988, the instruments found a new life. Former CWC student Frankie Anderson and Denver University ethnomusicologist John Trainor, along with percussionists Mark McCoin and Mark Fuller, arranged a musicians' collective to conduct a two-week intensive gamelan workshop with Wayne Vitale, a founding member (and later director) of Gamelan Sekar Jaya. Inspired by the workshop, a small group continued to play afterward, learning primarily from recordings. They traveled together to Bali in 1990, and on that trip I Ketut Madri of Pengosekan renamed the gamelan, thereby giving it a symbolic rebirth. The naming of a gamelan is important in setting the tone for the group; in the case of Tunas Mekar, it was also quite prescient. *Tunas* means "a bit of stored life force"; *mekar* means "to put forth." According to the annotated translation on the Gamelan Tunas Mekar website, the two words compounded carry a more detailed and poetic meaning: "a wayward seed, blown far from the parent plant and landing on unfamiliar soil that has nonetheless produced an amazing flower" (Gamelan Tunas Mekar 2013, n.p.).

That flower began to blossom with Lasmawan's arrival under circumstances that demonstrate that the artistic and the political, heavily mixed in Indonesia, could also be mixed in the United States. Dewi Sukarno—one of the wives of the deposed first president of Indonesia—had been imprisoned after slashing the face of Maria Victoria Osmeña, the socialite granddaughter of former Philippine president Sergio Osmeña, in January 1992. The gamelan in nearby Denver was commissioned to perform for her on the occasion of her release; Lasmawan was flown out from California to lead the group. After he rehearsed with the ensemble for only a day, they performed.

After that unusual beginning, the members of Gamelan Tunas Mekar brought Lasmawan to Colorado again. They borrowed previously unused gamelan gong kebyar instruments that had been donated to Naropa University in Boulder and put on a large concert at the Lamont School of Music. Yet as Tunas Mekar president Michael Fitts recalls, there were several blatant elements of unintentional cultural misappropriation that defined the performance.[1] Several years earlier, on the ensemble trip to Bali, members had commissioned and brought back performance uniforms (black satin-silk jackets and *kebaya*, or women's lace blouses), not knowing at the time that it was fashionable to wear the black garments at cremation ceremonies. In addition to the players' being decked out in these uniforms, ensemble member Dane Terry had decided to make a background for the stage. He had seen a temple gate that he had liked in a book, and so they had constructed an eighteen-foot replica of it and placed it onstage. Terry had not realized, however, that the gate he had copied was that to a *pura dalem*, which is associated with death rituals. "So," Fitts concludes in his telling of the story, "we had put up an eighteen-foot death temple and dressed in black, for a secular performance. I think he [Lasmawan] thought we were nuts! . . . And so we had learned a bunch of kebyar and angklung pieces and put this performance on, with the black shirts and the death temple. And after that Lasmawan was like, 'Yeah, I'm definitely going to come here.' He was literally exhausted and tearing up when he was onstage when we were all done. He just had some strong feeling." He had seen through the group's unintended errors and instead recognized the purity of spirit, energy, dedication, creativeness, and heart of the performers.

Nearly three decades later, Lasmawan still recalls that feeling, primarily in the symbolic relationship that he sees between his two homes, Bangah and Colorado Springs. "Bang" in Balinese denotes a scarlet red. The village of Bangah is named for the *teratai bang*, the red water lotus, symbol of the local temple Pura Pucak Teratai Bang, which sits, moss-covered and framed by palms, near the larger lakefront temple and tourist destination Pura Ulun Danu Bratan at Lake Beratan. Aside from its mountainous location in the shadow of Pikes Peak, the climate and geography of Colorado Springs could hardly seem more different from those of Bali. But then, there is the name Colorado; derived from Spanish,

Gamelan Tunas Mekar performs at the Bali Arts Festival, June 2019

it means "colored red." Red is an important color in the Balinese Hindu religion, along with black and white, and combinations of the three colors can be found throughout temple decorations in Bali. The colors represent the members of the *Trimurti*: Brahma, Vishnu, and Shiva, the creator, preserver, and destroyer of the universe. Red represents Brahma the Creator, the lord of speech and sound; thus, the central presence of red serves symbolically as the fostering of new creations, such as a career in teaching gamelan. Gamelan Tunas Mekar—whose three-decade legacy includes two tours to Bali, an offshoot children's group, Gamelan Anak Manik Galih, and countless performances in Colorado—is emblematic of this transnational legacy.[2]

A Network of Academic Gamelans

The community gamelan had first brought Lasmawan and his family to Colorado, but it was only due to work with university gamelans that he was financially able to remain. The primary funding came from Colorado College, where Victoria (Vicki) Levine, professor of ethnomusicology and specialist in Native

American music, had been teaching since 1988. She believed that establishing a world music ensemble course would be a crucial component of the program. Long fascinated by Balinese gamelan, she requested the help of her friend and colleague David Harnish to purchase a gamelan. With the additional aid of I Wayan Suweca, they were able to procure a Balinese gamelan angklung, whose small range and straightforward traditional repertoire were perceived as assets for instructing a beginning college-level group. Almost at the same time, in the fall of 1992, Levine learned about I Made Lasmawan. He had been invited to audition as the permanent instructor for Tunas Mekar and, following introductions at Colorado College, was selected to work with both groups, with Levine serving for many years as a partner in teaching. Lasmawan began teaching at Colorado College in 1993 and in short order revived Gamelan Eka Mudra (Gesture of Prayer) at Naropa University, finally putting the gamelan to full use; previously, only the gong had been used for the Buddhist school's ceremonies.[3]

At Colorado College, the gamelan ensemble and Balinese dance programs have remained at the core of the world music offerings since they were first offered in the spring of 1993. According to the college's block plan, students take one course at a time over the course of eight blocks per year. Both the music course (taught by Lasmawan and Levine) and the dance section (taught by Marni) run throughout the year, however. Having started with a single Balinese angklung ensemble, Gamelan Tunjung Sari (Essence of the Lotus Flower), the group now also includes a bamboo angklung set, a quartet of gender wayang instruments, a set of gamelan beleganjur instruments, and a Central Javanese court gamelan. Each is named and is used throughout the year by different groups of students depending on their skill levels and proclivities. Gamelan Tunjung Sari features all the current student players; Gamelan Santi Suara (Peaceful Sound), a gender wayang group, has met occasionally when there have been enough advanced students who are interested. The Javanese gamelan, a recent addition, is still played infrequently, most often in conjunction with non-ensemble courses and special events.

Students in the gamelan course may also study dance, but it is rare for students to take both courses at once. For those who do choose to dance, however, the college owns costumes for approximately a dozen different dances—enough for a full undergraduate education in learning new works. The pride of the college's Indonesian performing arts collections, however, are the costumes for two Barong, Bali's mythological protector spirits; they are perhaps the only two Balinese-made Barong costumes in the United States that reside outside the Indonesian embassies. Danced by two people, each Barong costume resembles one of several different types of animals. The college has a *Barong ket*—the most prevalent type, which is lionlike—and a *Barong macan*, the tiger Barong. The Colorado College mascot is a tiger; the corresponding Barong has been danced at every homecoming parade since the costume's arrival in the mid-1990s. The gamelan offers at least two formal concerts on campus per academic year in addition to playing for other events in the university community.

The Colorado College gamelan program has sent participants to study abroad in Bali for more than twenty years. At first, students were housed with Lasmawan's family in Bangah, but the program expanded so much that Lasmawan acquired extra land in the village during the Asian financial crisis and built a compound for the sole purpose of housing students. The program has run every few years since 1997, except in the wake of the Bali bombings in 2002 and for lack of participants in 2009 and 2013. It has run successfully several times since then, co-directed by Lasmawan and the ethnomusicology professor Elizabeth Macy, who has been traveling to Bangah since she was an undergraduate participant in the college's first study abroad program. Marni serves as the main director of dance, with Hiranmayena assisting in recent years. Not only does this field study program serve as an exemplar of the interdisciplinary, global, and engaged learning that is key to the educational objectives of the music department at Colorado College (Levine and Kohut 2017), but it also links together two geographically and culturally different educational sites.

Of the long-term Indonesian teachers who have worked in North America, Lasmawan has been especially prolific in establishing and supporting new groups. Colleagues have referred to him as "the Johnny Appleseed of gamelan in the United States," referring to the American folk hero who traveled the country depositing apple seeds. Lasmawan notes, "Before I move to the USA, there is no gamelan in the middle of America, only in California and East Coast—you know like, New York, Boston, Wesleyan, Washington DC. . . . [I Nyoman] Wenten was performing everywhere, you know." The epicenter of these new programs has been in the area to the north of Colorado Springs. In addition to the two ensembles at Colorado College, Lasmawan also regularly instructs Gamelan Genta Kencana (Holy Golden Sound, a five-tone gamelan angklung, with Jay Keister) at the University of Colorado Boulder and Gamelan Manik Kusuma (Jewel of Good Aura, a four-tone gamelan angklung, with Elizabeth Macy and Peter Cooper) at Metropolitan State University in Denver, visiting each of them approximately once per week. His weekly travel within the state also includes two rehearsals with Gamelan Tunas Mekar in Denver (four-tone gamelan angklung and semaradana).

Other gamelans in the region enter the rotation less frequently but still contribute to an active travel schedule for Lasmawan and those of his family members who come along to teach or perform. Gamelan Candra Wyoga (Meditation on the Meaning of the Full Moon, or Wyoming Gamelan; gamelan semar pegulingan, with Jordan Hayes) at the University of Wyoming in Laramie, a college-and-community group that practices on a weekly basis.[4] A cluster of gamelans in Missoula, Montana, receive visits from Lasmawan and his family on roughly a yearly basis. They include Gamelan Jaya Budaya (Victorious Culture; gamelan angklung, directed by Robert Ledbetter) at the University of Wyoming and in Missoula, a community group, Gamelan Manik Harum (A Powerful Force That Gives You a Good Feeling Like a Pleasant Aroma; gamelan angklung and beleganjur, directed by Dorothy Morrison), and a children's group, Kocong! (Wild Kid Energy), at Lewis and Clark Elementary School. The community ensemble Gamelan Raga Garnita (Joyful Heart, directed by Rodney Garnett), founded in 2017 in Black Hills, South Dakota, is the latest addition to this regional cluster of ensembles. More far-flung programs led by American teachers who have studied with Lasmawan round out each semester's schedule;

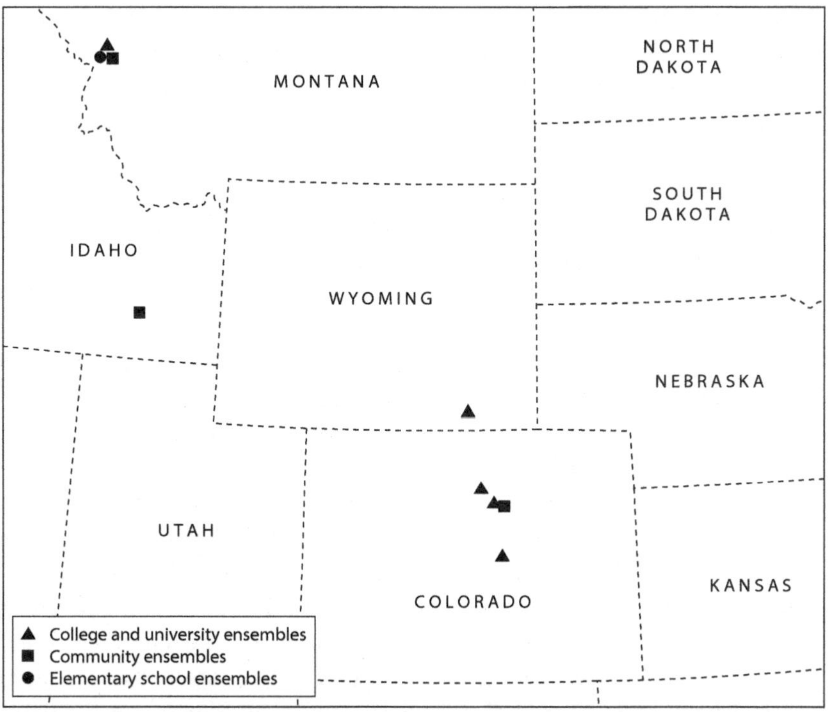

Gamelan ensembles taught long-term by the Tangkas family in the Rocky Mountain region. Cartography by Bill Nelson.

for example, he maintains connections to the gamelans at Emory University and at Wake Forest University that I initiated. Over the course of the past three decades, Lasmawan has worked with or established Balinese gamelan ensembles in almost two dozen states. Though he has begun to pare down his weekly visits to more distant groups and increasingly delegates more to local teachers, at earlier points in his career he drove up to one thousand miles per week, performing with various academic and community groups more than two dozen times per year—indeed, sometimes as much as two dozen times per semester.

Founding and Supporting Gamelan Programs

In visiting established gamelan programs such as many of those in the Front Range, it is difficult for an outsider to see anything but their successes—ambitious concert programs and dedicated and smiling students. Founding new gamelan programs and building a regular, dedicated flow of student or community musicians is not easy, however. Even for those who specialize in the Balinese performing arts the process of establishing a gamelan can be intimidating. From seeking approval to finding funds to finding performance space to encouraging new musicians to join, the process takes months, if not years, though sometimes it all comes together more quickly than expected. For example, the ethnomusicology professor Sonja Downing, who specializes in Balinese performing arts and who is married to the Balinese musician Dewa Ketut Alit Adnyana, told me that establishing a thriving gamelan had been a dream portion of their "ten-year plan" as a couple working together, and they were surprised and pleased that it instead happened almost immediately after she was hired at Lawrence University.

In recent years, external reviews from general or music-based accrediting bodies have proved instrumental in promoting non-Western music ensembles on campus. Adding a gamelan can provide a visible and audible answer to demands for cultural diversity. For example, Jeremy Grimshaw, founder of Gamelan Bintang Wahyu (Star of Vision) at Brigham Young University (BYU), who has collaborated regularly with Lasmawan, cited the university's response to a 2005 review by the National Association of Schools of Music as instrumental to increasing the number of non-Western music courses offered on campus, including the creation of his own position and the founding of their gamelan ensemble. He chose gamelan because he had played in one at Eastman University and subsequently founded a gamelan angklung group, Gamelan Dwara Udyani (Doorway to the Mountain), when he taught at Denison University in Ohio. This prior study of the music and practical, logistical university experience proved sufficiently convincing to obtain support for a new group at BYU.

The logistical difficulty of obtaining instruments, the cost, and the storage space all present challenges for Americans seeking to acquire them. The cost of purchasing and shipping a gamelan, though less than that of buying other equipment like a grand piano, can still run between a few thousand dollars for the small Balinese gender wayang to nearly fifty thousand dollars for a complete Javanese gamelan. Grimshaw recalls that he researched the possible costs of purchasing a gamelan, ranging from a small angklung to a large semaradana, which was his preference. He notes that when he presented that figure to the search committee when he first was interviewed, "they didn't even blink"; they were much more concerned about where the instruments would be stored and used. Grimshaw recalls, "It took me a few weeks to find the money to buy the gamelan. It took me a year, while they were making the gamelan, to figure out where we were going to put it and when we were going to rehearse" (2016).

The process of a new acquisition can itself be tricky. The instruments are first commissioned from one of the handful of major gong shops in Bali. Because keys and instrument cases are made to order, placing the order and negotiating the appropriate price, payment schedule, and construction schedule present the first challenge—one that must usually be accomplished in person. Payment in cash or by money transfer is common, since credit cards, though sometimes accepted, are not widely used in traditional places of business in Indonesia, especially for items as large as a gamelan. A busy gong shop may take months to begin and then complete a single large foreign order. After the order is completed, the instruments must be wrapped and packed in crates, routed through one or more Indonesian ports, and shipped to a port in the United States. Then, import fees must be paid and arrangements made for overland shipping of the crates of instruments to their destination. Even with the help of a native musician in haggling, arranging for payment, and transferring instruments, opportunities for costly errors lurk at every stage, especially at the customs office, where shifting importation regulations and lack of knowledge about the instruments can lead to misjudgments about the legality of their materials of construction and the estimation of their value.

Before their departure from Bali or after they reach their new home, the instruments are given a naming ceremony that includes a concert performed on them. The gong, which is believed to hold the spirit or soul of the ensemble, is officially bestowed with a name and ritually blessed before it is officially played for the first time. As incense burns, a ritual offering is dedicated to the gods and the officiant offers prayers for the instruments and sprinkles holy water over the instruments and the seated musicians. Then the concert begins, consecrating the ensemble with its own sound and introducing it to its new community. In the United States, the native musician who administers the ceremony often remains a sponsor of the ensemble, either teaching it regularly or assisting the primary ensemble leader from afar. In addition to ensembles that native Indonesians directly teach, the mentor relationship created by co-founding a gamelan provides another sort of social and pedagogical dependency within the American gamelan ecosystem.

Partners in Performance

Lasmawan and his work are the thread connecting all these ensembles; however, they could not have thrived for so long without the dedication and support of others. Each of the academic and community ensembles depends heavily on the work of partners who take care of logistical matters and perform cultural negotiation. Levine's initial advocacy and continued support was necessary to create a permanent teaching position for Lasmawan, find funding for new supplies for the Colorado College gamelan, help with visa issues, procure raises for him, and generally develop and maintain the ensemble course. Macy has arranged the logistical support for their recent co-taught study abroad programs. Fitts and Frederickson have housed the instruments and provided a free place for Gamelan Tunas Mekar to rehearse for more than two decades. Other Balinese and American musicians and teachers have served as guest performers, assisted in fundraising, and played other varied roles with respect to their own ensembles. Yet it is Marni's work, built on decades of transnational performance experience, that most strongly reinforces and sustains the musical and social lives of the ensembles.

Born in 1973 in the banjar of Kebon in the village of Singapadu, Ni Ketut Marni began to study dance with an aunt at the age of six or seven. Despite an inauspicious first performance at the temple—"I was still wearing my sandals! I forgot [to take them off] because that was my first time to perform onstage," Marni told me, laughing—she excelled in her dance studies. She began to travel at a young age with a local group that performed kecak at tourist venues along the island's southern coast, gradually working her way through learning the different roles, and continued to study dance more formally in middle school. At that time, she also joined the mixed-gender extracurricular gamelan class. Marni enrolled in SMKI, where she studied under Ni Ketut Arini (b. 1943), one of the most renowned dancers of her generation. In addition to dancing regularly as a form of ngayah in Singapadu, she had several prestigious performance opportunities, including dancing Legong and Tenun with the ensemble from Gianyar (the regency in which Singapadu is located) at the Bali Arts Festival.

It was alongside Arini that Marni took her first trips abroad in the mid-1990s, first to Japan, before her high school graduation, then for several longer periods to perform in Taiwan. Back in Bali, she taught dance alongside Arini in several banjar and at Sanggar Puri Saraswati, a Japanese-owned club in Singapadu that hosted as many as four hundred children on a weekly basis. Arini also proved to be the person who brought Marni and Lasmawan together. Before the couple met in Bali, Arini helped Marni make regular trips to a *wartel* (public phone facility) so that she could talk to Lasmawan. "He kept calling, kept calling me" perhaps dozens of times, Marni says, before they finally met, began to date, and married.

Lasmawan's current network of gamelans was for the most part established by the time Marni arrived in the United States at the end of the 1990s, but Marni's ability to teach and to perform as a dancer and increasingly also as a musician provided new artistic and pedagogical possibilities, as well as reinforcing those already available. Though she admits that she was at first afraid to go to social outings because she couldn't speak English well yet, teaching and performance proved to be less stressful. The students could "just follow" what she was doing, and since she had performed for tourists extensively when she was younger, the feeling of performing for American audiences was familiar. It was only trying to dance to the sound of the four-tone gamelan angklung that proved difficult; it is a common choice for American institutions owing to its small size and low cost, but it was unconventional in Bali (particularly a few decades ago) to use such instruments to perform dance repertoire intended for the larger gamelan gong kebyar.

Teaching and performing dance for all the academic and community ensembles is an occupation involving hours of rehearsal and costume preparation on its own. Marni also takes care of the traditional duties of a Balinese wife, however, including cleaning, ensuring that offerings are made for her household and for performances, and cooking for familial and community events. When time within her busy schedule has permitted, she has held outside jobs in hospitality, where her strong work ethic and job performance have made her much in demand. Finally, she has worked with Lasmawan to raise all three of their sons, who themselves have served as "ringer" musicians, dancers, and teachers with the college ensembles since the time they were old enough to hold mallets; as they have grown older, they have gradually had increased responsibilities in the groups.

I Made Lasmawan on kendang and Ni Ketut Marni (both front left) in performance with Gamelan Candra Wyoga

In Bali, it is the *sekaa* (club) that provides the most immediate support for a gamelan, but ultimately the sekaa depends on members of the banjar (for example, wives of male sekaa members) whose underlying support is necessary to maintain the ensemble community. In America, though there are no direct corollaries to the Balinese social and artistic structure, a modified version of this structure that incorporates the collaborative principles of both banjar and sekaa extends between and beyond the boundaries of individual ensembles.

Interdependency in a Network of Gamelans

The extent of the network of gamelans that Lasmawan teaches is extraordinarily large, but not anomalous in an artistic and educational world where teachers are few and far between yet demand is relatively high and consistent for native ones. There are positions for at least half-time gamelan teachers, for example, in academic institutions such as the College of the Holy Cross and the Robert E. Brown Center for World Music at the University of Illinois at Urbana-Champaign, or the annual residency offered by the semiprofessional community group Gamelan Sekar Jaya. But ensemble instruction is more often either considered a component of another academic appointment or treated as adjunct labor. As a result, other Indonesian gamelan teachers continue to work with a multitude of ensembles. For example, the Wentens regularly make a circuit to colleges and universities in California, albeit smaller than Lasmawan's, and I Nyoman Suadin travels a route that extends from Washington, DC, to upstate New York to teach. Others—for example, I Nyoman Saptanyana and I Gusti Ngurah Kertayuda, who are officially cultural attachés for the Indonesian embassies in New York City and Chicago, respectively—have also taken on teaching and performance work in their local areas. American professors of gamelan generally instruct only one or two ensembles as a part of their teaching schedule and rarely take on such travel-heavy teaching schedules, but they often rely on their connections to Indonesian teachers for collaborations or infusions of new material.

A gamelan network like the one connected to Lasmawan, though somewhat atypical in its geographic distribution and the variety of gamelan styles included, suggests a type of potential for the impact and relatedness of an academic world music ensemble that transcends the boundaries of the classroom, a type of symbiosis that allows gamelans as organisms to flourish to a much greater extent together than on their own. The presence of a professional who is willing to travel regionally allows ensembles to flourish in areas where they would face substantial difficulty otherwise, for example, in Montana. In addition, the connection of each of the academic ensembles to the more professional-level community ensemble Gamelan Tunas Mekar has benefits for student and community musicians.

The depth of this interrelationship between academic and non-academic ensembles appeared especially relevant to me in discussions about Tunas Mekar with members of that group. The ensemble is semiprofessional in that it can perform frequently and primarily performs paid gigs. Yet unlike some of its peer organizations in large urban areas, Tunas Mekar does not require auditions of its members, and players contribute monthly dues voluntarily, at a flexible rate, which is a point of pride for the group, one that, they feel, marks them as a true community-based ensemble. Instead, new members pledge that they will be diligent with their participation, including regular and enthusiastic attendance at the twice-weekly rehearsals and the regular performances that the group undertakes. Any fees earned from the performances go to expenses, Lasmawan's family, and payment of other guest artists. While this practice makes membership in Tunas Mekar more accessible, it means that ultimately the ensemble depends on its artistic directors' being able to make a sufficient living from sources of income other than directing the community group—historically, pay from university teaching.

Though sometimes paid for their assistance, the ensemble members frequently assist with the academic groups for fun or in thanks for the continued opportunity to play in Gamelan Tunas Mekar. Although he is technically a member only of Tunas Mekar, Fitts has also performed with many of Lasmawan's other groups. He notes, "At the beginning, when university groups weren't as well-attended, Tunas Mekar members were ringers to fill in student performances. He'd tell us just a few days before the performance . . . but people wouldn't know if they were going to play polos or sangsih, gangsa or reyong . . . they'd just be stuck in the holes, rehearse it through, and pull it off." Owing to the longevity of Gamelan Tunas Mekar, the availability of musicians to fulfill this role has remained consistent and even expanded. Highly skilled musicians who can play any part, including more difficult leadership roles on ugal or kendang, help teach the pieces that the college students are learning.

In return, the local academic programs serve as a crucial source of new members for Gamelan Tunas Mekar. Fitts notes:

> They're like AAA baseball, and we're the major leagues. . . . when [Lasmawan] finds somebody who's really switched on, he asks them, "So—do you want to come rehearse with Tunas Mekar?" [It is often] people who are really musicians and composers, really wondering what it's about.

The structure of the gamelan system in Colorado exemplifies interdependency in membership, but also an intriguing form of patronage and compensation that is a hybrid between typical American university pay structures, with a specific term of employment and a contract, and Balinese systems of exchange, in which long-term relationships are built on recurring cycles of favors. Lasmawan and Marni are supported primarily by a single patron, Colorado College. Secondary patrons include the other academic gamelan programs where they teach. Their income is further supplemented by guest teaching and performances elsewhere. These facets of this gamelan network are transactional and allow institutional support to subsidize the temporary nature of college careers. Yet more permanent members of the extended community, including members of Gamelan Tunas Mekar and Lasmawan's friends and colleagues at gamelan programs across the country, recognize that their relationship extends far beyond specific financial exchanges. Instead, a system of reciprocal favors has developed in which time, money, and various other forms of assistance contribute to creating not only a system of classes and guest residencies but an extended community.

Community Beyond Geography

Long-term members and supporters of the gamelans on the Front Range region of the Rocky Mountains, including Fitts and Levine, provide crucial academic and non-academic support for gamelan groups and teachers based on years or decades of collaboration in close geographic proximity to one another. Other groups, however, are linked to specific teachers owing to other sorts of long-term relationships. One of the most common is that between an Indonesian teacher and the groups that he helped establish: assisting in the purchase of instruments or in naming them. For example, the Emory Gamelan Ensemble performs primarily on the founding Central Javanese instruments brought by the composer Steven Everett in 1997 but plays a Balinese gamelan beleganjur (a marching gamelan), which I brought at the request of the Music Department when I taught there in 2013. (Also, a Sundanese degung ensemble that was donated to the university was in use from 2007 to 2013). The group has worked for decades with Midiyanto, a well-known Javanese musician and *dalang* (shadow puppet master); he continues to arrive once or twice per year to rehearse and perform a shadow play. Because Lasmawan helped import the beleganjur and named both the Central Javanese and the Balinese ensemble during a residency in 2014, he also has become affiliated with the ensemble. At least once, both teachers were in residence at the same time to work with a community of musicians who are one direct flight away from their Indonesian guest teachers.

A result of these differing degrees of kinship between ensembles is that musicians and whole ensembles, while related through direct lineages to specific teachers, have more distant musical and cultural relationships to each other, much as would individuals in extended families. This type of relationship was made particularly clear to me in October 2017, when I visited several of Lasmawan's Colorado groups and sat in with the collegiate ensembles during their rehearsals. At the rehearsal for the group at Metropolitan State University, I was sitting on *reyong* (a horizontally suspended gong chime) with a longtime Tunas Mekar player and professional percussionist, Jill Frederickson, who had been helping with the ensemble for the semester. The piece was "Baris Tunggal," a solo warrior dance, which in Bali serves as a foundational piece in the training of young male dancers. It is commonly performed among American gamelan groups as well, whether or not a dancer is present, because of its status as core repertoire and its fairly short and repetitive melody; the challenge of the piece is primarily in its fast speed and the complexity of following cues for the dancers. She and I had both played "Baris" dozens of times in different ensembles, but not necessarily on reyong, and never together.

Before she and I could gain verbal consensus on what we were playing, the initial drum strokes jolted us into action. We quickly discovered that the part that I was accustomed to playing contained eight beats of new material and lined up exactly with the eight-beat *gilak* gong cycle; the one that she had played most often consisted of a two-beat pattern repeated four times within every gong cycle. Both were correct elaborations that one could use for that piece, but whereas Lasmawan favored using the two-beat pattern with his groups,

Michael Bakan at Florida State University had usually taught the longer one; it was this pattern that I had learned first. Though Frederickson and I eventually reconciled our two parts, I took a moment afterwards to talk with her about it and apologize for not being fully on the same page. She smiled, shrugged, and said, "We're just from different banjars." The different ways in which we had worked with Lasmawan—she for almost three decades, in close proximity; I, for just over half a decade, from somewhat farther away except while resident in Bali—meant that although we shared some common musical ground, our positions within distinct branches of the musical family also created difference.

In addition to long-term bonds built through establishing or naming a gamelan, direct teacher-student lineages create strong bonds not only in terms of repertoire or guest artist roles but also in terms of truly familial relationships. Lasmawan's work with Elizabeth (Liz) Macy provides a prime example of this type of connection. Macy began her gamelan studies with Lasmawan during her first term at Colorado College in 1996 and the following year was among the first group of students to travel with Lasmawan and Levine to Bali. Although she played with the gamelan throughout most of her college career and traveled to Bali several more times, afterwards she lost contact with Lasmawan for a few years until he was a guest artist at UCLA, where she was then enrolled in the PhD program in ethnomusicology. Over the course of the next few years, she and Lasmawan increasingly had opportunities to teach together, first when Macy replaced Levine while she was on sabbatical, then when she was contracted to co-lead the college study abroad program in 2009 and 2011. The official founding of Sanggar Manik Galih in 2011 coincided with that study abroad program and crystalized the sanggar as an internationally oriented community.

Though the official headquarters for Sanggar Manik Galih is in Bangah, Macy's work with the sanggar has firmly extended it into the United States. When Macy began to teach gamelan at Skidmore College in 2014, it was Lasmawan's family who came to inaugurate the program; subsequently, in partnership with Lasmawan and his eldest son, Putu Hiranmayena, Macy co-taught a series of study abroad programs for Skidmore in Bali. The Balinese All Stars, a supergroup consisting of a shifting cast of Balinese and Balinese American performing artists from five families, grew from a Skidmore performance that featured many of these geographically distant artists playing together. Though Hiranmayena currently manages the All Stars' schedule, Macy has spearheaded other organizational aspects of the sanggar's work, including establishing the website and pursuing nonprofit status for the group in the United States.

Macy has chosen to formalize the relationship between the Tangkas family musicians and the collegiate groups and study-abroad participants that she has taught by specifically including them under the umbrella of Sanggar Manik Galih. For her, this choice was an easy one to make. "I was part of the sanggar from the get-go," she told me, explaining that she views her close work with Lasmawan and Marni over the years, particularly since she began to travel to Bali at least once per year with student groups, as an extension of the sanggar. Moreover, since Macy has been involved with the family since before Ade and Aji were born, she has watched all the members of the younger generation grow up and has, indeed, grown up with them, somewhat like an older sister, increasingly taking on responsibilities specific to that role. She concluded, "I am part of the family now, and that's going to be a life-long thing"—no matter what form that type of partnership may take in the future (Macy 2018).

Symbiosis in American Gamelan Groups

The gamelan ensembles and individual collaborators who have worked with Lasmawan's family for a long time provide distinctive models of the different ways in which parts of a widely dispersed gamelan community with both regional and national connections may grow and function. However, geography, population density, and overall availability of gamelans have made these constellations of academic and community groups interact in ways that are unique to each region. Areas such the Deep South contain too low a density of gamelans of similar types to make regular intraregional artistic exchange viable. On the other hand, areas like the California coast and the urban Northeast have historically supported stable ensembles and involved a large number of people.

California, for example, is home to the largest number of Indonesian Americans in the country. It is also the state with the largest number of gamelan ensembles of all varieties, at almost three dozen. Though this is not uniformly the case, some academic ensembles such as the Javanese gamelan taught at University of California, Berkeley, have the reputation of filling their seats quickly. Community ensembles of long standing such as Gamelan Sekar Jaya draw enough interest that they can require auditions to join some of their groups, rather than recruiting from the communities at large. With so many ensembles present, a plethora of skilled musicians and teachers available, and a large Indonesian American influence (and Asian American influence more broadly) in the culture of urban areas, sharing a single teacher and artistic vision becomes less of a necessity.

Similarly, in the urban Northeast, the high density of colleges and universities and high population density in general allow for resource-sharing between separate institutions that could not support full gamelans on their own but also allow for independent ensembles to thrive in relatively close proximity to each other. Like the historic, picturesque New England towns that appear to run seamlessly into each other in that part of the United States, liberal arts colleges of the region frequently foster their own localized cultures. Those that are geographically close to one another tend to share ensembles exclusively—for example, within the Five Colleges consortium consisting of Smith, Amherst, Hampshire, and Mount Holyoke Colleges and the University of Massachusetts, Amherst—whereas programs like those at College of the Holy Cross in Worcester, Massachusetts, and Wesleyan University in Middletown, Connecticut, have the resources to maintain full-time teachers on their own. In Boston and New York, the sheer diversity of cosmopolitan life means that gamelan ensembles emerge from and can be supported by the distinctive and varied cross-sections of the student bodies and city populations. Even as members are shared between academic and especially community groups, they are just as likely to be cross-country transplants or new musicians as they are to be students who have continued performing after college.

Each gamelan in North America was founded in a different time, place, and circumstance, and therefore each grows and develops differently. Some commonalities emerge, however, when we examine how ensembles are founded and maintained. Although academic gamelan groups can be maintained in relative isolation from each other, a certain amount of symbiotic exchange facilitates the sustenance of many such programs. In collegiate settings, it is often American partners who provide the impetus for starting an ensemble and then work with Indonesians on the potentially difficult task of acquiring instruments. These initial partnerships can form the basis of pedagogical, artistic, and personal relationships that last for many years, whether the primary Indonesian teacher and the new ensemble are close or distant geographically.

In regions of the country that support multiple ensembles, it is not uncommon for one teacher to work with multiple groups, in part owing to economic necessity and in part owing to the shortage of qualified teachers who are able or willing to instruct a single ensemble. Where academic and community groups near each other share physical resources or an instructor, they form bonds based not only on the sharing of those specific resources but also on musicianship. The network of gamelans taught by Lasmawan presents a particularly large and complex version of this model; although its shape and extent are somewhat anomalous, the vastness and diversity of this network makes it an ideal one in which to visualize the different possible interrelationships and complexities affecting individuals and programs.

It is fruitful to think of the ways in which in-group distinctions may be applied. The idea of sanggar and banjar carry a specific currency in a transnational setting, even as the words take on meanings that differ from their original usages. It is also important, however, to recognize that it is because of the actions of key members of specific communities that their ensembles are sustained at all. Even as academic gamelan courses are filled with students who, for the most part, may only participate in the group for a few months, there is always the possibility that, for one or more of the students, the relationship with their teacher or with gamelan as a way of life will instead last for years. These types of permanent relationships facilitate the more transient cultural and musical experiences that extend not only to experienced members of a core community but also to all who care to listen and learn.

CHAPTER 5

Teaching, Learning, Representing

It was almost time for the gamelan performance to begin at Wake Forest University, and backstage, more than a dozen musicians were fidgeting with unfamiliar items of clothing. A few women scratched themselves in a most undignified way; their lace kebaya, though elegant and much more comfortable than most, were itchier than they had expected. Unused to wearing any bottoms other than pants or shorts, the male students were moving carefully to avoid wardrobe malfunctions with their *kain* and *saput*, the two layers of cloth that had begun the evening tied around their waist at such a height that the bottom edges would neatly hit their calves. *This is why you always wear exercise shorts under your uniform*, I had admonished them the day before; despite my seemingly constant readjustments to student uniforms, a number of saput always seemed to want to creep southward. There had been enough of a delay in our performance start time that a few men had even taken off their *udeng* (cloth hats) for increased comfort. Suddenly, it was time to go. The words "don't forget your shrimp hats!" died on my lips before they were spoken; I remembered that I had not yet shared that wordplay (the Balinese word for that type of headgear, *udeng*, is phonetically close to the Indonesian word *udang*, shrimp), which had been a favorite joke at Florida State, with these new students. Nevertheless, the hats were retrieved and we emerged, more or less correctly clad in our black and gold uniforms, to showcase the work that a combination of students and community members had accomplished over the previous three months.

Some of the most contentious issues in gamelan performance in North America, or, indeed, any music taught to students outside its original performance context, have been related to artistic and cultural representation. From considering the pros and cons of wearing traditional uniforms to discussing appropriate methods for teaching American students and debating whether student groups should perform in formal venues, authenticity and representation have dominated the discussion about world music pedagogy (Moore 2017; Solís 2004). These debates are not without merit. Performing music for personal or institutional gain without adequate knowledge of, attention to, dialogue with, or respect for its original musical or cultural context (that is, musical and cultural appropriation) is a persistent issue. The specifically pedagogical purposes of playing within a classroom context heighten the need for care in this regard since every action can be interpreted as being explicitly educational.

In discussing pedagogical approaches to teaching gamelan in North America, I realize that I risk retreading on familiar ground covered by an array of published materials, most centrally Harnish's (2004) cogent descriptions of his own pedagogical practices and experience grappling with issues of transmission and representation. This issue is sufficiently important that it merits further examination, however, including the complex considerations that go into teaching Balinese gamelan and Balinese culture to American students, the creative adaptations that are sometimes required to achieve satisfying learning and performing experiences, and the diverse ways in which a close encounter with gamelan can teach students about Balinese culture while leading them to interrogate their own beliefs and ways of being in the world. Emergent issues in educational practice such as the use of new technologies in teaching, treatment of gender and the body in the classroom, and the potential roles for such "diverse" programming in educational offerings, are also treated briefly in this chapter.

The desired pedagogical outcomes for students learning Balinese gamelan can be seen as falling within two types of competencies: musical competency and cultural or intercultural competency. I draw on Brinner's definition of *musical competency* as "individualized mastery of the array of interrelated skills and knowledge" that is acquired in response to and deployed in accordance with specific musical and cultural environments (1995, 28). Musical competency is by its nature cumulative; individuals will gain certain degrees of technical and cognitive competency more slowly or quickly than others, with all gaining more skill as time progresses. One of the key challenges of teaching experience-oriented ensemble courses is that time within a single academic term is exceptionally limited; another, that all students will progress at different rates on the path to general or specific types of competency. Consideration of the types of competency that are crucial to achieving a satisfactory artistic or pedagogical outcome is integral in guiding how students are taught. Attaining intercultural competency is also central to collegiate gamelan classes, and one that requires time. I use the definition of this specific aim by the Association of American Colleges and Universities: that intercultural competency is "a set of cognitive, affective, and behavioral skills and characteristics that support effective and appropriate interaction in a variety of cultural contexts" (Bennett 2008, 97). Both types of competency, whether explicitly stated as such by teachers or not, are implicit in the pedagogical decisions that individuals make.

As stated in the introduction to this book, the pedagogical landscape in North America involves the use of gamelans in three distinct types of collegiate settings: pre-professional and music-oriented (the conservatory model), pre-professional and musical-cultural (the bimusicality model, aimed at ethnomusicology students), and focused on musical and cultural enrichment within a broader program of study (the liberal arts model). Gamelan has a place in all three models: as a globally influential music deserving of study as an art form, as a means for better understanding and being able to competently represent

I Made Lasmawan teaching at Metropolitan State University, October 2018

the music and culture of another group of people, and as a medium for general exploration and self-reflection. The subsequent discussion about teaching and learning gamelan, though applicable to all three models, is primarily concerned with the latter two, which are more common in the United States and are ones in which most of my informants were most deeply involved.

First, I address some basic musical considerations in teaching Balinese gamelan, from introducing students to the instruments and developing technique to programming a concert. I draw primarily on observations of and discussions with two Balinese gamelan teachers, I Made Lasmawan and I Ketut Gede Asnawa, supplemented by my graduate study with Michael Bakan (a student of Asnawa's and of I Ketut Sukarata's), observation of the rehearsals of or discussions with approximately a dozen other well-regarded Balinese and North American teachers, observations of rehearsals of Balinese groups of different proficiency levels in Bali, and my own experiences in teaching. For the sake of consistency, the discussion focuses primarily on material for gong kebyar and angklung kebyar ensembles unless noted otherwise; it includes some limited discussion of dance, a topic that merits further discussion in its own context. Ideas specific to one teacher are attributed directly, whereas those that I encountered widely are introduced without specific attribution.

I then focus on cultural considerations related to teaching and performance. In dialogue with a diverse cast of voices, American and Balinese, I examine how learning gamelan provides opportunities for students to engage with concepts of cultural diversity, including the cultural context of rehearsal and performance, sacred and secular approaches to music making, embodiment and gender, and the nature of community. Like Lysloff's concept of "worlding" (2016), in which he describes how musicians in Java consciously employ assumption and stereotype to position their works for specific audiences, I suggest that Balinese and American teachers alike acknowledge that gamelan is frequently perceived as exotic by American audiences, and they harness and transform this initial curiosity by drawing individuals away from being passive observers and toward being active and passionate learners.

I have regularly been told by Balinese teachers (as well as other Indonesian observers) that to see foreigners approach learning the Balinese performing arts with diligence and sincerity makes them feel proud of their own culture, regardless of the students' level of experience or skill, if their study and performance is contextualized. This chapter ultimately attempts to embody the seriousness, sense of humor, and warmth of spirit that I have consistently noted in observing teachers of Balinese gamelan in North America as they engage in musical and cultural pedagogy and dialogue with their students.

Instruments, Learning Progressions, Adaptations

Each instrument is crucial to producing the sound of a gamelan ensemble. Asnawa likens each of them to specific functions in the village, from the gongs that connect the ensemble spiritually (priests) to the plodding core melody played on jegogan or calung (village elders), the fast elaborating parts (young men), and the leading role of the kendang (the village head).[1] Each of these instruments has its own challenges, with some widely being perceived as more appropriate for new learners than others. Keyed metallophones that play the pokok (core melody)—calung and sometimes *penyacah* or *jublag*, with the lower-pitched jegogan playing an abstraction of the full musical line—tend to play evenly spaced rhythms that coincide neatly with the beat, either along with the beat or every several beats. These parts are easier to execute in terms of technique and therefore provide an approachable and common starting place for new musicians. The often long and abstract melodic lines make the parts difficult to memorize, however, unless players can understand and hear their part's relation to the others. Such listening skills, crucial to all gamelan musicians, are especially important for players to not get lost within the form of the piece.

The characteristic parts for gangsa (higher-pitched keyed metallophones) and reyong (a row of kettle gongs) are faster and less regular; they frequently subdivide the beat and play elaborative parts whose pitches are distributed between two or more players (kotekan and ubit-ubitan). The speed and especially the division of labor present a challenge for new musicians, particularly those who are not yet used to hearing and thinking about interlocking parts as being integral halves of a whole. On the opposite end of the spectrum of speed, the gong part, though seemingly simple, requires precise timing to play well. New players often wait too long before beginning their stroke to have the gong sound at the right time. In addition, gong players must have the ability to count for long periods of time, follow tempo changes, and conceptualize the entire form of a piece at once. Time-keeping instruments such as *kempli* (or *kajar*) are perhaps the most deceptive of all—after all, there is only one place to strike on these musical metronomes. Keeping a steady beat can be challenging in a group full of new learners; it requires a singularity of focus and the ability to mentally subdivide the beat. When one adds in the rapid and sometimes drastic tempo changes that are integral to much of Balinese gamelan gong kebyar music, keeping time can indeed require substantial attention and skill.

Instruments that cue tempo, dynamics, and changes in form and that coordinate with dancers provide even further challenges for student learners. Playing the ugal, a large keyed metallophone that much of the time plays a lightly elaborated version of the pokok, becomes far more challenging in portions of the music that engage the instrument in its true primary function: to provide cues for the ensemble. A good ugal player knows the whole form of the piece being played, can follow the kendang player (drummer), and wields his or her hammer-shaped mallet clearly to show the other instruments where to go. The kendang, which play the role of ultimate ensemble leader in gong kebyar, requires specific hand-drumming techniques that must be cultivated. The two kendang players share interlocking parts, except when the lead drummer plays alone (a rare place for true solo playing in Balinese gamelan); the parts, whether played together or alone, again subdivide the beat. In addition to such technical challenges, as leader of dynamics and tempo control and primary point of communication with dancers, the drummer also ensures that the ensemble stays together. Kendang players must be aware of every aspect of the performance at once, which is why the role is reserved for advanced musicians including the ensemble leader.[2] In Bali, not all musicians learn to play all instruments; in fact, though skilled instrumentalists can play most or all the gamelan instruments well, they generally specialize in one or two, which they play most of the time in their home ensembles. Relatively few musicians in a village gamelan play kendang at more than a rudimentary level; there is no need to do so, since their musical place is elsewhere in the group.

A director of a college gamelan in North America may not have the luxury of sufficient time to guide students through the different instruments or experienced players who can cover different parts or help their neighbors learn. Players of other instruments may be able to transfer their skills to certain instruments—for example, wind players to *suling* (bamboo flute), pianists to gangsa, or percussionists to nearly any of the instruments—but such transfer is not predictable, and novice players may adapt more easily to learning in the Balinese manner or to hearing kotekan as a single line rather than feeling overwhelmed by a part that seem to consist only of offbeats. Teachers like Lasmawan can tell the skill level and aptitude of new learners quickly after watching them try a new instrument, but the logistics of running the ensemble (for example, accommodating a student who signs up for the ensemble class very late or a student who is sick for several weeks while a new piece is being taught) can affect part assignments. Devoted students who study hard may also make more progress than peers who initially seemed more capable.

Even if a piece is at an appropriate level for student learners and they are placed on instruments that suit them, simplifications may still be necessary in order for students to present the piece effectively. Kotekan is one of the main types of figuration that may be simplified. For example, long passages containing *kotekan norot*, a type of kotekan in which gangsas anticipate and elaborate on the upcoming core melody note by playing an oscillating neighbor-note pattern, are often played at slower tempos and can be played undivided; that is, every musician plays the whole musical figure rather than dividing it between two individuals. At faster tempos, when, the part is split, passages of norot may prove more technically difficult for students who are striking mostly what they perceive to be upbeats; however, the pattern is still relatively simple to conceptualize. In faster sections with more difficult kotekan patterns, students on the gangsa can double strike on the melody notes rather than play kotekan to give a sense of movement; for example, if the calung is playing at the beat level (quarter notes), the gangsas can strike the same pitch twice (rendering it as two eighth notes). This option is easier than playing the kotekan elaboration, which might be interlocking at the sixteenth-note level. Another option is to have all gangsas play polos and only insert elaboration in select places, for example, when polos and sangsih are not interlocking but rather playing different pitches from each other in rhythmic unison. This harmonization, which frequently occurs four scale degrees apart (at an interval approximately the same as a fifth in Western music), adds a more substantive feel without adding substantive difficulty. The reyong, with its own idiomatic interlocking parts, can be made more approachable by choosing material that takes more advantage of the instrument's percussive abilities than its melodic ones.

One of the most oft-noted curiosities about American gamelan groups is how much the musicians switch between instruments in performance (Harnish 2004). Though sometimes a result of logistic issues with the ensemble as discussed above, moving students around may also be a pedagogical choice, made to allow students to experience multiple different perspectives in playing or to balance a challenging role given to a student on one piece with a more relaxed role on another, for example, trying a kotekan-heavy gangsa part on one piece but keeping time on another. Arrangements of pieces and repertoire choices, discussed below, depend on the number of players and their ability levels. Finally, some instruments may be introduced to students in a special session, even if none ultimately play them that semester—for example, having the leader demonstrate the kendang and allow students to try basic patterns without the pressure of being expected to lead. In performance, however, the kendang are left to their usual players or sometimes even player, singular; for example, without a ringer playing with him in a class group, Lasmawan generally plays kendang alone, in a hybrid pattern that blends both drum parts into one. Each instrument has a different role in the music but also presents its own challenges for learners, which is why teachers may encourage students to play a specific instrument to advance specific playing skills. Placing students on instruments so that they can both contribute well and expand their skills is an important part of group pedagogy.

Choosing Repertoire

In addition to placing students correctly within an ensemble, the pedagogical process entails technique in learning specific pieces and programming works to learn and present. Whereas newer American teachers or ones who are less familiar with Balinese music may work to replicate pieces they already know via oral transmission, notation, or video, experienced teachers (Balinese and American alike) have dozens of possible programming choices readily available, even if there is a shortlist of pieces that they teach often. A key consideration in choosing repertoire for a gamelan is the available instrumentation. Each type of ensemble (gong kebyar, angklung, semar pegulingan, beleganjur, and so on) has its own tuning systems, range of pitches, instrumentation, and historic repertoire. The number and playing abilities of the students, too, need to be taken into account. At last come dictates of learning time and final presentation: for example, whether there will be a formal final performance, how many hours of practice are expected to prepare for it, and how long it needs to be.

Though no educational ensemble is completely consistent in regard to these factors from semester to semester, recurring patterns in time and resources allow for instructors to develop some consistency in their choices. Lasmawan—who favors traditional and neotraditional repertoires, consistently serves as a skilled leader himself, and has long had the resource of family members to serve as dancers—regularly programs at least one instrumental piece, at least one dance piece, and some musical material that contrasts with those performed on the main ensemble instruments (for example, beleganjur or kecak). Although he composes pieces for some of the ensembles he teaches, Lasmawan often chooses pieces that are widely played across Bali. Regardless of the type of gamelan used, dance pieces are drawn from (and when necessary, adapted from) the gamelan gong kebyar repertoire, which for several decades has been the most popular throughout the island.[3] In addition, although his knowledge of Balinese gamelan repertoire is vast, Lasmawan will teach the same pieces to his groups, in Bali and in the United States.

There are several logical reasons for this consistency of repertoire. In Bali, gamelan music is a consistent part of the fabric of Hindu life. It is performed at major public ceremonies like *odalan* (temple anniversary celebrations) and *ngaben* (cremations), as well as more familial affairs; these performances and group practices can be readily seen or heard by local people. Balinese gamelan and dance are also taught at an introductory level in schools, and youth and adults may participate in recreational gamelan clubs with varying levels of proficiency and commitment. Though significant regional artistic traditions still exist, increased access by certain musicians or promoters to the radio, television, cassette, and VCD (videodisc) industries has elevated some repertoires and styles of playing over others. (The Internet seems to have reinforced this standardization in some ways—for example, having a specific version of a piece become the most-watched version on YouTube—while also allowing space for the revival of archaic recordings or the individual presentation of musik kontemporer or other nontraditional styles.) Other forms of official endorsement of specific works, such as being consistently requested for local or tourist performances, being taught at the conservatories, and being programmed as standard repertoire at the Bali Arts Festival, have accorded them the status of standards.

By learning works from the Balinese gamelan "canon" rather than pieces or exercises specifically written to teach foreigners, students can both learn how to play and become more musically literate. In programs that Lasmawan can teach on at least a weekly basis, this programming pattern is one that is both flexible and sustainable.

Lasmawan's decision to teach primarily from the same core repertoire is also a practical one. In working with so many groups, having some consistency and repetition helps his own teaching. He says, "In ISI-Solo, the teaching is not hard, the teaching Balinese [music to the Javanese students]. In teaching a Balinese course in ISI-Solo, we have like fifteen to twenty people, it's only a small amount of your time, not like here, you know [where Lasmawan may teach as many as 150 students at once]" (Lasmawan 2013). Playing these standard works allows students to learn repertoire that they would be able to perform other gamelan groups within Sanggar Manik Galih and beyond and need only adapt to the ensemble's playing style. This musical "transfer" includes students who have sat in with or joined another of Lasmawan's groups in America and new students, American and Balinese, that he teaches in Bangah. By teaching the same set of standard pieces to all his student groups, Lasmawan can maintain a musical and stylistic unity between them, despite the groups' being located in different places and performing on different types of gamelans that have different tuning systems and melodic ranges. Within the world of Lasmawan's gamelan communities, at least, sharing repertoire allows for an evenness of musical competency to be attained across the interlinked communities.

Maguru Panggul and Beyond

The hands-on approaches traditional to gamelan pedagogy have become an iconic part of world music teaching. The *maguru panggul* (mallet as teacher) technique, used in most types of Balinese gamelan learning, is a prototype for this type of aural-visual-tactile learning. In this method, musicians who do not yet know their musical part play along with those on the same instrument who do, gradually reducing mistakes as they learn individual parts and the whole piece. Or, as Asnawa refers to it, it is a system of "listening, watching, and doing" (Asnawa 2016). This method of learning has been extensively documented in Balinese communities by scholars of the past century examining a diverse array of Balinese performing arts repertoires (e.g., Bakan 1994, 1999; Dibia and Ballinger 2004; DeZoete and Spies 1939; Gold 2005; Harnish 2004; Heimarck 2003; Hough 1999; McPhee 1966; Sudirana 2018; Tenzer 2000, 2011). Rote memorization, though slower at first for most learners accustomed to reading scores, generally is quicker for achieving the ideal performance aesthetic, in which musicians have all pieces fully memorized and use no written materials. As Downing (2010) points out, pedagogy through embodiment serves much the same function in learning Balinese dance. Writing down the music may, indeed, be harmful to the learning process because it undermines the pedagogical focus on "repetition, imitation, and transmission" both as a learning technique and a method of respecting and coming to understand Balinese artistic and pedagogical values (Macy 2017). The use of maguru panggul means that "the interaction between teacher and student is not based on talking a lot.... It's based on watching, then trying to play with them, mallet to mallet, action to action" (Asnawa 2016). Just as American students often struggle to get used to learning by observation, sometimes without specific direction, Indonesian teachers must cope with students who are persistently asking questions instead of following (Harnish, Solís, and Witzleben 2004; Sudirana 2018).

While the maguru panggul technique is employed by Balinese gamelan teachers, and indeed, constitutes one of the most obvious differences between gamelan and Western classical notation-based learning, it is by no means the only "traditional" technique that master teachers use. Lasmawan, for example, breaks down the method further, emphasizing the equal importance of other "maguru" techniques as opposed to the kinesthetic learning that he sees most clearly embodied by maguru panggul. For example, in *maguru mata* ("eyes as teacher"), the focus is on observing; *maguru kuping* ("ears as teacher") likewise brings the focus to listening, which could either include critical listening to a specific piece or the general form of aural observation that can be achieved by accessing recordings but is better achieved by long exposure to live gamelan music.

Traditional methods such as maguru panggul remain at the heart of pedagogy in both Balinese and American educational settings. Yet adaptation and pedagogical hybridity are required owing to differences in the contexts of learning and performance. In general, all but the strongest of programs lack enough experienced teachers to concurrently model each instrumental part, and students have insufficient experience on the instruments to simultaneously grasp technique and musical structure. Slower-moving than the melodic elaboration layers and crucial to the structure of the piece of music, the pokok also provides students opportunities to become used to the striking and damping techniques of their instruments and to have a physical and aural sense of the musical superstructure of a specific section. To teach an entire pokok orally with but one teacher as a visual aid can be time-consuming, however; after several unfamiliar melodies are added to the students' repertoires, it can be difficult for them to remember them or distinguish between them.

Lasmawan, who generally works with each group of students only once per week, provides numeric cipher notation for musicians playing the pokok, with gong strikes indicated. He adopted this style of *kepatihan* notation from his time in Java. Though other Balinese and American musicians will sometimes use notation in a similar fashion, this practice is more common in Javanese traditions, where European-influenced notation systems had been used archivally since the end of the nineteenth century (Sumarsam 1995); it remains relatively uncommon in Bali, where written notation is used selectively by composers. Lasmawan prefers to use oral transmission for more rhythmically dense parts, usually providing written notation or video for gangsa and reyong only when he is sending materials ahead for a guest artist residency or when the material must be learned quickly. When he is serving as a guest, only present for a limited number of the groups' practices, sending written cipher notation (in which numbers represent pitches in the scale) ahead of time provides tangible documents for study, while preparation of audiovisual recordings helps engage visual and aural skills as well as potentially priming kinesthetic skills. If this use of methods is viewed as a compromise, it is one that is already common within Balinese conservatories; Asnawa notes that even in Bali, students today use notation on a blackboard and will sometimes sing through their parts before ever picking up a mallet. Direct transmission from teacher to student by watching or learning is nonetheless widely regarded as being the preferred method.

In terms of learning specific pieces, traditional modes of pedagogy or their adaptations form the core approach. Nontraditional methods are, however, sometimes introduced and appreciated by Balinese and Balinese American teachers alike. Adapting Balinese learning styles for specialized groups such as children may entail different types of modification (see chapter 8). A younger generation of teachers is also beginning to incorporate new approaches to teaching and learning with specialized as well as general audiences. For example, because of Putu Hiranmayena's varied gamelan-learning and -teaching background and his interest in and study of improvisation in and beyond Western musical genres, he has adopted his own pedagogical style. One experiment that he began while teaching at the Museum School in San Diego and later tried with adult learners was to include elements of Conduction (conducted improvisation), a system of free improvisation created by the jazz musician, composer, and conductor Lawrence D. "Butch" Morris in which the leader uses hand gestures to guide the musicians. By treating the initial approach to the gamelan instruments like a game—"putting the game in gamelan"—Hiranmayena found that learners were able to express their musical preferences and indicate their musical skills in a relaxed format, one that gave him insight into how to approach more formalized learning using the maguru panggul method (Hiranmayena 2016). For musicians with interests beyond gamelan, use of tradition is also fundamentally open to transformations that will better serve specific audiences of learners.

Another example of a Balinese performing arts teacher whose hybrid educational background has influenced his career and pedagogical approaches is I Nyoman Sedana. Educated first in the conservatory system in Bali, Sedana received an MA in theater from Brown University in 1993 and a PhD in drama and theater arts from the University of Georgia in 2002. He regularly pursues international residencies and publishes scholarly articles in international academic journals in addition to maintaining his regular teaching schedule in Denpasar. In personal communications with myself and others (Heimarck 2003), he often notes that his teaching philosophy is born of "Western theory and Balinese practice." One project, for example, included leading students at Butler University in a performance of Shakespeare's *A Midsummer Night's Dream* couched in the language of traditional Balinese music and dance. As for teaching his Balinese students, he cites his study of major English-language plays (Shakespeare), readings in anthropological theory, and lessons at the University of Georgia writing center as major influences on the way he introduces traditional Balinese stories and constructs new narrative performances.

The final step to truly learning a piece well is one that cannot be taught directly but must take years of study: understanding and being able to choose and replicate musical feeling and style. Correct feeling within a piece—for example, knowing implicitly where certain cues for dancers fall within a musical line or precisely when and where the tempo is expected to slow down or speed up slightly for emphasis—can be attained on a limited basis within a single semester, as students come to know an individual piece that they are studying. Replicating that same sense of expectation in new pieces of music often takes several years to achieve. Still more complicated is understanding playing style more broadly. Each area or village in Bali has different preferred ways to interpret elaborating patterns (kotekan and ubit-ubitan), drumming styles, form (*paileh*), and other musical structures. Balinese teachers may teach pieces in the style of their region, in the style that they learned at one of the conservatories (ISI or South Bali style), or another regional style that they particularly like—but much of this subtlety or level of choice-making is lost on even experienced American community gamelan players, not to mention new learners, who are still working on striking and damping correctly. The longer American musicians play gamelan with a single teacher, however, the more likely they are to adopt the nuances of his or her musical idiolect, the distinctive artistic signature that encompasses the aesthetic preferences of the teacher as well as those of his or her musical forebears.[4]

Although learning is a practical process, it can also be approached philosophically. Asnawa, for example, who views most aspects of gamelan playing and instruction according to Balinese Hindu concepts of the balance of threes, cites three key steps to learning gamelan. The first step, he says, is *wiraga*, which encompasses learning the basic technique on an instrument and specific instrumental parts. The second step, *wirama*, includes learning how these parts fit into the greater musical context, which happens in dialogue with the development of wiraga. Finally, *wirasa* (from the Sanskrit root *rasa*, meaning "taste or flavor") is developing musical sensitivity, which only happens when all the basics of the music are mastered.[5] This is "the most crucial step" of the three "wi's," Asnawa notes; at this point, true interpretation can take place, and as he says, "Then you are free!" Following the gaining of wirasa, the transitional stage between the physical action and higher-level understanding, he cites two further "wi's": *wicaksana* (wisdom; in Balinese, *elah*), which means that the players understand musical flow and structure intuitively, and *wibawa*, "charisma" and the level of professionalism. For American musicians, Asnawa cites Hood's ethic of bimusicality in noting that achieving wiraga, wirama, and just a little wirasa alone may take a long time. Yet the sense of masterfulness or flow through which musicians can attain taksu (divine connection) in their playing is possible for students who study deeply and with dedication, regardless of their background.[6]

Sincerity in approach, then, is perhaps the most important aspect of pedagogy. While much has been made about "authentic" replication in world music ensemble studies, Harnish emphasizes that teachers in Bali are "less concerned with 'authenticity' than with which style (for example, conservatory, region, or village) is taught to students by gamelan directors in America. In this sense, then, gamelan can become a non-contested area open to any ethnicity to become students, performers, and teachers" (2004, 129). I have certainly found this to be true. Lasmawan, when asked how he felt about the fact that most of the students he would teach in his life would not be Balinese, replied:

> That's fine! Because the concept of gamelan is universal, is not only for [the] Balinese, you know? Not only for [the] Javanese. It is good, you know? A good gamelan player can be from another country . . . from Canada, from England, or from Japan, or from America, or from Mexico, or from anywhere, because to study gamelan is just like to study other things, if you learn seriously, you get it. I'm okay with that. (Lasmawan 2013)

This style of openness and dedication to transnational education demonstrates the flexibility of both the musical traditions and its teachers in helping gamelan find new niches in North America.

A Buffet of Diversity for White Americans?

Artistic fidelity, adherence to form, and informed adaptational choices are important aspects of intercultural artistic teaching. Given that most American audiences have a limited understanding of Indonesian art forms, however, cultural identity and representation are perhaps more important. These issues, specifically with regard to community-based gamelan groups, are concisely addressed in a blog post by McGraw (2013b). Following a historical summary of the development of gamelan and its migration and adoption in North America, he positions gamelan's popularity among its presumed middle-class, white adherents as resistance against the effects of global capitalism, accomplished by musicians and composers favoring gamelan's unique tonalities over the hegemony of Western tuning systems, idealizing cooperative group organization and face-to-face interaction built on oft-idealized conceptions of communal, egalitarian Indonesian culture over the individualism and anonymity common in contemporary American social structures, and using gamelan as a chance to express cultural and musical affinity with an artistic genre other than those associated with ethnic whiteness. Just as gamelans have been tasked with representing cultural and musical diversity within the academy, representation through performance has long been considered a fraught issue. Should beginning-level musicians perform publicly? How should such performances be contextualized? What does it mean for a group of non-Indonesian students to represent Indonesian music and culture at an Asian festival or, in contrast, be denied such opportunities, despite being skilled, because they appear too white (Harnish 2004, 135–136)?

These potential issues become even more fraught in pedagogical settings, where instructors may have to selectively employ exoticisms to attract student attention or gain administrative support for a gamelan ensemble, even as they attempt to evoke what they know of Indonesian culture in an accurate and fair way to student learners. In contemporary discourse, gamelans have become a part of collegiate campaigns to offer the most diverse options to students for the sake of seeming inclusive; a colleague of mine characterized the trend as attempting to offer "a buffet of diversity" for white American students to consume. Students indeed often sign up for gamelan class for its sheer novelty, one in a large collection of odd college experiences taken on as much for the stories to tell people at parties as for aesthetic or cultural interest in the ensemble itself. Educators must take care to ensure that the tendencies of advertisers and artists alike to romanticize "the East" or treat "the Balinese" or "Indonesians" as a singular group does not creep into classroom spaces—or at least to ensure that such ideas are discussed and interrogated when they inevitably make an appearance.

In a comparative study of cultures, however, one could argue that inviting students to consider their reactions to different tuning systems or struggle to work together cooperatively are in fact desirable learning outcomes, ones that are facilitated naturally by learning to play gamelan. Furthermore, though certain types of colleges and universities—northeastern or West Coast liberal arts colleges, Ivy League schools, and major research institutions—are more likely to have gamelans than are others, the student bodies that are exposed to gamelan at such places tend to be diverse in terms of race, ethnicity, and sometimes (though not always) socioeconomic background. The ensemble experience speaks to students in different ways, informing them about Indonesian culture but also perhaps more about their own interests and abilities. It is telling that non-Indonesian instructors (Solis 2004) are usually the ones who agonize about the cultural content that they are presenting. Balinese instructors that I have observed and spoken with also regularly acknowledge and encourage studying gamelan and dance as a method of intercultural learning. Yet the focus is more often on fostering good feeling within the group, which includes clear communication, approaching both musical aspects and cultural aspects (like making appropriate ritual offerings) of performance with rigor, consistency, and sincerity, and creating a pleasant and positive environment for all involved.

My own position as a white, middle-class, female gamelan musician who primarily grew up and taught in the American South has deeply affected my views of how I approach gamelan, both as a musician and a teacher. I cannot help but identify with some of the aspects of American culture that McGraw has described. When gamelan arrived in my life, it largely supplanted my affinity with the musics of ethnic whiteness, mainly Irish and Scottish bagpipe music and Celtic rock, that my parents had reclaimed for the soundtrack of our home and the pattern of our lives. I have many times sold the concept of gamelan to colleagues and students by emphasizing the value of cooperation and hands-on music making. I have observed in my work with community gamelan members a tendency toward equating playing gamelan with other socially subversive practices in American contexts, such as living in communal housing. Finally, it is an uncomfortable truth that ethnomusicologists who research and teach about other cultures inevitably build their careers, if not also large portions of their identities, on portraying and humanizing so-called exotic practices and peoples; I have not been immune from this practice, especially when a little exoticism could be used to entice previously nonreceptive audiences to engage in more in-depth learning about Indonesian culture.

I cannot embody diversity for American students as an Indonesian musician would. But I can enact diversity by setting the best example I can for building intercultural relationships. I can evoke diversity by providing students with a multifaceted view of Indonesian culture. I can introduce them to my teachers' and colleagues' work in person, through listening to recordings and watching video, and by communicating online. I can invite them to think about why their university has a gamelan ensemble in the first place. Most of all, I can tell the students my own story—about how signing up for one music class when I was only eighteen led to becoming a part of a global community that I had not previously known existed. I can tell them about the deep and abiding relationships that I have formed through learning, playing, and teaching gamelan, and not just stories about the good times but also about times when those relationships required care and negotiation. I can own my story, my successes and my failures. I can tell them how I gradually realized that gamelan was not just a hobby or an effective means to an end within my profession, but that I truly loved it, and that when you love something and care about its well-being, when you come to consider it part of your vocation or dharma, then you will do your best to respect, protect, and care for it because it is a part of you. Devotion and sincerity do not prevent mistakes or misunderstandings, but such attitudes can transform them into opportunities to learn how to become a better representative in bringing new learners to understand one's art, one's community, and one's self.

Evoking Other Times and Places

The proscenium stage is a relatively recent import to Bali. Though specific areas are set aside for performances within temples, audiences can frequently view the performance from at least three sides. In wayang kulit (shadow puppetry), the screen onto which the puppets' shadows are projected provides a demarcation between the world of the audience and the world of the narrative, but audience members can easily walk around and watch from behind the screen or sit at the side, observing both the seen (*sekala*, the material world) and unseen (*niskala*, the invisible world, the realm of ancestors, deities, and spirits) elements that comprise the performance. Similarly, in topeng (masked dance) performances, the dancer prepares behind a set of colorful curtains, an area where clothing can be adjusted and masks donned or exchanged to evoke new characters. But when a performer passes through the curtain, often teasing the audience at the border by showing only his hands before coming through, he leaves the quotidian world and enters the timeless (yet timely) world of the story (Dibia and Ballinger 2004).

In using music to teach about culture, we attempt to bring students into another reality, with its own signs and symbols and relationships to space and time. Bali is, of course, no isolated timeless island, and I do not mean to imply that it is. Inasmuch as gamelan ensembles build cultural competency, however, it is because they invite students into other ways of approaching not only music and music making but also different ways of being in the contemporary world. This cultural immersion or dialogue also manifests in ways that are seen (stated or made explicit) or unseen (embodied as habitus). The richness of Balinese cultural practices that can be identified in gamelan playing in ways both obvious and subtle have made it a particularly attractive means of teaching cultural diversity.

The differences between musical contexts of practice and performance in Bali and those that support American gamelans are vast. Rather than growing up immersed in gamelan music, most American students have little or no knowledge about the gamelan before they begin to play. Their allotted time for learning is also short and conscribed. While Balinese musicians learn over the course of many years with opportunities for continuous improvement, American gamelan ensembles meet sometimes as little as once per week for two hours or less, with a semester-end performance as the only guaranteed opportunity to share their knowledge and experience. The ensembles themselves are unstable in membership, unlike the banjar-oriented groups in Bali in which musicians may play for their entire adult lives.[7] Teachers and students in the ensembles vary widely in experience, skill level, and ability to learn from more experienced performers, meaning that the ensembles, too, can vary widely in ability. Rather than being performed at temple ceremonies or in other contexts with audiences that are relatively knowledgeable about the music, gamelan in North America is performed almost exclusively for audiences who are relatively unfamiliar with the sound. For such audiences, a student performance may serve as metonym for Balinese culture as a whole—a heavy burden to place on a beginning group.

This metonymic relation between a Balinese gamelan and Balinese culture more broadly imbues every action with a potential representational capacity. Though true onstage, it is even more important in a classroom setting and is perhaps one of the reasons why gamelans have become popular pedagogical tools: the ease of making these musical and cultural connections. The instruments and how they are treated and played in themselves provide an important site of understanding Balinese Hindu beliefs and social practice. Cultural practices that students learn immediately in approaching the instruments, such as respecting the instruments' spirits by removing one's shoes to play and not stepping over them, reinforce Balinese cultural values. The male-female duality found in paired instrument tunings, the correspondence of cyclical gong cycles to cyclical conceptions of time (like those in Java, most famously presented in Becker 1979) and other points of reciprocity speak to other perceptions of the cosmos. The decorations on many Balinese gamelan sets, which feature carvings of scenes from Hindu epics, impart a sense of central religious and cultural narratives. The very physicality of the instruments and how they are treated embodies cultural difference.

The way teachers treat the ensembles and their players, too, shares cultural information. The concepts of providing blessings for the instruments is one important marker. In Bali, blessings and offerings are given at the naming ceremony for the instruments and on the holiday of Tumpek Krulut, but throughout the year, musicians often pray together before they perform. Balinese teachers adapt these traditions so that they serve as markers of difference that are especially educational, even as they represent a spiritual necessity for the Balinese (Grimshaw 2009; Talbot 2012). More secular Indonesian customs, such as the practice of *gotong royong* (community service) or eating a celebratory meal together, may be counted among the ways ensemble members experience cultural difference.

Teachers, whether Balinese or not, also communicate information about the performing arts and culture through their embodied presence and actions and by the stories that they tell, either about their own experiences or those of their friends, colleagues, and teachers. Although many non-Balinese teachers approach diversity via direct discussion of their own position with their students, working with a native musician can help students navigate intercultural relationships in other ways. For example, Ellen Koskoff has worked with I Nyoman Suadin, the director of the Eastman gamelan Lila Muni (Heavenly Sound), since the early 1990s. In her view, just working with Suadin is one of the most important ways students can understand cultural diversity. She says, "Diversity is not me sitting there and saying, 'Love and respect each other;' diversity is students having to deal with Nyoman [Suadin] yelling 'ngyaaah, ngyaah!' at them when they miss the gong!" (Koskoff 2016).

Downing sees students benefiting similarly when they study with her husband, Dewa Ketut Alit Adnyana, whose attitude toward making music reframes the way students view the cultural possibilities for playing music. She reports,

> It's such a huge benefit . . . it's such a wonderful thing for students to interact with Dewa. They value his musical expertise, but they also seem to value his approach to music—especially the music majors, where their own training is strict, where it's vocational training to become professional musicians. And to hear Dewa, who says, "In this piece, we play the intro, and then we stop and smoke a cigarette." . . . that just blows their mind. And they say, "Wait, what, music can be integrated into a casual social situation?" It's so freeing. It's so valuable. It's so valuable for them to interact with someone they respect musically but who can provide such a different perspective on the importance of the arts, the importance of interacting with each other in a creative way. . . . It's totally, ridiculously valuable. It's hard to show that on paper, to put it into words. The most gratifying thing was last spring when there was a visit day for prospective students and the current students talked about gamelan. They said, "Oh, my gosh, and then you can do this, and you can get Lawrence funding, and you can actually go to Bali, and then you can bring these amazing, valuable ideas into your own studio." . . . They had such a wonderfully holistic sense of how it was impacting their lives. (Downing 2018)

The atmosphere cultivated in a gamelan class can effectively bring students closer to experiencing a Balinese context than can other types of activities available to them short of studying abroad. In addition to entering a new aural world, students are given the opportunity to confront their own assumptions about time, spatiality, objects, and people, all of which can reshape their musical and cultural assumptions. Entering the gamelan room, they can leave the quotidian ways of their college life behind, if only briefly.

Taken further, it is this property of a gamelan rehearsal that is effective not only for evoking musical and cultural diversity but also for providing it in a way that is largely non-confrontational; gamelan can become a "safe space." This requires the type of apparent societal disconnect for which American gamelan culture has frequently been criticized by Indonesians and Americans alike. It is true that American gamelans rarely build strong connections with Indonesian American communities and that many exist in areas with few or no such communities. Further, curricular diversity initiatives in collegiate settings that are couched in terms of social activism favor teaching about topics or geographic areas that are contentious in American culture, for example, the continued legacy of inequity rooted in the aftermath of the American enslavement of African peoples or continuing American involvement in the Middle East. In these cases, an institution might view supporting a West African ensemble or a Middle Eastern ensemble as a sociopolitical assertion as well as a pedagogical opportunity. Though negotiating the Indonesian American political relationship helped establish gamelans in the United States in the 1960s, the relative lack of public concern about this relationship in the early twenty-first century means that gamelan does not address contemporary geopolitical issues in the same way. This very lack, however, can serve as an educational advantage by defusing the tensions that students might feel in approaching music associated with a currently sensitive cultural or political issue.

On the day of the 2016 U.S. presidential election, I taught kecak in my undergraduate world music survey class. Some of my colleagues in ethnomusicology might criticize this choice. Removed from the global social issues that provide more timely and contentious points of debate within musical contexts, Balinese vocal gamelan is particularly chameleonesque; generally simpler and more versatile than instrumental gamelan, it can become whatever students need it to be. On that day, my students needed a refuge. The angry, polarizing rhetoric that had blasted from every television and screamed across social media for weeks had produced a chilling effect on classroom discussions as students, unsure of the political positions of their classmates, increasingly fell silent owing to fears of social or physical reprisals.

At first, they were reluctant to enter the ensemble rehearsal space, despite having spent several previous class sessions at the gamelan instruments. But the change in atmosphere from the hallway to the classroom was palpable. They left the tension that had plagued our divided campus for weeks outside the door with their shoes. Suddenly forced to sit on the ground, to collaborate to chant interlocking patterns and wave their arms, they were temporarily spirited away from their concerns, their attention fixed solely on trying to follow my musical and choreographic cues as they embodied the kecak chorus. Meanwhile, with the help of a student who had grown up in a Hindu family, I interpreted the narrative of the Abduction of Sita, the story told nightly in a half dozen tourist venues in Bali, as a one-woman show.

Starting with Prince Rama's refined and confident stride, I transformed into his wife, Princess Sita, marked with swaying hips and a demure smile. In the story, Sita asks her husband to bring her the golden deer that they see on their walk in the forest, which I portrayed with forefinger antlers and a hopping gait. Rama draws a magic circle for his wife, leaving her in the care of his brother Laksmana, and then chases after the deer. The prince draws his bow—I turned right to mimic the action—and turning left again to become the deer, I am pierced by Rama's imaginary arrow and fall. Suddenly, Rama realizes he's been tricked. He goes back to the magic circle, but Sita is gone. In a flashback, I showed Sita sending Laksmana after Rama, then leaving the circle herself to bring water to a hunched, limping beggar man who—with great fanfare and a rise in volume and intensity from the kecak chorus—changes into the ten-headed demon Rahwana (Ravana). I uncurled my body to its full height and my limbs to their full width, widening my eyes as far as they could go. My bare feet slapped roughly against the ground as both the character Sita and I, the actor, became carried away. My antics, which were more energetic than polished, earned laughter and the shouting of suggestions from the students.

The appearance of Hanuman, the monkeylike general who leads his army of *vanara* (monkey-people) to rescue Sita, brought a more fervent tone to the production as the students divided into the two armies that must battle each other for the fate of the princess. They stood and pretended to attack each other as the battle raged from one side of the room to the other, but true fear and aggression had been forgotten. I gave them a fairytale ending to the story: Sita is rescued and reunited with a joyous Rama, who praises and rewards Hanuman for his loyalty and courage.[8] Though I expected more protests from class feminists such as those I'd received in the past (why couldn't Sita rescue herself?) it seemed like everyone was grateful to have a happy ending.

After leaving for the Society for Ethnomusicology conference the next day, I learned that the tensions that I had felt on campus the previous day had exploded in my absence. Some students interpreted the outcome of the election as an opportunity to run through dormitory hallways and yell racial and homophobic slurs. As a result, students who felt threatened fled to spend the night at the campus theater and in the LGTBQ center, knowing they would be safe there.

Amid this chaos I received an email from a student. She thanked me and stated that as a student of color, she thought that my class was one of the few places on campus where she felt included and safe. Though I was distressed that I could not be on campus to support my students directly, I felt glad that the last experience I had left them with was one that had brought togetherness and laughter rather than division.

I had programmed kecak for that day out of habit rather than any canny foresight into my class's social climate. Though the kecak-based Ramayana story is rarely performed as such in Bali except in tourist shows, it is a staple form for introducing American students to Balinese culture because of its approachability and vivid storytelling possibilities. I had long considered it to be a pedagogical magic bullet, in part because of the relative ease of teaching it and in part for how masterfully I had seen Bakan and Lasmawan use it to entice large and sometimes unruly or indifferent groups of students into enthusiastic music making. It took me a long time, however, to connect those experiences with that of my election-day kecak, to realize that because the diversity that students experience in gamelan felt so distant from their own lives, it provided a safe context for them to learn about others while they explored expressing themselves artistically.

Body and Belief: Challenging Students' Self-Conceptions

Within the extensive discourse about representation, it is easy to lose sight of one of the major reasons for students to engage with gamelan, especially with native teachers: as a form of cultural self-discovery and dialogue, existing both within and external to other dialogues of representation. Such experiences, for me, at least, have often taken forms outside the pedagogical structures that were intended to foster specific types of musical or cultural competency. When I began to study Balinese dance at Florida State, it did not take me many forays into group performance to realize the representational strangeness (at least in some respects) of what we were doing. As we got ready for a performance, the six or so women and the occasional man who were participating that semester would put on costumes in brilliant hues. We would lighten our faces and darken our eyebrows. We would put on the reddest of lipsticks (this part was generally a new experience for the male dancer), and we women would affix golden flowers and long dark ponytails to our heads—all except the dancer with the waist-length blond hair, who simply styled her own. Then we would get in our cars, seatbelts fastened awkwardly around our costumed torsos, and head to the performance. At events for the small local Indonesian community and at global and Asian cultural festivals, our moving bodies, clad in the symbols of another artistic world, became representative of Bali and Asian artistic diversity more generally. There was no mistaking us for Balinese, yet with our learner-level ability to dance, we were being called on to embody an entire art form that we both respected and could only understand through the lenses of our own limited experiences.

I did not realize until much later in my studies, however, the extent to which this foreign form of performing arts was an opportunity not only for us to learn about Bali but also for a multidirectional intercultural exchange. Though American gamelans have been cast as stereotypically white and middle-class, the dancers and the ensemble at Florida State drew heavily on the university's pan–Latin American student population, attracting students who were also active in the Andean and salsa ensembles. When the student dancers and our Balinese teacher were together, our default languages were English, Balinese, and Spanish. We chatted in rehearsal, in the car, at the venues, to the point where observers jokingly asked whether we ever danced!

Balinese dance was our medium of physical and artistic instruction, but our conversations became a deeper means of exchange as we shared from our own perspectives what it meant to be female at the turn of the twenty-first century. In some cases, we were recipients of unidirectional instruction on the art of being female. Our teacher Candra frowned at our slumped-over postures, created by carrying heavy backpacks—our walking was not at all *seksi*; how could we possibly attract or please husbands? The perceived relative weakness of our pelvic muscles was also a cause for concern, both for dancing and husband-pleasing applications; in addition to practicing our walk with swaying hips, we were also assigned squeezing exercises to strengthen and tighten the offending areas. It was certain that we needed to know how to hold our bodies and walk in an appropriately female fashion to be able to dance, if not also for other purposes.

As we grew to know each other better, however, we began to talk more about not only the art form but also life's deeper questions: What types of food or gifts are appropriate to bring to a party? What does it mean to be patriotic? What type of work, paid or unpaid, is important for supporting a family? How many children should one have? What should one do about an abusive romantic partner? What did we, a group consisting of a Balinese Hindu, a Mormon, two Catholics, a Protestant, and an agnostic, think about the existence of ghosts or about the afterlife? In this case, we became friends and confidants, each of us emissaries of our own cultural framework even when at first our thoughts and confessions were ostensibly couched in discussions of Balinese performing arts and culture.

Though the dancers found these discussions woven into our informal exchanges, there are ways in which gamelan itself can become a critical means of engaging such important philosophical discussions within a pedagogical community. For example, modern academic discourses of multiculturalism in the United States generally assume interaction within the sphere of secular humanism. Yet, for American students and teachers, part of the interpretation of new musical and cultural traditions is comparing the new information with their own worldviews. In a religious school, the gamelan may occupy discourse about sacred as well as secular themes. For example, Brigham Young University in Provo, Utah, which is part of the Church of Jesus Christ of Latter-day Saints, is the largest religious university in the United States, and aspects of Mormon belief and practice permeate life there. A Balinese gamelan ensemble with its embedded references to Hindu belief and attendant practices of giving offerings to the instruments would seem incompatible with an institutional setting so thoroughly devoted to another religion. For the past decade, however, a Balinese gamelan has thrived at BYU under the leadership of Jeremy Grimshaw, with regular visits from Balinese guests including Lasmawan and Asnawa. Based on institutional hiring practices that give strong preference to church members, Grimshaw explains that it would be difficult for a Balinese instructor to permanently join the faculty at the university. Yet under Grimshaw's direction, the ensemble provides students with a taste of a different musical, cultural, and religious viewpoint, one through which students may better understand their own worldview and faith. Because Mormon cosmology conceives of the physical and the spiritual as being contiguous—that God and heaven are physically embodied—Grimshaw notes that there can be "a certain kind of sacredness to detailed exploration of the material world," including studying the material culture and practices of other societies.

Grimshaw reports that the overt religious symbolism in the practice of gamelan is also a means by which students can consider their beliefs and those of others. In some ways, teaching in an explicitly religious setting highlights an ecumenicism that some view as being inherent in studying gamelan, since the ensemble members are trying to understand and approximate a sense of another worldview within their own language of belief and practice. These connections are potentially manifold; Grimshaw finds parallels between ngayah (voluntary devotional service) and what in Mormonism is called consecration, the principle by which believers voluntarily dedicate their wealth, time, and talents to enhancing God's kingdom. He says that he does not push this connection, however, believing it better for students to notice and ponder the similarities and differences on their own: "I personally think that if my ensemble contributes in a valid way to the religious mission of the university, it is because those resonances or homologies actually exist and stand on their own, apart from my pedagogical narrative" (Grimshaw 2016). In this way, musical practice and cultural practice become a distinctive opportunity for students to understand both views.

Performance of gamelan can also challenge student musicians' senses of identity or feeling of comfort in their body. The assumption of Balinese gender norms, if only in the immediate context of a staged performance, can present both challenges and opportunities for American college students who are struggling to be comfortable in their own bodies. Musicians must sometimes alter the way they sit when playing in the kebaya, corset, and kain (for females) or jacket, kain, saput, and udeng (for males) that characterize traditional performance uniforms; women are sometimes uncomfortable with the relatively constrained and exposed feel of the kebaya. The feeling of embodied difference is perhaps particularly true for those studying dance, in which they are either typecast or trained to alter their movements to embody a specific image. Ideally, *alus* (refined) male characters and most female characters are portrayed by dancers who are slender and slight, with precise but graceful movements; *keras* (coarse) male characters and many nonhuman characters are portrayed by dancers with larger frames and use stronger body language. Being forced into a type or having to learn to dance against body type can be a challenge.

Students' reactions to embodying gender in new ways are, not surprisingly, variable. Humor is a powerful tool in handling potentially awkward situations, such as the time one of my larger-chested female students was struggling to close the top of her kebaya. "Help!" she said, turning to me, the lacy fabric gaping open over her tank top. "The girls won't stay in." Carefully, and with apologies in advance, I helped her squeeze everything in and finished fastening up the front. For nonheterosexual or non-cisgender students, particularly those who are not publicly open about their identities, performing gender roles that are divergent from their usual public presentation can be a heightened experience with the potential to bring liberation or distress. It requires both a steady hand and a steady heart to help a young man who has chosen to dance to put on his makeup for the first time, to apply eyeliner and mascara around dancing, fluttering eyelashes and to paint bright red lipstick on nervous lips that may never dare to publicly reveal the student's true feelings about embodying such a visually different presentation of masculinity. Sometimes, however, as a director steeped in American liberal social consciousness, I have been forced to make difficult choices. What do you do when a student who has presented as lesbian or queer asks to wear a male performance uniform, but there are not enough male uniforms to go around?[9]

For Americans studying the Balinese performing arts, learning to perform a gendered role, considering homologies between one's own religion and Balinese Hindu practices, or renegotiating the way one navigates space and time comprises an education no less profound or of less importance than learning to play the music. In that gamelan can spark these experiences of self-discovery—often in a "safe space," one in which students feel less likely to be personally attacked owing to its relative lack of fraught geopolitical or sociocultural associations for American students—it provides an approachable way to spark such self-discovery and develop cultural competency. American students cannot understand gamelan in the same way as Balinese students, nor can a non-Balinese teacher embody a Balinese experience. Yet by providing a diverse set of experiences for students and thoughtful approaches to both music and culture, teachers can encourage students to thoughtfully approach gamelan on its, and their, own terms.

Learning from Gamelan

Gamelan has been embraced by educational institutions across North America as a means of fostering musical and cultural diversity. The art is particularly approachable because of the varied levels of technical difficulty of the instruments, the flexibility of repertoire choice in the hands of a skillful teacher, and the overt representations of difference (or perhaps exoticism) embodied by the instruments and by traditional methods of learning, which are capable of stretching students' inherent expectations and capabilities, no matter what they are. Though an ensemble setting is ideally focused on attaining musical and cultural competence, the current position of gamelan in most American institutions as an "experience ensemble" makes exposure to new ideas rather than technical achievement the most important learning outcome for students. However, such an outcome can be challenged by the requirement or precedent of performing at the end of every semester, though doing so limits both the ability to achieve musical competency and the time to develop and consider cultural competency.

Artistic integrity is important, but Balinese instructors consider teaching, performing, and presenting Balinese music in accordance with the principles of desa, kala, patra—with deep consideration of and adherence to what is appropriate to time, place, and situation—to be key to cultivating a good ensemble experience. Arguably, such flexibility is important for an instructor of any type of ensemble, but it has added benefits in an intercultural setting because it encourages continued growth and learning on the part of teachers as well as students;

making judgments of appropriateness relies on a deep understanding of both material and context. Balinese and American teachers may have different challenges in cultivating this appropriate experience; typically, American gamelan musicians need more attention in their early years of teaching as they learn technical skill and build understanding of repertoire, while Balinese teachers must work to select and translate their knowledge for new audiences. Though representation and appropriation are still of concern, having American instructors that are connected to Balinese arts practitioners, even to a small extent, helps mediate such issues. Continuing to foster artistic training for American teachers and a tradition of openness and sharing about adaptation and experimentalism moves pedagogy toward becoming a collaborative effort rather than an environment where artificially strict concepts of tradition and authenticity are imposed (or flouted) without consideration or discussion.

"Making a good feeling" in a performance group, as Lasmawan emphasizes, can take many artistic and cultural forms, whether using a Barong in a homecoming parade (the Colorado College tradition), taking beleganjur to a college protest rally (as Hiranmayena has done), or allowing students to enact their own traditions of dance-drama stories. Rather than being a threat to or a misrepresentation of tradition, thoughtful and sincere efforts to adopt and adapt Balinese arts for new educational contexts instead become yet another way of embodying the arts in accordance to desa, kala, patra.

CHAPTER 6

Americans Learning Gamelan in Bali

The sun rises early in the mountains in Tabanan. Although the American college students emerge from their rooms early by their own standards (between seven and eight in the morning), the Balinese members of the family and household staff have already been up for hours, especially the women, who have long since traveled to the markets and begun to prepare the day's meals. After a shower (featuring hot water since 2016), the students make their way to the front of the compound and the expansive dining area attached to the kitchen, where they are presented with the options of "kopi atau teh"—coffee or tea, two of the words that most of the students manage to pick up during their several weeks of music study. Back in the main part of the kitchen, Marni and one or more women hired from the village prepare breakfast, which is generally a twist on Western offerings like pancakes or French toast (rather than rice-based Balinese staples), often served with banana or papaya. With beverage and plate in hand, the students then either sit in the dining area or out on the edges of the balé to chat and eat. Sometimes, one of the students or Lasmawan's sons is up earlier, practicing gender or kendang even before breakfast appears.

After breakfast, when the sun was just starting to get hot at about nine or ten, the first rehearsal of the day begins. Sometimes it involves the full group on angklung or gong kebyar, learning a new piece or revisiting a tricky spot from the piece that everyone had worked on the day before. Sometimes it is an intensive work session on technique with kendang or gender, or sometimes the students work on beleganjur. After the first rehearsal come lunch (rice, meat, vegetables, and fruit, served much in the same manner as before), followed by the second rehearsal of the day. Late afternoon brings the arrival of the village girl dancers to practice their own repertoire; female foreigners who are studying dance might join in for extra practice, while others take individual leisure time or play soccer in front of the stage with Lasmawan's sons, creating a cacophonous scene as the ball sometimes is accidentally kicked up into the dancers' formations.

After the dancers leave people might rehearse some more or go straight on to dinner, right around sunset. Then the members of the women's gamelan come; at this point, the foreign students used to make a run to the now-defunct Internet café or the Indomaret convenience store, as much to avoid hearing the same two pieces again as to reconnect with the outside world. Then there might be night rehearsal, or not; there might be a chess game and drinking and smoking, or not. Almost every night, when the students and Lasmawan's nephews gather, there is trilingual teasing (Balinese, Indonesian, and English) and universal laughing. By eleven, everyone is in bed, ears saturated with gamelan, stomachs full of rice, ready to sleep until it all starts again the next day.

The program that Lasmawan runs in his compound in Bali, like the formal summer institute that I first attended with Gamelan Çudamani, represents one

Sunrise over Sanggar Manik Galih, Bangah

of the most common ways for foreign students and adult learners alike to gain their first substantive experiences studying in Bali. Such programs have existed since the 1970s, though they have arguably become more prevalent in the early twenty-first century. Catering to foreigners interested in learning Balinese performing arts forms, such programs accept beginners and more experienced musicians, though for many participants they are an intermediate step between beginning instruction in North America and pursuing more intensive study in Indonesia.

Programs devoted to such educational tourism, or edutourism, include a wide array of formats, from one-hour private music or dance lessons for visitors to multi-week intensive programs. Some are affiliated directly with academic study-abroad programs, while others serve a wider variety of college-age or older adults who wish to engage in a program of intensive study. With the stated goal of allowing students to immerse themselves in Balinese arts study including or featuring a perceived insider's view on Balinese culture, these programs embrace artistic, social, cultural, and economic characteristics that variously resemble conventional leisure tourism, collegiate study-abroad programs, and anthropological or ethnomusicological fieldwork. Such programs are hardly distinctive to Bali; Dor (2014), for example, notes that educational programs in West Africa constitute a significant aspect of the academic American African music scene. Because of the prevalence of gamelan in North America and Bali's distinctive orientation to tourism, however, the infrastructure devoted to teaching Balinese performing arts provides an apt example of relations between artistic study or research as a form of professional development, experiential programs, and leisure travel as outgrowths of a tripartite nexus of educational, financial, and political movements within Balinese, Indonesian, and transnational contexts.

Educational tourism programs that are tied to academic programs function in specific ways. Instructors who teach gamelan to non-Indonesian musicians largely agree that studying in Indonesia with skilled native musicians is crucial to students' ultimate understanding of the music and culture, or, in Susilo's phrase, being a "bridge to Java" (Harnish, Solís, and Witzleben 2004). In Bali, where groups of American music students are taught together more regularly than in Java, Lasmawan and a handful of other internationally connected teachers of his generation maintain study programs that can accommodate both formal academic study groups and individual visitors. As with language study, musical immersion allows students to accelerate their understanding of culture, musical theory, philosophy, and nuances of performance. Edutourists may also come away with other skills such as increased self-confidence, awareness of their own culture, and feelings of connection to their host culture (Dwyer and Peters 2004).

In this chapter, which expands on my previous work (Clendinning 2017), I examine the structure and impact of short- to medium-length (one-week to two-month) performing arts study programs in Bali that are, at least in part, marketed as academic experiences. By examining how students are integrated and educated within their Balinese host communities, I present arts edutourism as a specific mode of engagement between host and visitor, with intersecting facets of performing arts education, research, and leisure. I problematize the term *turis* (tourist) as applied to such foreign students because of their tendencies to both embody and transcend musical, linguistic, and other behavioral markers of tourists more broadly, and I examine how such programs promote visions of *kebalian* (Balineseness) as a cultural concept. Ultimately, I suggest that edutourism programs form an integral part of academic musical ecosystems in three ways: first, in their capacity to provide visitors with sustainable opportunities to contribute to local artistic communities, financially and through study and performance; second, by strengthening interest in and understanding of performing arts and culture in the host country; and third, by providing opportunities for musical and cultural study that are difficult to achieve in an American academic context.

Tourism and the Arts in Bali

> Impossibly green rice terraces, pulse-pounding surf, enchanting Hindu temple ceremonies, mesmerizing dance performances, ribbons of beaches, a truly charming people: there are as many images of Bali as there are flowers on the ubiquitous frangipani trees.
>
> —*Lonely Planet Indonesia*, 2010

There is something about the island of Bali that has driven writers, historic and modern alike, to indulge in purple prose. Yet the images touted in the guidebooks are largely accurate, if carefully cultivated. The lure of the island as a lush tropical paradise has continued unabated for the past half century; even the bombings of tourist areas in Bali by Islamist extremists in 2002 and 2005 and occasional disruptions due to natural disasters have barely stemmed the tide of visitors. Riding high on a wave of publicity from the popularity of Elizabeth Gilbert's *Eat, Pray, Love: One Woman's Search for Everything Across Italy, India and Indonesia* (2006), a boom in yoga tourism, and a rise in intra-Asian tourism, among other things, the Balinese tourist industry has expanded greatly since 2010. In 2016 more than 4.9 million foreign visitors descended on the island, a figure substantially exceeding Bali's population at the time, 4.2 million (Erviani 2012b). The island therefore serves as an interesting location in which to consider the impact of the introduction of tourism programs designed specifically to be educational.

Though Kuta Beach with its white sands, blue waters, nightclubs, and extensive shopping plazas remains the most popular destination for foreign visitors to Bali, a substantial number of visitors are also drawn to visit the island for its distinctive culture, including the "mesmerizing dance performances" touted in the Lonely Planet guide. They need not go far off the beaten path to see them. In Ubud, the town dubbed "the cultural heart" of Bali in twenty-first-century tourist literature, up to a dozen local music and dance troupes perform short concerts designed to attract non-Balinese viewers, who are expected to have no more familiarity with Balinese performing arts than that which can be gleaned from reading a guidebook. Like summer pops concerts performed by Western orchestras that are designed to please audiences that might otherwise attend classical music events rarely (if at all), the Balinese touristic concerts largely feature classic works that are aurally and visually dramatic. The kecak-Ramayana narrative perhaps best embodies this experience. In their current form, the forty-five-minute performances feature kecak paired with a secularized version of the *sanghyang jaran* horse trance dance. The performances often begin just before sunset, which allows the performers to become increasingly illuminated by only a fire in the center of a performance space, to dramatic effect.

Though applied to the island's tourist industry in its entirety, Vickers' description of Bali as a "paradise, created" via careful cultivation by regional, national, and international forces (2012) clearly applies to the creative arts. Just as with Balinese performances abroad, addressed previously, transnational collaborations between foreigners and Balinese performers in Bali initially were instrumental to developing Balinese traditional and innovative arts alike into marketable forms. Yet groups of Balinese individuals in positions of cultural and governmental power took early and relatively consistent action to tailor policies that would both reflect and protect Balinese culture. Cultural sustainability remains central to this artistic development.

The issue of sustainability first came to the fore during the Suharto presidency in the late 1960s, when Bali was chosen as a center for concentrated economic development, primarily tourism, by the national government (Ramstedt 1993, 73). Yet given the immediate and massive allocation of resources to tourist developments, in 1971 the World Bank predicted that by 1985 Bali's "cultural manifestations will probably have disappeared" owing to outside influences (Picard 1996, 48). In 1968 the Commission for Evaluating and Promoting Culture (Majelis Pertimbangan dan Pembinaan Kebudayaan, known as LISTIBIYA) was founded by the Balinese regional office of the Ministry of Education and Culture (Departemen Pendidikan dan Kebudayaan) to address the potentially conflicting priorities of developing tourist infrastructure and maintaining traditional culture. Its membership was composed of individuals with substantive experience in performing arts and politics, both regionally and internationally—including I Made Bandem, one of the first Balinese artists to study and teach performing arts in the United States—who met to decide how the arts could be protected and allowed to thrive. Subsequently, official guidance from LISTIBIYA and the Ministry of Education and Culture created a tripartite categorization of the performing arts repertoire using the Balinese terms *wali* (sacred), *bebali* (ceremonial), and *bali-balihan* (secular) based on the genres' traditional site and function, use of consecrated objects or trance, and intended audience. The commission promoted and regulated the performing arts, even requiring licensure for specific groups that wished to market their performances for tourist consumption (Umeda 2007, 51).

The official policy, though perhaps helpful for administrative reasons, may have been more useful as an impetus for communities to continuously renegotiate their own decisions rather than codify artistic and cultural practices. The externally imposed categories were an imperfect fit for the way many art forms had long been practiced. Performing artists had grown up immersed in the concepts of desa, kala, patra as central to their decision making, and they were already considerate and flexible in their choices of repertoire and the adaptations they chose to make for different performance contexts, touristic and otherwise (Sudirana 2019). Even as enterprising chauffeurs began to shuttle visitors out to local temple ceremonies in order to cater to a perpetual thirst for more "authentic" experiences, the long-held Balinese cultural concepts of flexibility, appropriateness to context, and importance of sustaining religious practice on their own created an environment that could be welcoming to outsiders without compromising the key elements of Balinese ritual and art. How to achieve this balance remains a central point of debate not only in the contexts of artistic and religious practices but also in all aspects of social and political life.

A Flower Blooms on the Mountain

Since the time of Kunst and McPhee, researchers and artists had traveled to Bali to learn more about its performing arts. Few visitors of any kind arrived during World War II or the initial years after Indonesian independence, but tourism again was on the rise by the mid-1960s; Bali's international airport, Ngurah Rai, was remodeled and expanded twice within a decade to meet the demand.

Graduate students and recent graduates of UCLA who had played in the gamelan ensemble such as Robert Brown and Gertrude Rivers Robinson traveled to Bali and Java to study and record music before much of this tourist infrastructure was in place. Like their teachers before them, these musician-scholars lived and worked closely with their host communities. They stayed for several months at a time and used their experiences as professional development.

Brown, in turn, founded the first organized performing arts–oriented study tour to Bali. In 1971 he became the director of the San Francisco–based Center for World Music, a nonprofit organization that began primarily as a site for studying Indian classical music and dance. By this time the center was hosting programs in performing arts traditions from around the world at different sites across the American West. At its self-proclaimed height in 1973, its programming at the University of Washington in Seattle brought together dozens of the most distinguished artists, performers, directors, composers, and teachers of the Asian arts of that generation, including American and Indonesian founders of Balinese and Javanese gamelan programs such as Nyoman and Nanik Wenten, who subsequently spent the following four decades teaching in California.

It was at this time that the center further expanded its offerings to include formal study programs outside the United States. The first of these was founded in Payangan, Gianyar, Bali, and was called Giri Kusuma, or Flower Mountain. Established as a collaboration between the Balinese Yayasan Seni Dunia Tradisional (Foundation for the Traditional Arts) and the Center for World Music, the program at Flower Mountain provided a space where a group of foreign students could study together.[1] Sets of instruments of more varieties than would likely be found in any single village were stored together onsite, and specialists were brought in to teach the different repertoires. Logistical matters such as food and laundry were arranged for students who paid a set fee that covered the cost of the experience. In March 1999 Brown announced the opening of a new compound for the program on the international gamelan listserv. Facilities at the compound included a three-story building with offices, dormitories, and a library and outdoor practice and performance spaces, all built on the land where the palace of the king of Payangan once stood. The location continues to be associated with the center and has hosted groups of students regularly for the past four decades.

The program at Flower Mountain, which partnered with academic and nonacademic institutions, was an outgrowth of the interest in learning gamelan and dance that had begun to be cultivated in American institutions of higher education. It can also be viewed as an outgrowth of the emphasis on formalized learning processes that had been introduced to the Balinese conservatories only a decade earlier. Finally, the programs offered an alternative to prior methods of studying the performing arts in Bali, which had required the development of personal contacts on the island and the time and temperament to devote to studying in a village setting. With a program that was designed for foreign students of all ages, it also differed substantially from the newly founded Darmasiswa program, which sponsored foreign students to enroll directly at Indonesian arts conservatories for up to a full year.[a] For more than two decades Flower Mountain served as the primary established site of its kind in Bali. The acceleration in dispersal of gamelan culture resulted in an influx of new programming at the turn of the twenty-first century, however—programming that combined intense artistic study and cultural immersion and that were cast more specifically as academic experiences.

Performing Arts Edutourism in the Twenty-First Century

Since the establishment of Flower Mountain, American students have continued to arrive to study in Bali, working either with that group or individually through connections forged with their teachers in the United States. Other Balinese teachers host individuals or private groups in their home villages, generally in partnership with one or more American universities. Since the mid-1990s, individuals and institutions have created formalized open-enrollment programs that may absorb both college students and other interested persons. These include Gamelan Çudamani, an internationally renowned performing sanggar (privately owned arts organization) in Pengosekan, Gianyar; Mekar Bhuana, a Badung-based conservatory, research center, and exporter of performing arts products; the Bali Module for the World, based in Denpasar and affiliated with the ISI-Denpasar and University of Essex; and Lasmawan's Sanggar Manik Galih near Baturiti, among many others. Other individual Balinese and American teachers work with Balinese performing artists to host student experiences in settings that are otherwise closed to the public. All these programs are organized by Balinese performing artists with substantial international performing and teaching experience and are generally maintained together with non-Indonesians.

Substantial changes in the Balinese social and artistic landscape around the turn of the twenty-first century likely influenced the founding of such formalized programs. Throughout Indonesia, the Asian financial crisis and subsequent political unrest had substantially disrupted foreign travel; the Reformasi government, coming into power in 1998, displaced the authoritarian policies that had been in place under Suharto and initiated new opportunities for international cultural exchanges. Concurrently, according to the Institute for International Education, rates of American students studying abroad in formal academic programs nearly doubled between 1998 and 2014. With the national interest in strengthening the programs of the Indonesian arts conservatories and the increasing ease with which Indonesian artists (via their own travel or via the Internet) could learn about and model different types of arts programs, codification of artistic study became increasingly common across the spectrum of performing arts education. In sum, increasing support for formalization and institutionalization of artistic study from all quarters was at least correlated with (if not the cause of) the establishment of newer programs that rose to diversify and meet a demand that could not be satisfied by Flower Mountain alone.

The explicit ties between some arts edutourism programs and academic institutions places them within a long history of educational travel that goes back to the Grand Tours that educated Europe's young aristocrats from the seventeenth to the early nineteenth century (Towner 1985). On such tours, young adults around the age of twenty-one from well-off families would travel a relatively set route through the political and cultural capitals of western Europe with the aid of a culturally experienced tutor or guide. The tours were not considered to be specifically scholarly or religious in nature, but rather combined leisure with education. In addition to making valuable social contacts and practicing language skills, the young travelers on such tours would encounter important works of art, architecture, music, and other forms of cultural capital at first hand—all experiences deemed necessary to becoming cultured adults. As such, the tours served as a capstone and a rite of passage for those who could afford to undertake them.

Grand Tours in their original form declined with the advent in the nineteenth century of mass tourism, which opened travel experiences to a wider array of European and American social classes and largely revolved around leisure venues such as seaside resorts and amusement parks (Falk et al. 2012). Yet certain aspects of the Grand Tour were reinvented for American college students and young adults beginning in the mid-twentieth century, again combining leisure tourism and education. In educational discourse, collegiate study-abroad programs have been heavily touted since that time in response to a perceived need for an increase in global preparedness in students (Lantis and DuPlaga 2010). Side benefits such as "becoming an adult" faster and "self-discovery" make frequent appearances in study program literature aimed toward students. Today, mass media enable them to gain a wider exposure to global culture than their ancestors had. Experiencing the art, architecture, culture, and food of the great cultural capitals of the world—not only in Europe—has become a marker of social status, one that can make appearances on students' social media accounts as easily as on their résumés. For individuals who missed such opportunities as undergraduates, cultural tours directed at specific age groups that cater to interests in history, art, or food and wine are available to fill the gap. Some program directors work to make study abroad or other edutourism programs accessibly priced. Programs based in colleges are often still only available to economically elite students, however—those who are attending a four-year university and whose families have enough financial resources to muster thousands of dollars to support the experience.

Programs in Bali that cater to college students and ones that have more open enrollment typically balance formal artistic study in a large group with guest master classes, individual or small-group lessons, and visits to important cultural sites and musical events. Programs such as those hosted by Çudamani, while sometimes absorbing the students of an American academic program, often integrate students and non-students of varying degrees of experience by providing open registration to adult individuals. In contrast, Lasmawan, who has formally partnered with educational institutions such as Skidmore College, Northern Illinois University, and Colorado College, has increasingly arranged for formal study-abroad program participants to be the only visitors to his compound during their stay; during other weeks with no formal programs, he hosts whichever of his students want to come to work with members of the family.

In terms of curriculum, such programs provide a wealth of opportunities for learning the Balinese performing arts unavailable anywhere in the United States. Considering only the programs listed above, between them the organizations offer fourteen different types of gamelan ensembles for students to experience, each with its own distinctive cultural history and repertoire, though most programs focus on one or two styles. Dance instruction in a variety of styles is available at all the aforementioned locations, including a range of solo and group study of female and male styles. All these programs either regularly offer or can arrange a focused or elective program of study in other Balinese performing and plastic arts, including *kidung* and *kakawin* (traditional song genres), shadow puppetry, mask carving, and puppet making. Taken together, the programs represent a broad spectrum of contemporary approaches to displaying what is musically important in the Balinese performing arts.

Given that cultural immersion is a major reason for students to travel to Bali rather than remain at home, it is important to consider how arts edutourism programs also provide different geographical and even logistical experiences of the Balinese lifestyle. Homestay-style accommodations that are purpose-built to accommodate students and home-cooked (catered) meals are typical for groups hosted in village settings. For programs located near tourist areas, such as at Çudamani and several private programs run by Gianyar-based teachers, students are housed in a local hotel, provided with one or two meals per day, and may walk or be shuttled through streets lined with tourist shops to their daily lessons. In either of these types of locations, students not only have access to lessons with regular and guest teachers but also experience the local cultural and religious life of their host communities. In addition to practical lessons, some academically focused programs also schedule formal lectures on Balinese history, culture, religion, and other topics to supplement the students' experiences. Finally, most programs incorporate significant aspects of cultural tourism via excursions to sites of cultural importance. Such trips both provide well-needed breaks from learning and show visitors important natural and cultural facets of the island. In addition to trips to the beach, a monkey forest, the islands' picturesque *sawah* (rice paddies) and waterfalls, or shopping districts—which are often directly contextualized for students as a part of the tourist industry—visits to important temples such as Pura Besakih and Pura Tanah Lot provide context for the experience of Balinese religious practice. Moreover, experiencing performances in other villages, at touristic venues in Ubud, and at the annual Bali Arts Festival provides an extended sense of the diversity of performing arts styles, venues, and philosophies in Bali in a way that is difficult to capture in an academic course in the United States.

Extended Pedagogies and Educational Results

In addition to the ability to plunge into a cultural context, study in Bali allows for an expansion of musical context in terms of pedagogical intensity and overall performing arts immersion. The maguru panggul technique, described in chapter 5, is common. In the United States, the technique is potentially supplemented by written notation or employed only in step-by-step instruction of one section of instruments at a time because of an insufficient number of musician-teachers (Harnish 2004). Different variants on the technique are practiced in programs in Bali, in part because there are frequently more experienced teachers on site. For example, in the Çudamani summer institutes, the gamelan students who enroll are directed by Dewa Putu Berata, assisted by a handful of members of Gamelan Çudamani. In rehearsal, these assistants initially serve as a musical mirror, sitting on the opposite side of each learner's instrument and playing the part so that the learner can follow on the same set of keys or gongs. Although they hear other repertoires and may progress to them at the end of the institute, all students start by learning *tari dasar* and *tabuh dasar*, etude-like pieces that are newly composed to include all the basic techniques in one piece. While the foundational pieces are pedagogically efficient, students must pursue further study in order to encounter canonical Balinese works, ones that employ the different techniques in a more naturalized setting.

In contrast, at Sanggar Manik Galih the experience is more variable according to the number and experience levels of foreign learners. Groups of visitors with whom Lasmawan has already worked tend to focus on pieces with which they are familiar, whereas new students begin to learn either on compositions by Lasmawan that are written at an easier level or standard pieces of gong kebyar or angklung repertoire, sometimes in simplified forms. Newer students joining in may look for guidance to the members of Lasmawan's family, village community, and other foreign visitors playing together, using the mirroring technique only for one-on-one practice sessions. Private or small-group lessons within any of the programs mentioned may vary in pedagogical style as teachers adapt to learners' needs.

In all such programs, students' increased exposure to Balinese performing arts—whether through watching local groups practice, attending temple ceremonies, or attending formal concerts—more clearly mimics the Balinese experience of learning music. Maguru panggul, though seized upon as quintessential by Westerners who have written about Balinese music, is only one aspect of what, Balinese teachers emphasize, constitutes learning. Musical competency cannot be achieved by learning individual parts in individual pieces. In Bali, the other techniques such as maguru mata (learning by watching) and maguru kuping (learning by hearing) are much easier to put into practice than in North America.

In part, an expanded understanding of the Balinese artistic world can come from playing different types of gamelan. Given that each gamelan produces a distinctive sound and requires slightly different playing techniques, the aesthetic and technical experience of study is also distinctive to each ensemble. For example, for a student who has only played the four-tone ceremonial angklung at home, the aural, physical, and mental experience of learning pieces for semaradana—a substantially larger, seven-tone bronze gamelan invented at the end of the twentieth century—would be entirely different in physical terms and would bring the student to understand an entirely different repertoire, set of artistic aesthetics, and portion of Balinese cultural history. More important, being surrounded by the music as played by the Balinese or by more advanced non-Balinese musicians (whether in temple ceremonies or other types of public performance) exposes students to types of artistic and social skills and senses of group feeling that teachers can rarely provide for them in person in the United States.

These types of expanded musical and cultural access are not available to all foreigners who might be interested. For students, the opportunity to continue their studies abroad requires several weeks of free time that are not otherwise devoted to study or work, as well as enough funding to pay for travel to Bali, tuition and housing, and incidentals. Scholarships are available for many programs but may leave out major costs such as airfare, which is often the single most expensive part of the trip. At the time of writing, these expenses could easily equal more than a month's income for the average American household or more than a year's income for a middle-class Balinese family. Like ensemble education in North America itself, this type of education is a privilege available only to a certain subset of the American population; impressions of egalitarianism that can be casually implied in gamelan ensembles in North America are exposed as illusions in an international context to a greater extent than they are in students' home contexts.

Performing arts edutourism programs provide foreigners with levels of access to Balinese culture that they might not experience in pursuing solo study, however. For example, young female students who might otherwise find their musical study options limited—or at least subject to inevitable incidents of miscommunication involving differing perceptions of gender roles in Bali and America—may feel more comfortable in formal programs and have a greater chance of socially integrating and taking on leadership roles than if embedded within a Balinese men's group, while still receiving more intensive instruction than they would in a Balinese women's group. More generally, students who might never have the confidence to travel or live by themselves in Bali to pursue musical study are able to feel supported in group travel. On the other hand, Balinese artists' exposure to American musicians in professional and artistic settings may also encourage a depth of social interaction and relationship-building that they might not otherwise find as performers.

The degree of access to Balinese life afforded to students in these programs extends to performance settings. In addition to observing local performances, groups studying in Bali often present end-of-term concerts. Their intensive period of study, freedom from an academic schedule, and ability to perform in a more informal setting contrast substantially with the American academic performance experience. Some shows are small and semi-private, limited to students, teachers, and other invited guests. Another option for visitors—advanced individual students or groups—is to play at the Bali Arts Festival. Because it is the primary artistic showcase for the entire island, however, performing there requires a high level of skill, making it a less common venue for visitors.[3] Village civic events offer other opportunities, as do temple ceremonies, where performance traditionally fulfills the function of making an important devotional offering, or ngayah.[4] Other programs, including Çudamani, provide this opportunity, but Lasmawan insists on temple performances whenever possible. He describes the benefits of this type of experience:

> Every time we play—I think every time we have sixty members—so we can play beleganjur, all the members combined from the village [with the students], we have a ceremonial thing. Close to a thousand people watch. That kind of thing, most of my guests think is better than in Denpasar [the Bali Arts Festival]. Because in Denpasar, my guests see after they play, there's just no connection. . . . If we play in the temple, after we play, everybody's like, "Ooooh, we want to take a photo with you, with the turis [tourists, visitors]." It's crowded, and almost everybody looks happy, and everybody enjoys their time. (2012b)

In a practical sense, performing at a temple ceremony is an ideal setting for the experience-oriented foreign student ensembles in that it provides a way for the learners to engage in an important social context with their adopted local communities. Though foreign musicians may or may not view their playing as a religious offering, in my experience, it certainly functions as a social offering, a sign of giving back to one's hosts. Similarly, although artistry in such performances is still valued, intention in presentation is also valued. While local audiences tend to laugh if they hear a major mistake or are faced with the sight of "giant" American women dancing a part usually reserved for prepubescent Balinese girls, such incongruities serve as part of the entertainment. The practice of foreign groups playing in temples is not beyond controversy, however—I remember playing once with a group that was moved to a remote area of the temple in order not to distract from other performances—the overall context for performance provides a way in which foreign visitors are able to demonstrate an appreciation for Balinese culture that is more than financially transactional.

Seeking the "Authentic" Bali

Before I visited Bali for the first time, a savvy colleague cautioned me to be critical of what was formally presented to me as Balinese culture. Although the exhortation certainly applied to navigating sites and resources maintained for general tourism, I quickly discovered that it applied to what I was learning from my teachers as well. Authenticity was not only sought by students but was also explicitly evoked by Balinese hosts. The description of a program's method of study, living situation, food, and cultural excursions as authentic served in part as marketing, intended to steer newcomers to choose a specific program of study rather than others—and the information deemed appropriate and important to transmit within the context of a program depended entirely on the teacher. Representations of the best version of a "real" Bali, therefore, can take many different forms. The tension between these seen and unseen motivations for the way culture is contextualized in these settings, and how students interact with such representations, reveals a complex negotiation of individual and group identity that in general exceeds the depth reached in conventional tourist settings.

Despite its extensive baggage in academic contexts, the trope of authenticity carries considerable currency in Balinese contexts. This value is most visible in Balinese discourses that interface with the outside world, such as the cultivation of specific performing arts forms for tourist performances and the codification of Balinese Hindu beliefs and practices to align with the Indonesian-state definition of a religion (Howe 2005). Within arts study programs, the concept of authenticity or realness is highlighted not only by participants but also by the teachers, who specifically tout the benefits of their location and program (living in the village or learning a certain type of repertoire) as providing the quintessential Balinese experience.

Like Bakan (1999), Gold (2005), and I, and anyone who has written about their initial experiences in Bali, the students in these programs experience several different ideas of kebalian, or Balineseness.[5] More vivid than the narratives that are carefully cultivated in an academic course, the sequence of planned learning opportunities in edutouristic programs presents a tangible impression of the "real" Bali, something more than could ever be found in books or videos, and definitely an experience believed to be more real than that of the typical tourist visit. That experience was summed up by Aleanna Collins, a student of Lasmawan's who had studied twice in Bali, who noted, "I'm staying with the people who live here, and I live in the village, and we get to see this women's group come every night and get to experience that part of everybody's daily life, for example, whereas the Rustic Pathways people [a high school service travel group] are going to go, 'Do activities'" (Collins 2012).

Elizabeth Macy, who wrote about her initial experiences of studying in Bali with Lasmawan in her dissertation (2010), says that her perception of the importance of that journey has expanded since she began to take her own students there. Although she at first assigned readings in the course, she quickly just let the students experience being in Bangah because "assigning reading means they're missing out on so many things." She recalls, "To me, participating in that class in college shifted a lot of the ways I felt about the world. . . . It sounds cliché, but it was literally a life-changing experience. . . . It means a lot to my students that this was something that *I* did at their age. They see that, long-term, they could maintain this type of relationship [with a teacher from another country] when they see me." She reports that one student even asked her, somewhat in seriousness, "How do I get to have a sixty-year-old friend who's Balinese?" (Macy 2018). The atmosphere that the Tangkas family creates in their compound, she believes, is something truly special in that the family can accommodate student needs in a way that also allows them to experience, to a large extent, the daily rhythms of a Balinese household.

Foreigners who visit Bali to study the performing arts simultaneously blur the distinctions between being students, researchers, performing artists, and tourists. Such turis rarely become true participants in the fabric of the Balinese reality, however, because of the relationships that they build during their time on the island. They often arrive in Bali on tourist visas and stay for a relatively short period of time. Because of the pedagogical style, the presence of multilingual hosts, and the short duration of their programs, few of the visitors learn more than basic phrases in Indonesian or Balinese, and that is insufficient for holding meaningful conversations with most of the Balinese people they encounter. Group study programs obviate the need for visitors to take care of transportation, housing, food, or most other daily necessities, and direct payment for these services cements the transactional nature of these visits. Finally, Balinese performing arts edutourism programs create a narrative of Bali for their guests by means of explicit pedagogical choices and implicit cultural narratives that visitors absorb through interacting with their teachers, going on excursions, and living locally. Such edutourists gain access to parts of Balinese life that many other visitors never see, but even those who stay in villages remain at least one step removed from regular Balinese life.

Despite the temptation on the part of the leaders of educational programs in Bali to show their visitors only the "best" and most authentic experiences of culture, most pedagogues realize that a layered approach helps students see a number of different authentic versions of Bali. In the 2014 "Experiencing the Arts in Bali" program hosted by Northern Illinois University, awareness of the student-tourist nexus was listed as an integral part of the program: "Students in this program are also encouraged to interact with other tourists to gain insights into the impact of tourism on the development of Balinese culture in the globalized era" (Northern Illinois University Study Abroad Office 2014, n.p.). Although Lasmawan used to limit student visits to areas like the surfer-and-nightclub center of Kuta, he has relented in recent years, and the kecak performances in

Ubud are always on the to-do list as a point of exposure to tourist culture. The juxtaposition of these with a visit to the Bali Arts Festival, temple ceremonies, and formalized study adds a sense of complexity to each student's impression of Bali.

As if exposing students to the differences between local and tourist performances is not enough for a three-week period, some American teachers who themselves have had several teachers recognize the importance of taking students to learn from multiple perspectives. Grimshaw, for example, purposefully engages with programs sponsored by three of his major teachers in a whirlwind, month-long dash that allows students to realize the individuality of each situation and location, all of which contribute to the Balinese educational and performance ecosystem. In each of these cases, students gain a more layered understanding of Balinese culture and performing arts than they might through casual observation at a single location.

The Sale of Kebalian

Contemporary visitors to Bali are confronted by symbolic markers of Balinese culture beginning at the airport. A Barong—a figure whose ritual versions are perceived to be so spiritually potent that they are stored with their masks covered—is displayed openly, with renderings of its face plastered on nearby t-shirts. Moving out into the island, it is easy to find aspects of Balinese ethnic identity that have been abstracted from traditional life to mark or market a sense of Balineseness. Temple offerings, rice paddies, cremation processions, and certainly the performing arts have been used as marketing images or tour opportunities presented for foreign consumption to generate revenue. In turn, these signifiers of identity are, in keeping with Comaroff and Comaroff, "at once essentialized and made the subject of choice, construction, consumption" by foreign visitors (2009, 150). Island culture is therefore packaged as a part of the "growing naturalization of the trope of identity" (ibid.) but also is used as an accessory for foreign visitors to convey status, now by posting exoticized and sometimes inappropriate selfies on social media with temples, rice fields, and other important elements of Balinese daily life serving as a backdrop.

Although visitors studying the performing arts in Bali still document their experiences, their education generally leads them to avoid such problematic excesses. Yet their experiences are still bounded within a type of economic exchange. Indeed, the transactional nature of world music study in general is more apparent in study-abroad or edutouristic settings than in regular college settings. In the United States, for example, students in academic gamelans generally enroll as a part of a course, the actual costs of which are obscured by lack of transparency of faculty salaries, the differing ways in which ensembles are credited between and across colleges and universities, and the fact that in many private institutions full-time tuition is the same for students no matter how many courses one takes, so there is no specific cost to participate in the ensemble. As a result, any funds paid to the institution to support a gamelan ensemble may not come directly from its participants. At any institution, unless the ensemble instructor is employed only for that course, the financial remuneration for the teacher's instruction in Balinese music or culture is also obscured by the panoply of other duties accorded to faculty.

Direct monetary payment for lessons in music or dance is no longer uncommon in Bali, both within the official conservatory system and in private contexts; in this sense, the distribution of student fees is, perhaps, as transparently transactional as in North America. Yet the fact that arts edutourism programs are designed to be culturally immersive, too, complicates the situation. In Bali, musical study was traditionally embedded within a larger framework of reciprocal social exchanges—and this is still possible for foreigners who have made long-term commitments to Balinese communities, but is not feasible for first-time or short-term visitors. On one hand, direct payment allows fees for instruction to make their way much more directly into the hands of the Balinese, with American host teachers generally taking a cut as co-instructors or facilitators. And students can experience Balinese culture and art without as many levels of mediation as are present in American contexts, with cultural immediacy that presents opportunities for building true connections. On the other, when students pay teachers directly, the boundaries between professional obligation and personal commitment from the Balinese instructors are not clear-cut.

Whereas students who stay in Bali for a limited time cannot contribute to the well-being of a single family or community in the more traditional model of a long-term exchange of favors, many study programs officially and openly provide substantial support for their Balinese host communities, including funding the preservation of historic artistic repertoires, teaching local children for free, or contributing financially to general village infrastructure. Making these connections explicit highlights the way money is being transformed back into social action. Macy, for example, explains to students over breakfast, "We're here, and that's why this kitchen got built," and tells them that their tuition funds, furthermore, sponsored the stage that now hosts dozens of village children who can study traditional arts every week for free.

Finally, presenting the performing artists' teaching as work compensated directly through monetary payment can also be interpreted as a source of valuation, a point of pride in Balinese artistry and heritage that is not found in other aspects of the tourist industry. At the annual Çudamani Institute program concert in 2015, organizer Emiko Saraswati Susilo highlighted this point about the Balinese teachers who have long worked with the program. Since they are formally employed and paid wages, the instructors are treated as the professionals that they are rather than as mere entertainers for tourist audiences. Their artistic talents are recognized not as a vacation diversion but as being at a level that is aspirational for students—an advanced level of skill that it would take a lifetime to achieve.

Whereas the economic outcomes are relatively fixed, the individual interpersonal outcomes of such systems largely depend on the attitudes and actions of participants. If they chose, foreign students could plant a few grains of rice, visit a few performances, take some pictures, and go home, having used their experience merely as a chance to enhance their résumés and social media feeds. Likewise, Balinese community members, particularly teachers, could ignore students once the official programs are over. Although this does sometimes happen, it is relatively rare. Photos from the groups are often instead displayed with pride on social media with all participants, Balinese and American alike, gleefully tagged. The rice that the students planted, once green and grown, will almost inevitably reappear in photos online that are posted by the Balinese hosts, with all the planters tagged. Even though economic exchanges are a key component of how arts edutourism programs are run, the potential for identity to be for sale is ameliorated by both the formal educational context and the potential for professional and personal exchanges.

Conclusions

Combining elements of academic study-abroad programs, professional arts intensive workshops, and other forms of cultural tourism, Balinese performing arts edutourism programs provide a distinctive way for foreign gamelan students to connect to Balinese communities. With populations that sometimes overlap with those of academic arts researchers or semiprofessional American gamelan groups who tour to Bali, the edutourism programs occupy a specific niche in that they highlight experiential and immersive learning rather than performance, and they interact with Balinese communities accordingly. In doing so, such programs represent an artistic option within the ever-increasing variety of American collegiate foreign study programs and provide a place for novice and experienced musicians alike to experience Balinese arts and culture.

The programs' recent addition to the transnational Balinese performing arts ecosystem complicates traditional artistic systems of remuneration as well as the transactional relationships common in conventional tourism programs. Such programs allow visitors not only to consume the experiences of ethnic authenticity but also to enter this liminal space between student, tourist, and temporary local community member, thus transcending the role of a conventional tourist. Although the negotiation and representation of cultural identity and achieving appropriate financial remuneration remain concerns for this pedagogical community, the ability of such programs to extend reciprocity beyond the purely monetary sphere offers Balinese teachers an opportunity to be paid fairer wages for their work than those available in other tourist contexts and to be valued directly as the skilled artists, teachers, and cultural guides that they have trained to be. In programs oriented around living in the village such as that at Sanggar Manik Galih, moreover, the youth of the local community also reap the benefits of international exchange as they interact in formal and casual spaces of learning with their American peers.

As for the Americans, contemporary performing arts study-abroad programs can fulfill a much wider set of aims for their student participants. Some become performers of Balinese performing arts in their own rights, eventually building skill and expertise that rests comfortably alongside those of Balinese artists. They will have achieved greater musical competency—certainly more playing ability and experience—than the average nonmusician Balinese and may even serve as primary teachers or culture bearers in their own communities. Others, though adequate performers, may primarily teach at a basic level or facilitate the Balinese performing arts in their home contexts. Some will incorporate what they learn into their own original artworks. Others still will work in other fields inside or outside Indonesian contexts but maintain an appreciation for the Indonesian performing arts. Whether as a form of pre-professional development or, more commonly, a form of personal enrichment, these programs further the goals of liberal education above and beyond a classroom setting.

CHAPTER 7

Kembali: To Return or Change

In the summer of 2019, Gamelan Tunas Mekar made its second-ever appearance at the largest arts festival in Bali: Pesta Kesenian Bali, or Bali Arts Festival. The preparations had begun several years earlier, with new pieces being written and choreographed—including music by Hiranmayena, Wijaya, and American ensemble member Kendall Burks—and practiced for months. Because of their festival performance and subsequent tour of the island, the musicians became minor celebrities who were recognized on the street. A video of Burks's composition that was posted to YouTube, titled "Bule Ganteng Amerika Jago Megambel di PKB" (handsome foreigners from America are champions at playing gamelan), received over 1.4 million hits within the first six months of its posting.

The first time the group performed at the festival was in 1996, less than five years after Lasmawan moved to Colorado and before his youngest two sons were born. The ensemble only had a set of the smaller four-toned angklung instruments at that time, so the repertoire they had played consisted of interpretations of technically complex gong kebyar pieces on those instruments. As reported in the Balinese magazine *Gatra*, the ensemble's approach had proved surprising to listeners, since the angklung is more closely associated with ritual and especially funeral music than with *kreasi baru* ("new creation," new compositions in semitraditional formats) (Suartaya 1996). Limited by the small range of their instruments, the group was forced to interpret pieces in a new way. As

Lasmawan noted in the article, "We want to awaken the Balinese, especially composers, to examine angklung more closely" (ibid., n.p.). Now, returning to the stage as one of the oldest community gamelans in the United States, they impressed audiences not only with their novelty but also with their ability.

The Bali Arts Festival was the brainchild of Ida Bagus Mantra, the Indian-educated former governor of Bali (1978–1988) and former director general of culture (1968–1978). It was founded in 1978 and organized in conjunction with officials from political and arts institutions (Yamashita 2003, 47–48). Held in the center of Denpasar, the festival runs for one month every year from late June through mid-July. Three spaces in the Taman Werdhi Budaya Bali Art Center, the largest of which seats six thousand people, host approximately five performances each day. The programming features invited performers of music, dance, and theater; *lomba* (competitions) in music and other cultural activities; and special exhibitions and lectures, as well as a full array of vendors. Despite having dates that are fixed in accordance with the international Gregorian calendar (as opposed to being based on the Balinese Hindu calendars) and being free to all attendees, the festival attracts relatively few tourists from outside Indonesia; instead, it largely embraces its founding purpose: to be an exhibition of Balinese culture for the Balinese. Though it is sometimes criticized for attracting audiences that are as interested in socializing or shopping as in hearing music, the festival is the largest consistently held arts event on the island. For a foreign gamelan ensemble to be invited to perform there, particularly to play music that is innovative albeit built on deep understandings of Bali's musical history, is quite an accomplishment.

Gamelan Tunas Mekar was not the first gamelan from North America to perform at the festival; Gamelan Galak Tika (from Boston), Gamelan Dharma Swara (New York), Gamelan Gita Asmara (Vancouver), and Gamelan Sekar Jaya (Berkeley) have also performed there as a part of widespread tours to Bali. It was Gamelan Sekar Jaya's initial tour in 1985, however—the first tour of an American group to Bali—that marked the forming of a dialogue or exchange between the Balinese and American worlds of gamelan rather than a unidirectional relationship. This trip, documented in the film *Kembali: To Return* (1989), was notable for being the first large-scale exposure of the Balinese people to performing arts groups from outside Bali. Gamelan Sekar Jaya has since conducted five other tours to the island in conjunction with the Bali Arts Festival and was awarded the Dharma Kusuma Award, Bali's highest award for artistic achievement, in 2000. The ethnomusicologist and former U.S. consular agent to Bali Andy Toth claims, "It is no exaggeration to say that most of the 2.8 million Balinese [the population of Bali at the time of the initial tour] have seen Sekar Jaya in live performance and television broadcasts" (Gamelan Sekar Jaya 2017, n.p.). The 1985 performance was particularly notable, however, because it redefined Balinese people's expectations of their own performing arts. As Wayne Vitale, a founding member and former director of the ensemble, recalled,

> The Balinese were totally stunned by what we were doing. Our performance was broadcast all over the island, and it was a sensation. It was also kind of a wake-up call. We were foreigners who were passionate about gamelan, when many young people there were more interested in Western music. Traditional dance and music is thriving in Bali now, and we're an important part of that story. (A. Gilbert 2014, n.p.)

The narration of the documentary film adds additional insight to the importance of such tours:

> The Balinese were surprised that Americans would value their culture in the way that we do. It seemed fitting that it was the blending of Western and Balinese forms that turned out to be the most popular. Time and time again, in newspaper reviews or in person, people would mention how much the tour meant to them, how it had made them proud of their Balinese heritage. That made us feel good and made the whole trip seem worthwhile. (Adler, Mayer, and Rogers 1989)

Gamelan Sekar Jaya's impact, however, was not limited to demonstrating foreign interest in Balinese music. Other elements of the Americans' performances, such as having men and women play in the same ensemble, provided distinct points of cultural and musical disjuncture and at least in part inspired substantive changes to the Balinese performing arts—in this case, the rise in popularity in women's gamelans in the late 1980s (Downing 2019).

Used as a verb, the Indonesian word *kembali* most closely means "to return"; it is frequently used to describe the pilgrimages of foreign musicians to Indonesia to study or perform gamelan. Yet, used as a noun, the word can also mean "change" or potentially "renaissance." The artistic, social, and cultural exchanges caused by the return of Balinese culture from America to Bali fall at the nexus of these meanings, because a trip to Bali by Americans or the return to the island by Balinese American artists contains aspects of both pilgrimage and renaissance, ultimately changing all involved. This transnational artistic exchange has also affected the way Balinese institutions function, but perhaps more important, it has changed the way Balinese teachers have approached their careers, pattern of travel, and relationships with non-Balinese partners in performance and teaching.

Although it touches on institutional changes, this chapter focuses on the ways in which three generations of Balinese and Balinese American musicians—those born within the same date range and who share similar cultural experiences—are negotiating personal and professional lives that have substantively spanned two continents, two systems of institutionalized higher education, and a gamelan world increasingly shaped by transnational exchange. Following a brief overview of the types of institutionalization that have come to define Indonesian American pedagogical and artistic exchanges, I approach each generation roughly in order from oldest to youngest. Given that this discussion involves individuals born and working in two countries, I group individuals on the basis a combination of factors, including American generational designation (Pew Research Center 2019), familial status (marriage and children are particularly important social markers in Bali), and stage of career at the time of writing. The oldest generation is roughly equivalent in age to the American baby boomers, born from the mid-1940s to mid-1960s; they became adults during the Suharto era, have adult children themselves, and began transnational teaching and performing careers in the 1990s or earlier. The intermediate generation involves artists who are roughly the same age as Generation X (born between the mid-1960s and early 1980s), whose children are still teenagers or younger and whose international teaching careers took off after the turn of the millennium. Finally, the last generation consists of young adults born in the late 1980s or after who grew up primarily in the United States, have no children, and are still completing their educations.

Each generation has approached the premise of "return"—whether that be physical return to Bali or to North America to establish artistic and pedagogical niches for themselves, supporting their families, or navigating the perils of intercultural assumptions and misunderstandings—in different ways. The eldest generation, that which helped define or embody the role of "culture bearer" in teaching world music ensembles (Trimillos 2004, 36), was the first to attempt to balance maintaining long-term social and professional obligations that spanned Indonesia and the United States; it helped construct the institutional architecture that exists today. The subsequent generation of artists grew up in an explicitly international artistic world in part shaped by the previous generation, but it demonstrates new approaches in the way its members navigate transnational careers as performers, composers, and educators. The youngest generation is the first to embody 1.75- or second-generation immigrant experiences, here defined as those characteristic of children whose parents are immigrants and who were born in the United States or brought there in early childhood (Rumbaut 2004). Taken together, their stories demonstrate a transformation in the Balinese American artistic landscape that could not have taken place without the interlocking developments of both nations' artistic and educational institutions.

Negotiating Institutions, Defining an Indonesian American Career

The institutionalization of Balinese educational credentials has long been an influential factor in the types of careers that performing artists have been able to pursue. Bakan (1999) discusses at length the career implications of choosing to be a part of the conservatory system or remaining a seniman alam ("natural artist") in Bali in the 1990s. In contrasting the educational backgrounds and careers of his two major beleganjur teachers, the conservatory-trained Asnawa and I Ketut Sukarata, a well-known seniman alam in Denpasar, he illuminates the complexity of the situation. Sukarata, a successful composer and musician, perceived that he had been marginalized, overlooked in the awarding of official markers of musical success; he had substantial difficulty in obtaining recording contracts and felt ignored in the selection of committees to judge beleganjur competitions (Bakan 1999, 179–184). In contrast, Asnawa had by that point received degrees from KOKAR (1974) and ASTI (1980), held graduate degrees from ISI-Denpasar (1985) and the University of Maryland, Baltimore County (1991, advised by Mantle Hood), and taught on the faculties of KOKAR and STSI starting in the 1980s. Asnawa eventually left the Balinese conservatory system and has been teaching in the United States for nearly fifteen years as a full-time visiting professor at the Robert E. Brown Center for World Music at the University of Illinois at Urbana-Champaign.

Patterns of institutionalization of musical pedagogy in Indonesia and in the United States have also shaped the types of transnational opportunities available for Balinese artists. We have seen how the nascent Balinese conservatory system influenced Lasmawan's early education in chapter 3 and how LISTIBIYA influenced the modern structure of performance tourism in Bali in chapter 6. The series of Indonesian American cultural exchanges that brought Cokorda Mas and Gandera as well as dozens of gamelan instruments to universities in the United States represents another facet of this institutional infrastructure. Yet the emphasis on standardization and national accreditation through the conservatories also has shaped musicians' and educators' careers. Formal degrees from the Balinese conservatories, even if at the high school level, have proved to be prerequisites for Indonesian teachers pursuing long-term academic employment in the United States.

Obtaining an American graduate degree in music has also become increasingly instrumental for Balinese to achieve success within official musical channels in Bali such as serving as an instructor in the conservatories, acting as a competition judge or as a board member for the Bali Arts Festival or more regional lomba, or working as *pegawai* (mid-level civil servants) in governmental bureaus of culture. Many senior professors and top administrators at the Balinese conservatories of the past few decades such as I Made Bandem, I Wayan Rai, I Wayan Dibia, I Nyoman Sedana, I Nyoman Catra, and I Nyoman Astita have received graduate degrees in ethnomusicology or related fields in North America. The necessity for artists to obtain both locally and internationally recognized credentials broadens such administrators' levels of international experience. It also reifies social power structures that are already in place, including those related to gender, hereditary caste or social class, and geographic region, privileging male teachers of the socioeconomic middle class or above who have prior access to international contacts.

On the other hand, in North America, the system of Balinese musicians' enrolling in accredited graduate degree programs while simultaneously teaching performing arts seems to have been mutually beneficial. It aligns the goals of American music programs—hiring knowledgeable gamelan teachers, maintaining contacts for their own pupils to study in Indonesia, and claiming high-ranking foreign graduates as alumni—with those of Indonesian programs seeking to hire individuals with an international perspective on education and the attendant prestige that brings to the institution. On an individual level, the contact between young musicians and scholars is also beneficial, giving rise to sometimes lifelong friendships and artistic and scholarly collaboration.

The benefits reaped often are inequitably distributed, however. American ethnomusicologists historically have leaned heavily on their foreign counterparts for their own career advancement. Although there is a growing population of ethnomusicologists who pursue fieldwork "at home" (within local communities or those to which they already belong) or "online" (Nettl 2015; Barz and Cooley 2008), the markers of professional competence and job marketability as an ethnomusicologist (grants awarded, languages learned, world music ensembles taught) often depend to a great extent on making and maintaining international research connections, something more easily achieved by those who have classmates or teachers already skilled in their artistic tradition of study. At the same time, while Indonesian students receive important and marketable international experience overseas, they are largely ineligible for the same type of research and travel support as Americans or Europeans are and are more often overlooked for permanent professional positions in North America. Although they can lead to collaboration, such imbalances can also lead to tangled relationships of power.

Many American academic programs desire to have expert non-American performers on their faculty rosters; these culture bearers bring a sense of diversity and prestige to the institution. Yet most teaching opportunities for such artists remain part-time, without the benefits of full-time employment. In addition, teaching in locations isolated from the full range of artistic opportunities found in their home countries can limit foreign faculty, because they must specialize in teaching groups of beginner and intermediate students without many opportunities for advanced creative work. Maintaining personal and professional relationships in two countries and in two artistic and cultural contexts presents distinctive challenges. As the longest-established generations of U.S.-based Balinese musicians have built comfortable if complex lives balancing their transnational obligations and opportunities, the younger generation has presented different ways of attempting to address similar issues.

Keeping up Appearances

Many of the benefits and challenges of the foundational generations of Balinese musicians who have taught substantively in the United States have already been discussed in this book. It is worth briefly highlighting here other considerations and challenges that have come with a transnational living pattern, specifically those having to do with establishing status and negotiating different patterns of life in multiple locations. Returning to consider Asnawa's life and work following his move to the United States showcases the personal and professional benefits and costs of conducting a career between Indonesia and the United States. One issue faced by both expatriate teachers and those who have returned to Bali full-time is keeping up with modern life as it manifests itself in both places. The differences are particularly striking for those who, like Asnawa, spend most of their year in the United States, then return to Bali. "When I was younger," Asnawa told me in 2016, "All I could hear was crickets. And now this," he said, gesturing to the traffic noise still audible from his home, located just a few blocks from Jalan Gatot Subroto, a four-lane thoroughfare where *sepeda motor* and transport trucks zip anarchically by the knock-off Apple Store and the real twenty-four-hour McDonald's.

Asnawa's home, originally a show house meant to embody his elevated position at KOKAR (Bakan 1999), has seen some renovations in the two decades since he bought it as a young teacher. Some of these changes reflect a globalized emphasis on technology as a standard of comfort and success. For example, inside, a flat-screen television hangs on the wall in the sitting area near the expansive kitchen that contains a full complement of appliances. Select areas of the house have ductless air conditioners that provide some relief from the region's relentless heat and humidity. Standard for middle-class or upwardly mobile Balinese, checking the Internet is accomplished on a cell phone or by traveling to a public Wi-Fi hotspot. Yet a recent and more fundamental change to the living space is purely Balinese in design. Outside, the small family temple present in all Balinese permanent residences has been reconstructed to be more properly elevated and more accurate in its *kaja* orientation, that is, toward Mount Agung, the most sacred direction. Placement of temples is a common problem in contemporary urban Balinese architecture because there is rarely sufficient land to re-create traditional home designs. The move also allowed the family to have more extensive space for chatting or playing music outside in the artistically paved and manicured courtyard garden.

In the United States, Asnawa and his wife live comfortably. One of their three adult daughters is married with children and takes care of their Denpasar house during the year; the other daughters, twins, have stable jobs in nearby cities in the United States. For them, growing up in America has brought some advantages, particularly for one of the twins, who had scoliosis and required a course of surgeries that would have been unavailable in Bali at the time. Yet Asnawa misses the artistic activity and the community feeling of Bali, particularly the ability to connect with his neighbors. In the late 1990s, as he reflected on his brother's career, which consisted of working within the banjar, at the university, and in government, Asnawa said, "I think you risk losing something. . . . I don't want to lose touch with the common people. I think that there's a danger of that happening. . . . [Komang's] job creates a distance with the people of the banjar" (Bakan 1999, 196). Yet having moved so far from his community in Denpasar, Asnawa is also distant from the banjar for most of the year and must make a special effort to maintain a profile in Bali by aiding the banjar and continuing to judge contests, perform, and compose. His efforts, however, have been acknowledged: in recognition for his continuing contributions to Balinese cultural life, Asnawa was awarded the Dharma Kusuma prize in August 2017.

For those who have navigated the institutional system carefully, residing and working in the United States can have substantial rewards. When I spoke to I Made Bandem during his stint of several years at the College of the Holy Cross in 2012, he commented on how relatively peaceful life was in America. Although the American academic world still had its issues, there was "much less bureaucracy" than in Bali, including the Balinese musical and educational institutions that he had helped shape. The music and dance course that he was teaching at Holy Cross was full of enthusiastic undergraduates and always had a long waiting list. He and his wife Suasthi shared a full-time academic position with a generous salary and therefore did not need to worry about seeking further teaching engagements for financial reasons, although they did make regular guest visits to neighboring institutions to lecture or teach. Unhampered by extensive Balinese social obligations, they both were finally able to focus on their research—he, writing a book about the history of Balinese gamelan (Bandem 2013); she, translating obscure *lontar* (ancient palm-leaf manuscripts) concerning musical performance. It was logistically simpler to work with American musicians, one example being a collaboration with two ensembles, JACK Quartet and Lightbulb, conducted in 2015. Moreover, they habitually returned to Bali twice each year during university holidays. In the winter they put on a lavish arts production for tourist hotels in Ubud and Kuta, Bali's two major tourist meccas; in the summer they lived in Singapadu, taking care of family religious obligations, performing, and fielding a never-ending stream of guests. Very rarely, Bandem had an American student come visit him at home in Bali.

For Balinese artists who return to the island on an annual basis but spend most of their time in America, returning "home" feels good, but it comes with a few challenges. For Lasmawan and Marni, ensuring that their duties to the community in Bangah are fulfilled requires continual monitoring from the United States and intensive periods of work upon arrival, especially in case any of their arrangements for maintaining their home have fallen through. For Marni, in particular, life in Bangah can be exhausting as she adds preparation for the arrival of foreign guests to her expected role in managing the household; although some of her duties follow her even to her childhood banjar in Singapadu, visiting her own family feels like a vacation. American amenities like certain types of shopping, television, and facilities for sports and entertainment must be given up upon arrival, to be regained when the family returns to the United States in August.

Balinese teachers must also negotiate others' perceptions of their social status, which fluctuate widely depending on the context. In American classrooms and on the stage, Lasmawan and Marni are introduced and treated as expert artists. Like other visibly nonwhite people in the United States, however, Balinese artists must deal with individual and systematic racism in encounters lacking recognition of the person's actual race, ethnicity, religion, or educational background. For example, with most of the country's population having no specific reference for what a Balinese person looks like, Balinese artists outside their professional context are visually summed up as anything from South Asian to Middle Eastern to Latin American. Right after the terrorist attacks of September 11, 2001, Lasmawan found himself subjected to increased racial anger and discrimination although he was neither Middle Eastern nor a Muslim. Without the context of the classroom or the stage, the personal and professional merits of expert musicians are often challenged.

The status accorded to international teachers and artists, too, is highly variable depending on the circumstances. Although Lasmawan's name is not known to most of the younger artists studying at the Balinese conservatories, for example, to artists of his own generation in Bali and in Java he is still well known. In Bangah, he is regarded in at least some circles as a hometown hero, the local son who connected the banjar to the world. Outside such specific contexts, however, artists' close relationships with foreigners, often colleagues and students, can be looked on with suspicion. On a day trip with some of his students from BYU to Karangasem, Lasmawan enthusiastically paid the admission fee to enter the Tirta Gangga water palace and joined us to swim at the cold spring water pools in the back of the complex. When it came time to visit the nearby Ujung water palace, however, he declined to enter. "I've been here before," he noted. Then, after some hesitation, he added that the last time he had tried to enter with foreign friends, he had been scolded by the site's staff for acting as an unlicensed guide. (Hired Balinese guides are expected parts of foreigners' visits to historical or sacred sites, whether guide-drivers who transport visitors for a whole or half-day's worth of sightseeing or local guides who are officially or unofficially affiliated with a specific site. In either case, guides' behavioral protocol—and method of earning commission—are fixed.) Lasmawan's protests ("These are my friends!") were to no avail, and the staff demanded that he "stop explaining" the history of the site—evidence that forging an international career can bring increases in power and status but also can expose Balinese teachers (and their American colleagues) to sticky encounters with race, ethnicity, and power that are obscured in the classroom.[1]

Redefining Transnational Careers and Partnerships

Lasmawan's annual pattern—spending academic years in the United States and summers in Bali—is the most common one for long-term expatriate teachers of Balinese performing arts, mirroring that of other American academics who travel only during breaks from classes. Guest artists pursuing residencies of less than a year's duration rarely return with such frequency and thus lack a regular annual schedule of international travel. The Pengosekan-born composer, musician, and teacher Dewa Ketut Alit (b. 1973) challenges both this annual model of travel and the need for a permanent academic position. His innovative situation, in which he has composed for and regularly worked with Gamelan Galak Tika at MIT for two months per year, has allowed him to have a sustained relationship with a specific American program while also sustaining a full musical life in Bali.

Alit's co-founding of Gamelan Çudamani (with his brother Dewa Putu Berata) in 1997 and subsequent work as an internationally renowned composer has been previously documented (Tenzer 2011), but his work as a teacher and the way it has fit into his artistic profile is less often discussed. Born to a musical family, Alit played music from a young age but often felt "very bored" playing the same set of pieces repeatedly in the banjar, at school, and with Gamelan Semara Ratih, which performs weekly tourist shows in Ubud. By the time he was sixteen, composition became one of his chief forms of entertainment. Yet, he notes, "You know, composing in Bali, you can't make money." It was by selling his paintings, the fruits of a hobby that he uses today to relieve stress, that he was able to support himself through high school and college at Bali's conservatories.

His first teaching position abroad was with Australian children in 2000. Although he reports struggling at first with figuring out how to teach a general-level foreign student body, he soon developed his own teaching style in working with more musically focused children in which he incorporated his compositional practice and new works into the classroom. This residency was closely followed by a year-long residency at University of British Columbia (UBC) with Michael Tenzer in 2001, which allowed him to more fully develop his pedagogical practice. As a teenager, Alit had marveled at Tenzer and the other "white guys who just got on the gangsa and played some kotekan" when they appeared in Pengosekan, and they had become friends. The year-long residency in British Columbia, the first of several, provided Alit's first experience with seeing how Western musicians learned (as well as his first opportunity to see snow, the inspiration for his composition "Salju"). It was Alit's growing international renown as a composer starting at the beginning of the twenty-first century, however, that eventually led Evan Ziporyn to invite him to work as a composer and teacher with Gamelan Galak Tika at MIT.

The pattern of Alit's teaching work has been closely allied with Ziporyn's development of Gamelan Galak Tika as a distinctive performing ensemble. Using the same instrumental resources as MIT's introductory gamelan ensemble course, the main performing group (which consists of advanced-level students and community members) presents classic repertoire, classic repertoire with unusual twists (such as performing the dance piece "Puspanjali" with electric guitar instead of gangsa), and presentations of new compositions. As an "in-house" composer for the ensemble, Alit has written new pieces for it and sends notation, recordings, and other resources to the players in the fall.

He arrives every year in the late winter and stays in residence for approximately two months to rehearse with the ensemble before performing the new works in the spring; he may also travel in the United States for other, shorter residencies at the same time. He is comfortable teaching introductory-level or standard Balinese repertoire, but his self-perception as a composer and performer first and a pedagogue second makes for a comfortable fit for him since he focuses primarily on work with his own pieces with Galak Tika. Though this pedagogical activity is important, he believes that simply the cultural experience of working with a Balinese artist is more important than any specific musical instruction. When his performances and workshops are completed for the year, he can return home to Bali and continue work with his own ensemble, Gamelan Salukat, or pursue other projects.

Alit notes that it is difficult for him to be away from his family (particularly his children) for several months every year. He has not seriously considered either seeking alternative employment in Bali's conservatories, however, or seeking a year-round position in North America; the dictates of a full-time university position would disrupt his compositional work and prevent him from continuing to work regularly at MIT, and though he has become increasingly more comfortable staying in Massachusetts, Bali still feels most like home. The transnational arrangement that he has constructed over the course of the past decade, however, has allowed him to support his family financially as well as remain artistically stimulated. He says, "Now, I don't worry about money because I teach overseas, and I get money there and I come back to Bali and make music here." Alit's distinctive annual teaching path is a relatively rarefied one, a pattern of guest work that is unlikely to be financially or logistically possible at most institutions that only offer gamelan as an introductory course or in community gamelans without substantial financial resources. This pioneering partnership, however, has neatly filled a niche that satisfies both the artistic and teaching requirements of his American hosts and Alit's personal and professional aspirations.

The decision of whether to pursue careers in Indonesia or abroad can be a difficult one, in logistic and artist terms, for Balinese musicians who have studied and lived more extensively in North America. The career path of I Wayan Sudirana has exemplified the in-betweenness that younger artists report feeling as they weigh the potential benefits and drawbacks of basing their careers in either location. Born in Ubud in 1980, Sudirana was a founding member of Gamelan Çudamani and graduated from ISI-Denpasar before completing master's and doctoral degrees at the University of British Columbia in 2009 and 2013, respectively; he also served there as musical director of the university's

Gamelan Gita Asmara with Tenzer. His time in British Columbia gave him the opportunity to perform and study a variety of traditions, including Korean samul nori; a composition of his featuring Japanese taiko and bagpipes was chosen to be performed at the 2010 Winter Olympics, held in Vancouver. On graduation he returned to Bali as a lecturer in composition at ISI-Denpasar rather than seeking employment abroad, in large part to be able to support his family both financially and by proximity. His own compositional work, however, is as likely to be commissioned for pan-Indonesian or international audiences as it is for Balinese ones. The time that Sudirana spent in formal study in Canada had given him a distinctive perspective on Balinese and Western styles of teaching, learning, composing, and representing music.

Sudirana's composing and performing career is largely centered around creating new styles—he believes that composing new works in old styles "merusakan tradisi" (ruins tradition), whereas traditionalists might argue that deviating from the older styles at all does the same thing—and he chafes at some of the dictates of his work in the conservatory. On one occasion when I met with him in Denpasar in 2016, he had gone beyond the official casual Friday attire worn by all the other male teachers and administrators (chinos and a batik collared shirt) and was wearing jeans, which he defiantly told me was in violation of the dress code. As it turned out, his dress was merely symbolic of more fundamental disagreements that he and others of the younger generation have occasionally had with the educational and performing status quo in Bali. These disagreements extended to the bureaucratic method for appointing teachers, which prioritizes formal qualifications over talent and experience, the lack of opportunities to present serious music (nontraditional new compositions) for attentive audiences, and the didactic insistence on theory rather than creativity in teaching composition students. Though in a junior position at the time, he staged small rebellions against the perceived bureaucracy. For example, in planning a performing arts festival, Sudirana scheduled invited government dignitaries to speak near the end of the program rather than at the more traditional spot at the beginning, after which the speakers generally left without honoring the performers by viewing the performance. He reports that one of the officials later thanked him for the chance to finally enjoy the whole show.

Since his graduation from UBC, Sudirana has been able to cultivate a career that balances teaching commitments to ISI, hosting and teaching gamelan to foreign musicians, and working on commissions for groups in Indonesia and abroad. He has also consistently pushed for new pedagogical models and opportunities for transnational research for himself and his colleagues even as he maintains his service commitments (which he deeply values) to his banjar. Yet, like Lasmawan in his encounters with racial or ethnic bias, Sudirana's career status is often invisible to the tourists who flock to Ubud, including those who stay in his family's rental properties or, seeing him giving a ride to a foreign friend, assume that he is a hired driver. Though he brushes them off, such encounters, which are routinely experienced by Balinese musicians and teachers, serve as reminders of the disjunction in power structures within and outside academic contexts that are often invisible to foreign students and forgotten by foreign colleagues who are used to working together in only particular types of contexts.

Certain aspects of Sudirana's ideal modus operandi for teaching and composing might be a better fit in Western institutions than in those in Indonesia. Yet the structure of most American collegiate music departments, with their emphasis on Western music theory and compositional styles and treatment of gamelan as an experiential part of broad-based teaching in ethnomusicology, would also be an imperfect fit for him to continue to pursue the type of goals that he has developed in Indonesia. Though well qualified to hold academic positions in several locations, artists and scholars like Sudirana continue to find themselves caught between two worlds, professionally speaking.

The work of Sonja Downing and her husband Dewa Ketut Alit Adnyana, who teach at Lawrence University, exemplifies another way of being caught between two worlds. As Downing told me, "There's the model of the ethnomusicologist who teaches gamelan, and the model of the outside specialist who comes in." With relatively few models of how to negotiate the logistical, cultural, and interpersonal relationships that their bond entails within a single family and, indeed, within a marriage, they have had to "be both," to figure it out as they went along.

Adnyana, whose life path is discussed in more detail in chapter 10, grew up in Pengosekan, Bali; he first met Downing in 2000, when Gamelan Sekar Jaya toured to Bali, and again in 2002, when Çudamani toured in California. He accompanied and helped Downing when she began studying gamelan as a part of her graduate research in Bali on children's gamelans. Their relationship deepened and, following three weddings—two in Bali (one for legal purposes, followed by a larger traditional wedding) and one in America—Downing began work at Lawrence University as a postdoctoral fellow on a two-year contract, which was extended and then transformed into a tenure-track position. While Adnyana "drove all over Denpasar" to get vaccinations and proper documentation to move to the United States, Downing borrowed instruments from the University of Illinois at Urbana-Champaign (Bob Brown's original set) to start the gamelan group. They spent the first year in a "text message marriage" until

Adnyana received his green card, was hired, and officially began to teach the gamelan.

For Downing and Adnyana, the exercise and representation of expertise in the classroom requires constant negotiation, if it is also grounded in respect and affection. Downing notes that it was "a relief" when Adnyana arrived and began to teach; in particular, she lauds her husband's clear musical cues and engagement with the students. For his part, Adnyana proudly calls her "Professor Sonja Downing" even when it is not necessary in a particular social situation. For Downing, not undercutting Adnyana's authority in the classroom is extremely important, though sometimes difficult. When the gamelan class first began, she tried to establish herself on equal learner status with the students, an approach which, she thinks, ultimately confused those who knew her from other university contexts. She notes that it has also been an internal struggle to not jump in and explain when students are confused by some element of Adnyana's instruction, but after several years, she learned to "shut up or ask" about the situation, speaking in Balinese or Indonesian. On the other hand, since Downing has withdrawn from playing with the class consistently to care for their daughter, Adnyana has missed her being there to play and support the group in rehearsal. By each "being both" ethnomusicologist and native instructor within their teaching relationship, Adnyana and Downing literally embody the types of cultural and educational negotiation that are endemic to the world music ensemble enterprise.

The Next Generation: Dual Culture Bearers

American Balinese musicians who have grown up in the United States face a different set of benefits and challenges than do their Balinese counterparts—in particular, because they have lived in an environment where gamelan was a very specialized pursuit, one tied in everyday experience as much to American classrooms as to Balinese performance contexts, which they predominantly experienced only when returning to Bali in the summers. Still, for Putu Hiranmayena and Ade Wijaya, Lasmawan's two eldest sons, musical immersion was a part of everyday life. Hiranmayena states that gamelan "just happened" to him. Born in Surakarta to a Javanese mother, he moved to the United States with his family when he was about one year old and has spent most of his life in Colorado, despite not being an American citizen; he now constructs his identity as being American, Balinese, and Javanese. He has been learning and playing gamelan ever since he can remember. "There's a picture of me, about age three, sitting on my dad's lap while he played gender," he laughed during one of our talks. When he was not much older, he began to sit in on the rehearsals for his father's various performing groups. Although he spent his free time pursuing a diverse set of hobbies—soccer, roller hockey, snowboarding, skateboarding, and chess, among others—playing gamelan, Hiranmayena says, gave him "a uniqueness" among his peers, who would come to his performances and learn a bit about Balinese culture through those experiences. As a teenager, however, he would just as often sit through rehearsals on the sidelines, headphones blasting Western popular music, and ignoring his surroundings.

Like Balinese children, Hiranmayena inherited a background in gamelan. Yet ultimately choosing to play gamelan as an adult, like many other college students, gives him a different type of perspective on it. After earning his undergraduate degree, Hiranmayena moved to San Diego. There, he worked with his adopted uncle Alexander (Alex) Khalil, an ethnomusicologist and one of Lasmawan's students from SDSU, to teach the children's group Gamelan Giri Nata (Mountain Sage), a program that Brown's Center for World Music helped found. Soon afterwards, he began to co-teach with the ethnomusicologist David Harnish at the University of California, San Diego, thereby absorbing yet another teaching method. Deciding that he was interested in pursuing music, he earned his masters in integrative studies from UCSD in 2013. That program allowed him to combine his interests in improvisation, metal music, and gamelan, all of which have made various appearances in his work as a musician, scholar, and teacher.

In 2015 Hiranmayena began working on a PhD in ethnomusicology at the University of Illinois at Urbana-Champaign, where he performs with the university gamelan, organizes the multigenerational Balinese American master performing arts group Balinese All Stars, and guest teaches other gamelans in the region, as well as continuing to compose and play in his other favored musical styles: jazz and math metal. For Hiranmayena, growing up in a family that has played the role of culture bearer has at times been beneficial and at times felt frustrating. He reports that, on one hand, it felt as though the relatively tight-knit community of ethnomusicologists and American gamelan musicians who were his parents' longtime friends understood their lives and work better than did most other Americans he met. On the other, he also encountered a frustrating tendency for people to judge his identity on the basis of the interests and accomplishments of his family members and to impose their expectations of a gamelan musician from Indonesia on him rather than recognize his individual interests, pursuits, and approaches. Hiranmayena has noted that for most of his life, he has been instructed by his parents to *benen mua* ("fix his face") in response to being confronted with such assumptions (Hiranmayena 2018). The role of ethnomusicology student has also proved challenging for Hiranmayena, since his theoretical interests and pedagogical and artistic pursuits do not lie neatly within most traditional paths of study. With his hybridity of experience and approach, however, he stands a chance of challenging disciplinary narratives of the native expert musician and disrupting the static models of musicianship and scholarship.

Ade Wijaya, who graduated from high school with honors in 2018 and enrolled with an academic scholarship at the University of Denver, is already preparing to pursue a career in ethnomusicology or a related field that will allow him to carry on the musical tradition of his family in the United States. He grew up assisting his parents in teaching and performance but had a turning point in his understanding and appreciation of gamelan in the summer of 2015 after he received divine inspiration from staying in the taksu temple in Bangah overnight. Since then, he has honed his skills as a musician and a teacher, even transcribing a difficult competition piece by the well-known composer I Nyoman Windha from a recording and teaching it to Gamelan Tunas Mekar and co-founding Anak Manik Galih, a children's gamelan group, with Elizabeth Macy in 2019. Before enrolling in college, when he was still seventeen, he began to sketch out his plans for graduate school in ethnomusicology, asking advice from me and other professors who are family friends he knew about what classes to take in college, figuring out how to balance student loans, and how to prepare for graduate school. "They've worked so hard," he said of his parents. "I need to be able to support myself. I need to prepare to keep doing the work they started."

The Balinese All Stars performing at the Richmond Folk Festival, October 2016

Wijaya's enthusiasm for gamelan is at this point unshakable; he listens to the music incessantly on his headphones, and at one point took to keeping a gangsa near his bed so that he could practice when he first woke up in the morning and just before sleeping. Yet as college applications began to loom, the full implications of what it would take to gain the credentials to become a faculty member in music in the United States began to become more immediate than they had only a year earlier. He had investigated undergraduate course requirements for music majors and seen that they universally focused almost exclusively on Western classical music and held few opportunities to study, compose, and perform in Balinese styles. Enrolling to study Balinese performing arts full-time at ISI-Denpasar seemed like an attractive alternative, but it would potentially put him at a disadvantage in applying to and doing coursework in American graduate schools. Graduate school itself was a key consideration. He had watched his older brother and family friends struggle with the tough initial years of graduate coursework. He had watched those in the generation before him, now in their thirties and forties, struggle to find jobs and sustain their careers.

Moreover, as Wijaya highlighted in college admissions essays, he had mixed feelings about the way in which his family's work had been represented and remunerated. In performance and teaching contexts, the Balinese American musicians and teachers were respected and even revered for the distinctive culture that they brought with them. In others, they were viewed simply as members of a minority group—not Balinese, not Indonesians, not Southeast Asians, but Asians, with all the stereotypes that American culture has ascribed to anyone hailing from this vast region that contains more than half the world's population. He had witnessed his parents' unfailing hard work for nearly two decades as they not only taught courses within prescribed start and end times but also opened their homes and their lives to their students. Though he stopped short of describing this work as turning their home into a "living museum," the situation contains clear parallels. They had created a community so real that few realized how much had been put on display—and how relatively little even conscientious visitors had compensated the family for the privilege of entry.

Very few Millennial children of Balinese artists resident in North America have chosen to pursue music as their careers. Hiranmayena and Wijaya, however, are poised to have specific and substantial advantages if they continue to pursue careers in ethnomusicology. Having grown up immersed in Balinese performing arts and speaking conversational Balinese, both can navigate artistic settings in Bali and in America, even if they do not feel entirely at home in either place. They can serve as culture bearers in American contexts (and in Balinese ones) without having to negotiate the linguistic barriers or visa paperwork that present difficulties for non-American teachers. Hiranmayena's distinctive hybrid musical pursuits and affirmation of his ability to forge new American Balinese musical traditions may challenge artistic and scholarly assumptions. Wijaya's musical interests, which currently are relatively more focused on innovation within tradition, may help him more comfortably meet expectations for cultural representation. Both brothers stand to offer distinctive contributions to Balinese performance and ethnomusicology as they continue to carve out their own paths as performing artists, teachers, and scholars.

The House That Bimusicality Built

Though arguably less visible to the Balinese (and American) publics than specific international tours or performances such as American groups' appearances at the Bali Arts Festival, the transnational academic system constructed by support of gamelan in academic institutions has had far-reaching impacts. Its effects have shaped educational and employment structures for internationally minded Balinese artists who, though a minority within the transnational gamelan scene, still exercise substantial influence in their professional circles. Each generation of artists has approached the question of finding and fulfilling specific niches in different ways. The first generation discussed here (those primarily born in the 1960s and earlier) established several distinctive patterns of living and teaching as normative, including the pattern of using American graduate educations to advance careers based in Bali (dominating the governance of Bali's conservatories, among other things, for decades) and the model of the U.S.-based culture bearer working in one or more American educational settings. As heads of households with grown children, those who remain overseas for a long time have negotiated balancing responsibilities to communities on two continents; this balancing act can bring economic, professional, and personal benefits but also stretches their capacities to devote time to extended family and community.

The generation following them grew up in an artistic world that was defined by a new sense of transnationalism. This feeling of globalism was in part due to the increased circulation of foreign recordings of many musical genres, an influx that in some ways mirrored the sudden flood of "world music" into North America at the same time. More important, however, Balinese artists growing up primarily in the late 1970s to late 1990s who would later pursue transnational careers were aware as children that there were foreigners who were serious gamelan musicians and composers. Recurring visits from individual gamelan scholars who have maintained a presence on the island since the late 1970s or early 1980s (such as Tenzer and Lisa Gold), tours by American groups that were subsequently broadcast on television, and recordings and performances of compositions for Balinese gamelan by American composers like Evan Ziporyn and Wayne Vitale affirmed that gamelan was not only locally important but could also be a site of substantive international exchange and collaboration. It is unsurprising, too, that the three artists of this generation featured here were founding members of Gamelan Çudamani, the most prominent independent organization of its time to foster high-quality performance with an explicitly international focus. These formative experiences increased the options for what a transnational artistic career could mean in terms of education, institutional and non-institutional employment, and models for collaboration. The members of the youngest generation of Balinese artists (Millennial or Generation Z)—not discussed in depth here because they have not yet developed substantive presences in North America—are also able to build on these career models, their sense of transnationality further enhanced by online opportunities for communication and collaboration.

Finally, the youngest Balinese American artists—among the first to grow up primarily in the United States, cognizant of the degree to which academic institutions are the key supporters of gamelan ensembles—have been able to look to both countries' models for pursuing a career that includes gamelan. Though they do not play the role of Indonesian culture bearers, their growing up with gamelan as a part of family life in the United States has placed them in the distinctive position of being able to (and having to) negotiate the opportunities, drawbacks, and expectations of two artistic, educational, and social systems. Their future work, with its potential to enhance and challenge conventions of practice in both locations, offers hope for the idea of continued sustainability for American academic gamelans and increased (and increasingly fruitful) transnational collaborations.

Even as their paths differ, the members of these generations face some shared challenges, including cultivating lives that balance artistic richness and stability, creating or maintaining presences in North America and Bali, and negotiating complex systems of racial or ethnic bias outside the gamelan world that alternatively can lend cachet (the much-sought-after diversity desired by American academic institutions) to and obscure their individual accomplishments. These challenges are in part born not only by artists but also by their American collaborators. Moreover, the relatively rare opportunities to work abroad have historically not been equally shared. Most notably, female Balinese artists, though certainly present in American contexts (primarily as dancers), have rarely traveled or lived in North America on their own without taking part in a tour or initially following their husbands' careers. Even as dancers like Nanik Wenten and Suasthi Bandem have received independent commissions for choreographies and Bandem has been recognized for her scholarly work, their situations are more exceptional than normative. Growing transnational artistic collaborations among younger generations of gamelan musicians—female and male, Balinese, American, and Balinese American alike—as well as continuously shifting assumptions of what constitutes female roles in Bali suggest that this picture will also look different in future decades.

Overall, new opportunities and challenges have emerged in both structural and personal terms for individuals who build transnational careers. Just as formal academic systems give prestige and benefits to those who participate in them, they also create new areas of competition, tension, and potential misunderstanding. On a personal level, the situation provides rewards but also complicated patterns of professional development, relationships, and senses of identity. To kembali, to return—whether to Bali or to the United States—is a tricky proposition for many teachers whose lives must bridge two continents, three languages, two cultures, and multiple pedagogical systems.

CHAPTER 8

Bimusicality and Beyond

Hands lifted above the level of their heads like those of taiko drummers, two elementary-aged children gleefully brought their mallets down to strike the raised center bosses of the reyong. Behind them, a mother and a daughter carefully picked out the core melody on their calung instruments, and across the room, a mother guided her first-grade-aged son at the gangsa while her younger boy looked on, eyes wide. It was a Saturday afternoon at Lawrence University in Appleton, Wisconsin and, despite missing children who had games with their extracurricular sports teams that day, practice proceeded in good spirits. Seated at his kendang, Dewa Ketut Alit Adnyana grinned widely as he showed a new part to the girl seated behind a smaller drum next to him. How was teaching American children different from teaching those in Bali? Although he acknowledged that Americans had less aural exposure to the music, he contended that he teaches "the same way" he had in Bali, where he had specialized in working with youth groups.[1] In both places, the instruments and sounds fascinate children who—in Bali, at least—clamber on their parents' laps to begin picking out melodies at a young age.

The creation of the first American community gamelan ensembles in the 1970s in California and Massachusetts had already brought larger and more varied audiences to gamelan than the undergraduate and graduate students who initially participated in the early world music study groups. While gamelan classes are commonly incorporated into programs of study in ethnomusicology and are open to the general student body, however, there is relatively little formal connection between these ensembles and related areas of study including performance, music education, and music therapy, or indeed, anthropology, folklore, or religion. Teachers of gamelan know that the experience of playing can speak to students across disciplines and, indeed, to students of all ages, yet disciplinary and curricular structures often preclude such cross-pollinations from taking place.

This relative seclusion of gamelan within certain academic disciplines also limits the opportunities for American music students to learn skills in gamelan class that apply to their other musical studies. For example, conducting students assigned to cue the gamelan ensemble from the ugal (a keyed metallophone that plays a leading role) may find that the task reinforces their focus on clarity of gesture. Music education students can learn about and practice new types of nonverbal teaching and receive new perspectives on their training in the Orff Schulwerk method, an educational approach commonly used in American elementary music classes that originally was inspired in part by gamelan. Some students will take the initiative to explore such new musical worlds on their own, but these potential connections are often quietly neglected rather than being officially recognized and encouraged. Where such interdisciplinary connections within music happen, however, gamelan can foster musical and cultural competence in new ways among a wider set of audiences.

By examining how Balinese gamelan has been integrated into college-level programs in percussion and composition and into elementary music education settings, it is possible to understand how inclusive initiatives have impacted student and community education outside traditional ethnomusicological settings and contexts. In this chapter I discuss how training in gamelan can intersect with these three related areas, drawing on the stories of members of Lasmawan's (and my own) extended gamelan communities to illustrate the challenges and rewards of pursuing such programs. Creating room for gamelan in already full music curricula presents logistical challenges for those who bring gamelan to new audiences, as does finding instructors with enough training. Yet the results of this extended education and collaboration are well worth the trouble because they produce students with a broader sense of musical competence and knowledge of and respect for their own classmates and other world cultures. If gamelan enthusiasts—and indeed, advocates for global musical genres as a whole—hope to create greater opportunities for awareness of different musical genres, access to musical learning for diverse demographics, and possibilities for deeper respect and collaboration with non-Western musics as a focal point, the areas detailed below provide excellent opportunities for doing so.

World Percussion in College Music Education

Of all the instrument families, percussion instruments (membranophones and idiophones) have long been considered among the most approachable for new learners because of the ease of producing sound—any sound—before having to develop extensive playing technique. This property of sound production has meant that percussion instruments from around the world have found their way into Western music-making contexts, whether as played in the genres originally intended, as a new source of timbral color, or somewhere in between. The jazz drum kit and instruments such as the claves, maracas, and cowbell were added to standard percussion lineups beginning in the 1930s with the introduction of jazz and Latin repertoire into orchestral settings. Always on the hunt for new timbres, individual percussionists are often also scavengers, collectors who are forever experimenting with new instruments and techniques to incorporate into their own performance repertoires. It is perhaps unsurprising, then, that the most numerous non-Western music ensembles represented in American universities—gamelan, steel pan, and West African drum ensembles—are all largely percussive. Unlike individual foreign instruments that have been incorporated into general percussion training, however, such large ensembles, which are distinctive in their full form, have for the most part remained separate from mainstream percussion practice. Their historical and logistical similarities and differences, including who teaches them, what repertoire is performed, and how they are culturally connected to their college or university, illustrate the complicated relationship between world and Western percussion in the academy, as well as delineating where gamelan does and could fit into this picture.

Trinidadian steel pan has become a popular choice for music educators in the United States during the past half century owing to its relatively swift and direct introduction to school systems, the relative ease of acquiring the instruments, and the perceived approachability of the music. Steel pan music developed from a series of African-Trinidadian musical traditions that were banned by the colonial British, including the tamboo bamboo bands of the early twentieth century, created after the colonial ban on playing skin drums. In this music, sound is created by striking the ends of large pieces of bamboo against the ground and striking the bamboo with sticks. These male-dominated orchestras switched to all-steel instruments by the 1940s, with the modern oil-drum steel pan coming into standard use after World War II. The genre's introduction into North American contexts occurred in the early 1960s, when the legendary pannist Ellie Mannette (1927–2018) was commissioned to build up the U.S. Navy Steel Band and built instruments that were used by generations of children in a New York inner-city youth music program. He became a major supplier of instruments to colleges, universities, and community groups across the continent for decades (Tiffe 2007), forming one of the almost two dozen companies that make or ship steel band instruments within North America. Today, though sometimes taught by ethnomusicologists or steel pan specialists, academic steel pan ensembles are also commonly taught by percussion faculty.

Academic African drumming ensembles in the United States began to gain popularity at the same time as steel pan, about the end of the 1960s, because of their perceived cultural relevance and musical accessibility. Most such ensembles in the United States focus on West African genres, particularly those from Ghana, Guinea, and Senegal, as well as Afro-Cuban styles. Like steel pan ensembles, West African drumming ensembles in North America are associated with musical cultures that were once banned by white American plantation owners in an effort to subjugate and de-culture enslaved peoples. The invigoration of such drumming traditions entered American culture specifically in association with black pride movements and a burgeoning academic interest in African culture (Dor 2014).

Though hardly simple, as European observers originally thought, West African drumming styles can be approachable for students who learn first to perform specific rhythms in unison before playing more complicated versions or taking leading roles. Stratified, layered musical textures built on ostinatos and played by multiple musicians allow new players relatively low-stakes entry points to playing, perhaps compensating for the unfamiliar rhythmic complexity and primarily percussive (not melodic) textures. Musical arrangements can grow to be quite complex. Without the strict dictates of melody and form that make a steel pan or gamelan piece recognizable (or not), however, drumming patterns can be simplified relatively easily to fit the level of the musicians.

Study materials for certain West African styles are also particularly accessible. Teachers of such ensembles sometimes study within a teaching lineage, but they also work with published materials or pedagogical video recordings, including demonstration videos on websites such as YouTube. Formalized learning programs such as the Tam Tam Mandingue international school founded by Guinea's Mamady Keita provide a clear path for teachers to learn and become formally credentialed. Finally, instruments such as the *djembe* have become a part of broader participatory drum culture, with instruments made in natural and synthetic materials easily purchased from companies such as Remo. So many mass-produced and video-based materials are available that many teachers never go beyond them in their studies, despite the exhortations of master teachers to study in person. West African drumming groups are also regularly associated with pan-African or African American university and community groups that have reclaimed this music as a part of a pan-African heritage, even if they are taught by ethnomusicologists or African instructors. According to Dor (2014), such cultural connections make the ensembles particularly attractive to African American students, as well as interesting and approachable for broader groups of students.

In comparison to steel pan and African drumming ensembles, gamelan ensembles are more culturally distant from the racial and ethnic tensions caused by the legacies of American settler colonization, enslavement, and systematic inequality whose echoes haunt society to this day. Though this distance can be viewed as disadvantageous since it does not offer opportunities to unpack these fraught cultural circumstances, it is also advantageous in that it allows for students and instructors to explore musical and cultural difference in a subject area where they may have fewer preconceptions. The continued near-necessity of learning gamelan through oral tradition also differentiates it from these other popular ensemble types. While there is some published gamelan notation—for example, Sorrel's (1990) book on Javanese gamelan, select publications of works for Balinese gamelan within other academic materials (e.g., Tenzer 2000), and a growing smattering of scores and video resources on the Internet—there are few systematic and comprehensive learning resources that are publicly available. Because instruments and musical material are relatively more difficult to acquire, teaching the ensembles requires some specialized training and continuous connections to other American ensembles or to Indonesian artists for new source materials. Finally, although the sound of and learning methods for gamelan may be more of an acquired taste for students more familiar with other genres, exploration of this new sound world can be rewarding for students.

Balinese Gamelan in Percussion Education

Gamelan ensembles can accommodate students of varying musical proficiencies, providing learning opportunities equally for a mixed group containing both novice and experienced percussion players. Given that gamelans are often the largest unified sets of percussion instruments on a university campus, it seems logical for them to be put to use by percussion programs, at least as a method of providing exposure to a diversified set of sounds. Yet based on the limited time available for percussion students to master core Western percussion techniques and the fact that gamelan and other world percussion ensembles often remain firmly rooted in the ethnomusicology area of music programs, potential lessons that percussionists could learn from playing in the groups—such as cultivating their active listening skills, gaining new performance techniques, and expanding principles of intra-ensemble communication—are often treated as ancillary rather than central to their education.

The relative ease of adopting world percussion by percussionists and by percussion-savvy ethnomusicologists for pedagogical settings has proved helpful in solving one of the issues of sustainability in such ensembles: what to do with instruments that are inherited or acquired without a teacher. Nonspecialists generally either assume that such foreign instruments require instructors to undergo years of specialized training before they can begin to approach teaching them, or alternatively, that the ability to produce sound (without consideration for cultural context, repertoire choice, or understanding basics of musical style) is sufficient to become a teacher. Both assumptions are widely dismissed by gamelan teachers, Indonesian and American alike, who seek to find a middle ground that encourages balancing initial, unstructured experimentation with more serious instruction or co-teaching for gamelan courses.

The ecumenical approach to world percussion on the part of both percussionists and percussion-oriented ethnomusicologists has led to gamelan's being approached in some institutions as a part of a broader world percussion scene rather than an outgrowth of ethnomusicology. For example, Robert Ledbetter, director of percussion studies at the University of Montana, has integrated gamelan and other world musics to shape what he terms "one of the premier comprehensive programs in the Northwest" in percussion since his initial appointment to the university in 1990. The Balinese gamelan angklung unit that is guest taught by Lasmawan constitutes a core element of the students' world percussion opportunities, which also include steel drums, West African drumming (from Guinea, Mali, Ghana, and Senegal), Afro-Cuban percussion, Brazilian percussion, a Mexican marimba ensemble, and a salsa band, each of which is taught in collaboration between university faculty and visiting artists. The program offers breadth rather than depth—gamelan, for example, is taught as an intensive program for no more than six weeks, every two years—but it provides a basic exposure to the music that, in Ledbetter's view, improves his students' musicianship and opens opportunities for further musical study and for job opportunities.

Ledbetter is able to support the program because of his own musical training, which involved a large and varied amount of experience playing in world music ensembles. He was first introduced to steel pan music in the early 1980s as a master's student at the University of Akron; he recalls, "My advisor had just bought steel drums and had no idea what to do with them, and I didn't either, and he said, 'Well, we're going to figure it out together' . . . and I've been doing it ever since" (Ledbetter 2012). Subsequently, while working on a doctorate at the University of North Texas, he studied West African drumming and played in the Central Javanese gamelan ensemble. It was a "kind of hand-me-down experience," he noted; without a skilled Javanese music teacher present at the time, the ensemble's learning was based primarily on resources handed down by each subsequent generation of musicians.

His training in a number of world percussion ensembles, which is still a hallmark of the University of North Texas program, was a boon to Ledbetter when he began teaching at the University of Montana. In coordination with Dorothy Morrison, who was teaching world music as an adjunct there at the time, Ledbetter first acquired instruments from Guinea and Ghana. The gamelan arrived in 2002 through Morrison's prior connection with Lasmawan and was named Gamelan Jaya Budaya (Victorious Culture). Now the ensemble constitutes a portion of the World Percussion Ensemble course, one of two studio courses in which percussion students must enroll.

Although it lacks a permanent gamelan instructor, the shared teaching situation, and the fact that the ensemble consists entirely of percussion majors, who are used to intensive rehearsal on rhythmic parts, makes the experience substantially more dynamic than Ledbetter's original experiences with gamelan. Teaching from notation, Ledbetter prepares the students in advance of Lasmawan's arrival. Lasmawan then rehearses with them over the course of a week before the concert. Every four years, Ledbetter leads students to study with Lasmawan in Bali. Echoing the sentiments expressed by students who study in Bali, Ledbetter says of his time there:

> [I get a] deeper sense of appreciation for the music, more of a sense of the culture, so when I teach it, I can be even more respectful of it, which allows my students to get even more of an experience than just sitting in the world music room, playing world music instruments. I can be a better teacher and conveyor of the culture around the music. It's really a lot different when you do it from a cultural perspective, you know, not just "I can play this on my drum set." Although we do that, too.

Working primarily with students who intend to become professional percussionists, Ledbetter emphasizes different reasons for studying gamelan than those emphasized in the literature of bimusicality or the rhetoric of diversity within liberal arts institutions. He notes:

> Nowadays, world music is becoming more and more expected; . . . job qualifications are ridiculous. You have to be able to do drum set, and steel band, and gamelan, etc. That's the advantage—because in my program, all of my majors

> have to do it. If they go to the University of Montana, they have to play steel drums, they have to play gamelan, they have to play African. . . . I want my majors to get the experience so that when they leave, they can say, "Yeah, I know how to do that." . . . I feel like it's a really good training ground for people to go off and do graduate work.

The particular choice to offer gamelan paired with other ensembles is not a common one, but it can have utility outside a pre-professional setting. Exposure to gamelan in a program such as that at the University of Montana can increase students' awareness of the music, as well as provide some basis for potentially co-teaching if required in the future. It is important to note that students in Ledbetter's program whom I met while they were studying in Bali in 2012 did not have the impression that their newfound proficiency in a limited repertoire of gamelan music meant that it was simpler than the Western percussion that was at the core of their studies; instead, working in the new musical genre increased their appreciation of the skill level of the Balinese musicians.

Although educational institutions across the country increasingly are offering courses in world music (including ensembles) and percussionists increasingly are required to earn undergraduate degrees in music, students often are presented with world percussion as an elective—and not even a recommended elective—rather than a required course. In some cases, world percussion ensembles and the percussion program are separated into different administrative units, making cross-study nearly impossible. In other cases, where there is mutual support between percussion and ethnomusicology programs, logistical issues make regular cross-enrollment of students difficult. For example, the College of Music at Florida State University hosts both substantial curricular offerings in world percussion (including Balinese gamelan, steel pan, and African drumming ensembles) and a prestigious and competitive percussion studio, but the number of core requirements for the percussion degrees and the overlapping timing of rehearsals means that it takes active interest on the part of the student to pursue study in both areas. Similarly, at the Eastman School of Music in the University of Rochester, while students pursuing music degrees do enroll in the Balinese gamelan, few of them are percussionists. For those who are interested, however, combining intensive training in the percussion program and in world music can lead to culturally and musically enriching results, for example, the careers of young, up-and-coming percussionists such as Megan Arns.

Arns, an assistant professor of percussion at the School of Music at the University of Missouri, has incorporated non-Western percussion into her studies and teaching since she first traveled to Ghana to study Ewe drumming the summer after her senior year of college. She counts that experience as "a turning point for [her] in [her] life as a musician because of the concept of learning music orally, not writing down what you learn, not learning from paper, and also learning the rich cultural traditions behind it" (2017). In addition to her master's work in percussion performance at Florida State University, she managed to continue her exploration of world percussion by participating in Balinese gamelan and in steel pan, Irish, East African, and West African music ensembles. A subsequent orchestral residency and teaching position in Jordan afforded her the opportunity to study Middle Eastern percussion instruments as well. By the time she was pursuing a DMA in percussion at Eastman, she made the decision to study world musics more formally, adding a master's program in ethnomusicology to her coursework. While there, she played consistently in the Zimbabwean *mbira* group as well as becoming, first, an ensemble member and then a teaching assistant in Eastman's gong kebyar ensemble, Gamelan Lila Muni (Heavenly Sound).

Despite an initial intent to focus primarily on her studio percussion work, Arns found herself drawn into the Eastman gamelan by two friends, Jordan Hayes (who would later study and teach with Lasmawan) and Emeric Viani (who later taught and played with Gamelan Galak Tika in Cambridge, Massachusetts), and by her memory of the "powerful, magical" experiences that she had had when first hearing gamelan at Florida State. At Eastman, by arrangement with her primary advisor, Arns was able to switch her teaching assistant position from the percussion studio to the gamelan, where she worked closely with the ethnomusicologist Ellen Koskoff (the founder and organizer of the gamelan) and Nyoman Suadin, the group's longtime Balinese teacher. Since Suadin was in Rochester only one day per week—he lives in Maryland and travels a full circuit every week to teach at the University of Maryland, Swarthmore College, and the community gamelan Mitra Kusuma in Washington, DC—Arns was responsible for helping with Gamelan Lila Muni's weekly Saturday rehearsal, as well as coaching ensemble members during a midweek rehearsal. The responsibilities grew even greater during the semester of the most compelling of the group's performances, the one at the Smithsonian Institution in Washington, DC, in 2015. She notes that while percussionists have a head start in acquiring the mechanical skills necessary to play Balinese gamelan, its complexity and virtuosity, and the memory required to play it well, mean that "even the most skilled Western percussionists are challenged by it" and that the experience greatly expanded her musicianship.

At Missouri, Arns's teaching load does not currently include gamelan, though it does include co-direction of the Mizzou World Percussion Ensemble (steel band, Zimbabwean mbira, and Ghanaian West African ensembles); at the time of writing, she was also seeking to purchase a Balinese gamelan for the university. She credits her experience in world percussion with preparing her for the position, which had been expanded to focus on world percussion by her predecessor. Yet she agrees that formal relations between percussion and ethnomusicology programs to create shared ensemble experiences are "almost nonexistent," which is problematic for several reasons. One is that many of her colleagues, even those whose coursework includes world music seminar courses, are "intimidated by world percussion performance because they don't feel qualified" to teach; it is difficult to determine one's own proficiency in a musical style without the types of formal accreditations familiar to percussionists from other areas of their music study, and potentially difficult to find and approach qualified teachers. This helps explain why, when the university is able to bring in master musicians, Arns insists that her students take part. The styles are "so colorful, and interesting, and amazing," she says, "and if you have it there at your fingertips, especially if you have access to a native teacher, it can be an incredible experience. To me, it's like a gold mine—why wouldn't you embrace the experience?" Forming these connections within the discipline of music may be key to continuing to integrate world music into not only ethnomusicology curricula but also collegiate music programs as a whole.

Composing for and from Gamelan

"Please?" Shawn begged. It was the beginning of the spring semester in 2013, the first time I had taught a gamelan class entirely by myself. Shawn Havery—perennial student, perennial gamelan player, and professional computer programmer—approached me with the idea at the beginning of class, right as the other musicians were filing in. "We could do it with beleganjur, and the bamboo angklung, and write a new rap and do the choreography and everything."

I hesitated. Although we had performed it five years earlier, I still remembered the choreographic chaos of a new piece that Shawn had written that had involved our slipping around in stocking feet to enact elaborate *gerak* (choreography) while trying to play beleganjur instruments to a thirteen-beat pattern. (Playing an interlocking ceng-ceng part in thirteen is not easy for a first-semester gamelan player.) "Please? . . ." Shawn asked again, shifting impatiently from foot to foot. A graduate composition student who was standing nearby piped up, "I could transcribe the melody for you."

I turned to the ensemble members. "Do you want to do this?" Following enthusiastic cheers from all involved, I finally relented. "OK, yes. We can cover

'Gangnam Style,'" which had recently become the most-watched video globally on YouTube. At its one and only public performance three months later, our rendition, "Gamelan Style," which indeed featured bamboo angklung, beleganjur instruments, a newly composed rap describing the experience of playing gamelan, and an interpretation of PSY's iconic dance, was met with wild applause.

Creating new arrangements (discussed in chapter 5) and, indeed, new pieces for gamelan is a critical element of American academic gamelan practice for instructors and students alike; far from expressing the concerns about cultural appropriation that continue to haunt American gamelan teachers, many Balinese musicians encourage respectful and informed innovative work. Composers have long been among the musicians most interested in gamelan, attracted to both the instruments' distinctive sound palettes and the mathematical, theoretical aspects of gamelan practice. Compositions by non-Indonesians have played an influential part in building the transnational creative gamelan scene (J. Diamond 1992; House 2015; C. Miller 2005; Sorrell 2007), though distinctions in function should be made between Western works influenced or inspired by gamelan and those written for gamelan, deriving from deep study of the instruments (Tenzer 2000, 388–389, 434–435). Compositional interests have also influenced some of the most important theoretical literature on Balinese gamelan in the English language (McPhee 1966, xiii; Tenzer 2000, 8–10).

Yet composing for gamelan in classroom settings is underdiscussed, and as an activity, it has largely remained outside the scope of introductory gamelan classes for several reasons. First, some instructors may feel that having students create new compositions disrupts the bimusical intent of the ensembles (Becker 1983). Second, though Indonesian gamelan teachers frequently arrange music, they may or may not consider themselves to be composers or teachers of composition; likewise, American teachers may not have the knowledge, skill, or interest to encourage composition. Most practically, there is little class time for compositional activities when students are still working on basic playing techniques and understanding of idiomatic musical structures. As a result, when students do compose for gamelan, it is generally as an independent project. Despite limitations on time, knowledge, and skill, there are ways for instructors to bring new composition into the classroom, and doing so is an important way to establish Balinese gamelan as a living tradition rather than a static one. Hadley (1993) and Christopher Miller (2005) posit categorizing approaches to transnational gamelan composition in terms of where the "software" (musical ideas) and "hardware" (instrumentation) lie on the continuum between being Indonesian and non-Indonesian. Although defining the word *Indonesian* or even *traditional Indonesian* is an impossible task because tradition is always in the process of transformation, theirs is still a useful model for establishing a basic consideration of how different types of compositional activity might be embraced in American academic gamelans.

In terms of writing for gamelan, creative arrangements of extant non-Indonesian melodies (like "Gamelan Style") provide some of the most straightforward opportunities for creative work. Because their melodic and rhythmic content is preexisting, the primary tasks for arrangers include transferring this content to Indonesian instruments and often light additions of non-Indonesian musical ideas, such as turning a non-Indonesian ostinato into the pokok and adding a gong cycle. Such arrangements or adaptations might emerge from group interest in a piece or the instructor's discovery that a melody works reasonably well with the pitches present on the gamelan instruments. With audience recognition and enjoyment of the arrangement as the primary goal, such arrangements need to be made recognizable to audiences by keeping many of their musical ideas intact. Thus, arranging is an activity that is relatively approachable to those versed in the relevant non-gamelan musical idioms.

Working with new compositions written in hybrid styles that mix gamelan and non-gamelan instruments and Indonesian and non-Indonesian musical ideas is also an approachable way to work with students to compose for gamelan. Familiarity with the gamelan instruments (as well as any other instruments being used) is an essential prerequisite, however, for students who wish to compose in hybrid styles. Although this seems basic, it is important to ensure that students know each instrument's melodic range and the types of playing techniques that fit well with the instrument type. Misunderstanding of common playing techniques can make new compositions difficult or unpleasant to play; for example, whereas idiomatic kotekan patterns will fall easily under an experienced musician's hands, an individual part that switches between the usual roles of polos and sangsih (the two interlocking roles) is uncomfortable and more difficult to perform. Composers can also learn to experiment, however, even as they borrow concepts from traditional gamelan composition such as re-creating gong cycles using non-Balinese instruments, playing with the ensemble's paired tuning, or mirroring traditional interlocking patterns on non-Balinese instruments.

When successful, such pieces are not only musically interesting but also excellent educational tools not only for the gamelan musicians but also audiences. For example, in 2018 my former student Thomas Little composed a piece called "Shadow Waltz" that featured grand piano and two *curing* (high-pitched keyed metallophones from the gamelan angklung tradition) in order to have "something fun" featuring gamelan instruments in his senior composition recital at the University of North Carolina School of the Arts. The back-and-forth play of trading patterns idiomatic to each instrument was notable not only to those versed in gamelan but also to student audience members who had had only introductory exposure to the instruments. They were impressed that someone their own age could write and perform such work. One student reflected in a review assignment, "The crowning moment of the night for me was the performance of the piano and the gamelan. The way the two instruments interacted, which, on the surface, do not seem to have any overlapping musical elements[,] was extremely surprising."

On the other end of the spectrum is teaching students to write in a fully Balinese musical idiom (Indonesian instruments, Indonesian musical ideas), an activity that falls outside the mainstream of academic ensemble instruction because of limitations on depth of knowledge, time, and resources on the part of students and sometimes instructors. Balinese musicians often arrange traditional works but may not wish to compose for or with their students. Though some American gamelan musicians do compose in traditional styles, they are relatively uncommon; for those who direct academic ensembles, acquiring and learning extant repertoire is often already very time-consuming. The prerequisite musical knowledge that students need to compose in Balinese instrumental styles is more extensive than that which even experienced instructors can impart within a few semesters. Generally, it is long after students learn to play different types of kotekan that they can intuit what will happen next in accompanying a melodic line. Understanding other musical conventions, such as where and why *angsels* (cuing sequences) are placed within the elaborated melodies in late twentieth-century female "welcome dances" such as Gabor and Panyembrama, is difficult for the many students in programs with little or no access to observing or embodying live dance. Finally, as with composition in other styles, students need to have substantive technical knowledge and experience with all the instruments to be able to write for them compellingly, and this, once again, is something rare within the limited number of semesters that most students spend learning to play.

Instructors who wish to encourage composition for gamelan can take the advice of experienced Balinese musicians in doing so. For example, Asnawa, who has written well-known pieces for gong kebyar and beleganjur as well as in the neoclassic *kreasi lelambatan* and nontraditional musik kontemporer styles, advises new composers to begin with the pokok, the core melody—and with it, the gong cycle. From there, if writing in an established musical style, one can add melodic and rhythmic embellishments that are standard and appropriate to the style. Providing a standard melody and gong cycle and soliciting students to compose an idiomatic embellishment or simply add idiomatic rhythmic accents on ceng-ceng or reyong could be a step toward such more advanced work. Perhaps the most approachable ensemble type with which to do this is gamelan beleganjur, in which the standard eight-beat gilak gong cycle, the two-pitch melodies played by the *ponggong* (hand-held gongs), and the relatively idiomatic patterns of reyong and ceng-ceng provide substantive and clear creative ground rules from which students can build.

Compositional work does not always require producing a finished product. Providing opportunities for students to play freely with the instruments rather than learning a set composition can help students understand their own instruments better and encourage ensemble creativity as well. For example, drawing on his background in jazz and experimental Western and popular genres as well as in Balinese gamelan, Hiranmayena has encouraged sessions of group composition in which both idiomatic Balinese and new musical ideas can flourish. Such sessions foster experimentation and creativity without the formal pressure of preparing a full new composition for performance.

Perhaps most important for cultivating gamelan as a more integral part of training in composition is helping learners experience and acknowledge new composition for gamelan by Indonesian and non-Indonesian musicians not only as a part of the "world of gamelan" but also as a part of the world of new composition more generally. Having a Balinese composer as the ensemble director or initiating the type of long-term annual collaboration that exists between Dewa Alit and MIT's Gamelan Galak Tika, though certainly not sustainable with the resources allotted to most academic gamelans, allows the musicians to experience the compositional process from its initial stages through workshopping with the composer to performance. In the age of the Internet, remote collaborations such as one undertaken at Wake Forest are possible and can be rewarding.

In the fall of 2018 the gamelan at Wake Forest had its first opportunity to work with a new commission by a Balinese artist. Several composition students in the ensemble had heard and were intrigued by one of Sudirana's works-in-progress, and he in turn expressed interest and willingness to write a commission for the ensemble. The American students recorded sound samples that were sent to Bali via email. Over the course of the following weeks, new parts of the score and audio renderings of the composition arrived, ready to be learned; recordings of the rehearsal were messaged back instantly to the composer for commentary.

The name of the piece, which was only given near the end of the fall semester, was the subject of much speculation among members of the gamelan (the "Ring of Fire Suite," for example, was discarded for being too reminiscent of Johnny Cash); Sudirana bestowed the final title, "Dirghagati" (A Long Journey), in hopes that the piece would expedite a long journey into the future for foreign students in learning Balinese gamelan.

Sudirana was on the other side of the globe when the piece was rehearsed and premiered, but it was clear that those in both places felt connected through the immediacy and continuous development of the project. Ensemble members eagerly awaited news from the composer and arrival of new material for the piece. Sudirana, for his part, commented that he sees the globalization of his tradition as integral to "bringing people together" and that it provides opportunities for new creative work that reflects the global perspective of both composer and audiences—in the case of this piece, applying musical augmentation and retrograde approaches that are often thought of as being Western in ways that instead fit Balinese aesthetic principles. Students from outside the ensemble who watched the performance (which was accompanied by a short artist statement video) also commented on how much it made them feel that they were a

Dewa Ketut Alit Adnyana teaching children's gamelan, October 2018

part of a vibrant, contemporary artistic world, one that was not limited to Bali but spanned the globe. One student wrote in a reflection assignment:

> After hearing opening remarks as well as watching the video excerpt from the composer, I began to think about how interesting and exciting it was that a university in the United States could send sound bites of our gamelan's distinct timbre to a composer in Bali, and then to have it be turned around and performed through a mutual understanding of the instrument and its idiosyncrasies. I think that being able to reflect on the gravity of such a relationship is important—most people in the U.S. do not have the exposure to the sounds of somewhere as far away as Bali; yet for us, on the night of the gamelan ensemble's performance, we got to see an original Balinese composition performed on an instrument also from Bali that was written to highlight the anticipated evolution and adaptation of the art form. It makes globalization and its impact on a fast-changing society become a more immediate cause for discussion.

By bringing students into the process of new creation, gamelan music has the potential to feel vibrant and accessible rather than stagnant or exoticized, to be a place of potential musical dialogue and collaboration, both across campus and across the world.

Balinese Gamelan and Music Education

One striking outcome of the proliferation of community gamelans across North America has been the number of American children who have grown up learning gamelan with their parents, either by repeated exposure as observers of adult rehearsals and performances or by playing as young musicians. Even as millions of children are exposed to similar principles through the Orff Schulwerk system, adults who have the resources have also begun to create gamelan programs for children. Gamelan has been touted as a practical model for developing general pedagogical approaches (Bakan 1994; Talbot 2012), a way of aiding teachers in approaching cross-lingual pedagogy (Wharton Conkling 2015), or simply as an important and interesting subject to teach to children (Bakan 2010). Education programs that allow children to experience gamelan at first hand have grown across the United States since the 1990s. Today, such programs are often outgrowths of the musical resources of extant collegiate or community programs such as those at Swarthmore College, the University of Rochester, Lawrence University, Gamelan Sekar Jaya in California, Gamelan Galak Tika in Massachusetts, and the Metropolitan State University of Denver Department of Music and Sanggar Manik Galih in Colorado.

Although Balinese American and American children may grow up playing gamelan alongside their parents, as Lasmawan's sons did, groups intended for children offer a learning environment that is adapted to their needs. Such programs are often offered as workshops or have more limited terms of involvement than do academic or community groups; if they perform, the concert often is an informal one or a small part of a larger concert with the affiliated adult group. The rehearsal format is often shorter and less formalized than that for adult rehearsals, reflecting what Downing told me: "Kids don't want to stop and rehearse sections. Kids just want to play." The children often learn specific parts more swiftly than do adults, but their overall attention span is unpredictable. For example, Downing elaborated, "Like the five-year-old we have in our group . . . half the time, he can imitate anything that Dewa throws at him—like boom boom pak, boom pak—but the other half of the time, he's writhing on the floor trying to take his clothes off!" (Downing 2018).

Another challenge for those leading children's gamelan groups is consistency of enrollment. While parents in urban, coastal locations particularly value and seek out cross-cultural activities for their children, more traditional activities such as violin lessons and after-school sports may take precedence over gamelan. Such challenges are solved when gamelan becomes a part of students' regular schooling, a rare but growing occurrence. One of the oldest such programs in the country was founded at the Museum School, a public charter school in San Diego, in 1999 as the result of a collaboration between Alex Khalil and Bob Brown, who worked together to revive the world music in the schools program that Brown had led for a short time in the 1970s (Khalil 2016).

Since its founding, the curriculum of the Museum School has placed creative activity at the heart of student learning as part of the vision of its founder, former orchestra conductor Carl Hermanns. The school's first gamelan, which was lent to it by Brown, was originally meant to serve only as a part of a single two-month program; its popularity led Khalil and Brown to apply for and receive funding from the National Endowment for the Arts to expand the world music in the schools program. After the loss of the school's instruments when Brown died and his assets were transferred to the University of Illinois at Urbana-Champaign, a new set was bought from Lasmawan and the program continued. Currently, gamelan is taught in music class and is offered as an after-school activity. Though the school's gamelan program is successful, this model is not replicated widely elsewhere; it was only through the work of strongly committed individuals devoted to procuring and sustaining financial and artistic support that the gamelan has continued to be played for twenty years.

Gamelan in noncharter private schools, less common still, often comes about only on the initiative of individual teachers. For example, every year for a month during the spring, Lewis and Clark Elementary School in Missoula, Montana, is host to a unique "guest": a four-toned Balinese gamelan angklung. Brought to the school by its music teacher, Dorothy Morrison, the set provides the opportunity for five hundred students from kindergarten through fifth grade to study gamelan for six consecutive years as a part of their primary school education. Morrison also leads an after-school gamelan ensemble for a select group of the Lewis and Clark fourth and fifth graders called Kocong! as well as the Missoula community group, Gamelan Manik Harum (A Powerful Force That Gives You a Good Feeling Like a Pleasant Aroma).

Morrison's interest in gamelan predated both her residence in Montana and her role as an elementary school music teacher. She first encountered gamelan as an undergraduate at Wesleyan University when, unable to get into the perpetually full African drumming class, she enrolled in the Javanese gamelan ensemble, taught by Sumarsam and his wife Urip Sri Maeny. Falling in love with the music, she continued to play and dance during her entire undergraduate career in addition to studying for a year at the University of Michigan in Ann Arbor while her husband pursued a graduate degree. There were no gamelans in Montana when she moved there a few years later, but concerts that she arranged at the University of Montana that featured Gamelan Sekar Jaya and a collaboration between Jarrad Powell of Gamelan Pacifica (a Javanese group specializing in contemporary works) and the UMT percussion ensemble were received by full, enthusiastic audiences. The area was primed to host more gamelan ensembles.

Morrison tried next to bring in Michael Tenzer from Vancouver. She recalls that he said, "Well, you could bring me, but you should really bring a Balinese person, because Made Lasmawan is in Colorado Springs, in the Rocky Mountains, you should bring him." She describes what happened when she called Lasmawan:

> He was very friendly, and right away he said, "Well, you should just buy a gamelan!" The first time I talked to him—"You should just buy a gamelan!" And I said, "Well, I don't know, we don't have anywhere to keep it." And he said, "It's not that much money, and it's small; you can get the angklung and it doesn't take very much room to store." (Morrison 2013)

The UMT gamelan, as described above, arrived in 2002. Soon afterward, however, Morrison left the university owing to the instability of her adjunct position teaching world music and instead became certified to teach public school. But, she says,

> I knew I was not done with the gamelan. I knew I still had more things that I wanted to do and one of the first schools I taught at, somebody had donated a

> Balinese drum. It was a kendang, and I thought, "Ok, this is a sign; this is telling me that I need to have Balinese music in my life." So I called Made again, and I said, "I want to be able to buy a gamelan, for me, now." My husband and I decided that we would buy it for our own use and share it with the community in Missoula.

She started teaching the children at her school and formed a community group, Manik Harum, within that same year.

For most of the year the gamelan is stored in Morrison's living room; she told me, "I always say, my eldest daughter moved off to college and the gamelan moved in." The community group practices regularly at her house and performs several times per year throughout the Missoula area at a wide variety of venues, including public schools, farmer's markets, the Garden of One Thousand Buddhas near Arlee, Montana (for a peace festival), and for a New Year's Eve First Night concert in downtown Missoula. Approximately once per year Lasmawan joins them for an intensive workshop, and every few years core members of the group travel to Bali for further study.

Every year Morrison engages in intensive teaching of gamelan angklung to her elementary school classes. She says, "I can't believe how successful it's been with children kindergarten through fifth grade. It's unbelievable how much they love it. They *love* it." Starting in kindergarten, the students learn the very basics of history, culture, and gamelan technique, which they build on using similar repertoire every year throughout elementary school until they are able to play simple interlocking kotekan parts by the end of fifth grade.

Morrison's pedagogical use of the gamelan in class overlaps substantially with the themes and principles that she would employ with those age groups using any instrumental genre. With the youngest, in particular, she says, "I focus on teaching about the instruments themselves. At that level you are teaching about how size influences sound—if an instrument is *big*, as opposed to if an instrument is *small*, how is the sound different? Gamelan is *perfect* for that type of teaching. The keyed instruments all look the same, except there are four different sizes." In large part, Morrison teaches the same musical repertoire across the different grades. Often starting with Balinese folk songs and musical games or other songs reflecting Indonesian culture, she will teach the children to sing first, then add in gamelan parts as they progress through the grades. Here, she describes the process of teaching a simple song:

> In kindergarten, I teach them a song I learned from James Harding, who used to play with Sekar Jaya. James is a member of a national music organization—as I am—called the American Orff Schulwerk Association, and I met him through

> that. He taught a song called "Selamat Pagi," and it's a very simple song. There [are] only four phrases in it. The words are "*Selamat pagi, selamat siang, selamat sore, selamat malam*" (good morning, good noontime, good afternoon, good night). The children learn a little Indonesian language, and it has a very simple gong structure.
>
> The kindergarteners take turns playing gong on the parts of the song and they also do movement for the times of the day—the sun rising in the east, high in the sky at noon, setting in the west and hiding at night, in a continuous cycle. Meanwhile I'm teaching them that song, they're hearing it over and over, and I think by third grade they are ready to play "Selemat Pagi." They're ready to play it on the melody instruments with the gong parts. By fourth and fifth grade, I start teaching the kotekan that goes with the melody. So they've heard the song since kindergarten, and by fifth grade, they're playing the interlocking kotekan rhythms with it.

Teaching technique on the instruments, especially to the youngest of the students, whose motor coordination is not yet well developed, is difficult. With the children of the same grade level (and gamelan-playing experience) all in classes together, there are no more advanced players to imitate; Morrison combines gamelan playing techniques with other principles for primary music education to teach them the basics. She says:

> Going back then to the beginning, I have to teach the technique of "squeezing (damping)." That has been one of my biggest challenges—how do you teach kids to do that technique? So I use a song that combines singing and playing [with the notes numbered one through four]:
>
> Here's what we do
> One-squeeze-two-squeeze-three-squeeze-four-squeeze
> When we play the gamelan
> One-squeeze-two-squeeze-three-squeeze-four-squeeze
> Squeeze the metal keys
> One-squeeze-two-squeeze-three-squeeze-four-squeeze
> That will stop the sound
> Four-squeeze-three-squeeze-two-squeeze-one-squeeze.

Even this exercise is adapted to the relevant skill level; younger children try first by squeezing numbered, folded pieces of paper in time while they sing the melody, eventually transferring the motion to instruments. (This pattern of instruction, which focuses on developing students' gestures first, then working with the instruments, closely aligns with the introductory approach that Adnyana developed for his children's groups in Bali.) The first and second graders will add gong and basic reyong; the third graders will add the "byong-byuk" patterns on the reyong and play the notes smoothly, damping one key at the same time they strike the next. Finally, the eldest children will both sing and play, in addition to composing short melodies in the instrumental sections.

Although the children play throughout their time at the school and may give mini-performances, it is the fifth graders who primarily work with Lasmawan when he comes and give larger performances at school assemblies. The children need more time to learn the pieces, however, and Morrison only brings the gamelan to the school grounds for the one month of intensive work because it is too distracting otherwise. Instead of practicing on the gamelan, she has found other ways to teach them in advance:

> Being an Orff Schulwerk teacher, I have a lot of mallet instruments in my room—xylophones and metallophones. We use those instruments for a makeshift gamelan. We start on the music, but not on the real instruments. By the time the gamelan month comes around, which culminates in a performance with Made, they've already learned the music and we just transfer it to the gamelan instruments, which they like much better. Until then, the students will constantly ask, "When are we going to play on the real thing?"

Because the students have already practiced the music for a long time and because Lasmawan's time with them is so short, the students are basically "ready to go" when he arrives at the school. Morrison says: "He meets with each fifth-grade class for about forty minutes on the piece that they will perform for the school. And then we do a performance, which is about a forty-minute performance with him in the gym. Although the music is pretty much ready to go when Pak Made arrives, it just adds that authenticity to their experience . . . and the minute he does a drum solo, they're just, 'WHOA!'" As much as when watching Lasmawan, the students would be fascinated when he brought his sons up to perform with the elementary group. Morrison told me, "When they were in elementary school, they [Lasmawan's sons] would go to school with my son—Ade and Aji would hang out at the school and then Ade would come out after being at the school, go to classes, play on the playground, and all the kids would say, 'They're so nice and friendly.' Everybody loved them. Then Ade would come out in the performance as the Baris dancer, and the kids, their jaws would just drop. They think that's pretty cool." After playing with the group for a few years, some of the children had become particularly interested in continuing their gamelan studies. To fill this need, Morrison started an after-school program for a select group of fourth and fifth graders featuring gamelan players and "movement specialists" (a name for "dancers" that will not scare away the boys). The group practices and performs at events across the city, sometimes alone, sometimes with Gamelan Manik Harum. As a separate ensemble, they also requested a separate name:

> They're called "Kocong!" and *kocong* means "wild kid energy." At first I asked Made, "How do you say 'children of Manik Harum?' And he said it's Rare Manik Harum. Two years ago, . . . I told the group, "Ok, your name is Rare Manik Harum," and they said, "We don't want to be part of Manik Harum!" They didn't like it, so I said to Made, "What's another name, what do you call wild kids?" And that was perfect; "KoCONG!"

Despite the general enthusiasm of Morrison and the musicians in the groups that she directs, there have been some difficulties. Once they enter middle school, the children in Kocong! tend to leave the group behind. Finding funding to bring up Lasmawan to teach is also an issue; Morrison has managed to receive grants from the Montana Arts Council to sponsor Manik Harum as well as regular small sums for the school gamelan from its parent-teacher association. During the first two years, Morrison wrote to the Indonesian consulate in Los Angeles and it granted funding; one year, it sent up a delegation to watch the students perform. Finally, Morrison reports of her elementary school students, "As their teacher, it gets really tiring on your body. It's six hours a day of gamelan! It's a lot of sound. Seriously, this last year, there were times I couldn't sleep."

Yet the benefits seem to far outweigh the drawbacks. Although Morrison acknowledges educational benefits for the adult musicians of Manik Harum and their audiences, the lessons that she teaches via gamelan seem much more apparent when they are revealed by her elementary school students. She says,

> We'd sit down all together at the same time in the V-formation, so they're facing each other, and one second grader says, "Ah! I feel like I'm part of a group!" That's when I realized that part of the gamelans' power is that the class is doing something, all together. It's powerful. And we're all sitting on the floor, cross-legged; I make everybody sit that way before we start. Using the gamelan is highly structured—taking off your shoes, sitting crossed-legged, not picking up the mallet until you hear the drum cue, playing the gong in the exact right spot. Kids really respond to that. I'm talking about all kids. It's safe, you know. It's a safe space where you know what to expect.
>
> And those kind of lessons—like the lessons about respecting the instruments, and what it's like to be part of a group, and how your part fits in with other parts, you know, and just playing the gong the one time, it's just so awesome for the kids, you know? They can't wait to get to the gong. So those were the lessons

> that I didn't expect initially to show them—and I've learned actually that there [are] all of those powerful lessons about being a good person, and being a part of a group, and waiting for your turn, and all of that, so . . . yeah, there's some sort of very positive energy that emanates from the gamelan.

Of all the lessons, though, perhaps the most important one that Morrison imparts to her group is the idea of respect and continuity: "I spend a lot of time teaching about respect of the instruments. I tell the students how special they are, and how I want the instruments to last for their children! And," she continues, "they do treat them respectfully."

At least as much as pre-collegiate students, elementary-age students can reap the benefits of intercultural learning from playing the gamelan instruments and interacting with teachers and musicians from another culture. While adults find their sense of musicality challenged by the complex rhythms of Balinese music and the technical demands of playing, the more fundamental necessity of developing the fine motor skills and coordination required to grab and squeeze the instruments' keys after striking to damp the sound challenges younger students. Morrison's year-by-year presentation of slightly harder material on the gamelan also provides an explicit structural progression for the whole group that mimics, with more guidance, the adult individual learning process highlighted in chapter 4. Khalil, working with the Museum School, also has observed that "the ability to synchronize in an ensemble setting—regardless of other musical abilities—seemed to correlate strongly with ability to 'pay attention' or maintain focus, not only in music class but in other areas as well" (2016, n.p.). The community structure also reveals fundamental lessons that can be learned via gamelan including working as a part of a group, treating objects and individuals with respect, and respecting musical and social order. All of these factors lead to the creation of an ordered space that feels safe for cultivating musical, cultural, and personal development.

Cultivating Related Communities

Like many of my colleagues, I have long been uncomfortable with the trope of American music buildings containing a "gamelan room" or a "world music room" where instruments are stored away in their own space, unable to be seen and (less often) unable to be heard by anyone who is not studying them. In Bali the village gamelans are proudly displayed in the open under the roofs of *bale* (elevated covered pavilions) for the community to see and curious children to sneak up and tinker with the keys, even if restrictions remain regarding who can play in certain ensembles. The result of physically segregating gamelans from other instruments and, in many cases, positioning the ensemble as ancillary to other parts of the music curriculum in American universities is that a restricted portion of the university music community knows that the ensemble exists, and even fewer realize that it might be a logical and indeed important part of study for students across the disciplines, something that they could bring into their future work as artists. Though this issue was described in this chapter through consideration of musical production alone, it is also relevant for the broader teaching of the Balinese performing arts and particularly theater and dance in North America.

The task for American gamelan leaders is not to re-create the way music is practiced or played in Bali—a truly impossible goal—but rather to fit gamelan more comprehensively into existing American social and musical structures. For the most part, American children do not grow up immersed in any type of musical practice as much as children are exposed to gamelan in Bali; neither is there the cultural or social imperative for them to continue learning or specialize in the art form. Yet when children learn to sit and "squeeze" keys and listen, they gain not only new technical skills but also tangible experience in a physical and artistic activity that other children their age are learning halfway across the world; in an educational atmosphere that otherwise emphasizes testing the individual, they are given the safety, comfort, and motivation of working within and for a community.

College-age percussionists may also find gamelan helpful in continuing to develop motor coordination, physical technique, and focus and cognition; improve their listening skills; and expand their concepts of artistic collaboration or group social skills more generally. Though students do, as Ledbetter admits, learn how to jam in their own ways on gamelan instruments, the immersion in a new musical-cultural environment that they need their full skills to approach and master makes learning about "cultural diversity" a tangible experience that allows them to challenge and expand their own musical and cultural competency. Direct work with Indonesian musicians, when possible, also instills the real possibility for cross-cultural professional collaboration in their future work as performers and teachers.

Finally, even as there are still good pedagogical reasons for American students to learn classic or canonical works for gamelan, encouraging informed artistic experimentation with gamelan instruments and forms allows students to become a creative part of the gamelan community. Having the entire ensemble study new compositions or work with Balinese composers inspires their understanding of gamelan not as a geographically limited "traditional" art form but as a global musical heritage whose future paths depend on continued musical interest and practice in Indonesia, as well as in the global realm of new musical works. It provides nuance to the idea of gamelan as a communal practice by highlighting how the work of individuals—including, potentially, young American gamelan enthusiasts—can change the course of the art form.

If ethnomusicologists and other advocates for globally oriented ensemble practice are truly serious about "decolonizing" musical practice, gamelan must first be taught in North America by more means than through its use by Western composers, a status that has largely already been achieved. It must be taught not only as an experience-oriented, "diversifying" ensemble within the area of academic ethnomusicology but also as a distinctive and versatile art form that is capable of speaking to individuals' musical and social needs and that is accessible to them regardless of their age or level of musical experience. Finally, the future of gamelan in North America must be allowed to develop collaboratively, in dialogue between American and Indonesian musicians who work co-creatively to experiment together on the front lines of performance, composition, musicianship, and education to create mutually productive artistic experiences.

Like playing the gamelan itself, this is not a task that can be accomplished alone. Whereas specialist gamelan teachers are often skilled musicians and educators, dancers, composers and arrangers, wranglers of costumes, and promoters of ensembles, most American gamelan teachers are not specialists—and most specialists have little time to support other instructors outside their own immediate programs. It will require the efforts of those who care about the gamelan to not only develop their own programs but also to stretch their own abilities and find the resources and level of encouragement necessary to broaden the diversity of spaces where gamelan is taught and performed. While the benefit of gamelan playing is at the level of the community, much rests on the decisions of individuals to make ensembles flourish.

CHAPTER 9

Sustainability and the Academic World Music Ensemble

In the introduction to *The Ethnomusicologist*, Hood presented American and Balinese musical and societal structures as polar opposites, two systems that seemingly would be impossible to reconcile:

> Viewed as a total society, the United States regards the arts as nonessential, low on its scale of values. The hero of the day is in orbit in outer space or tunneling into the bowels of the earth or exploring the ocean floor. The poet, the painter, the musician, the dancer, the writer, the actor manage a tolerable acceptance as nonessential members of an affluent society. . . . The island of Bali, to the best of my knowledge, has more artists per capita than any other society. Here, where religion pervades every aspect of living, the creation and performance of music, dance, various forms of theater, sculpture, painting, and decoration are such an indispensable part of religious devotion that the arts, too, have become a way of life. . . . There is no word in the Balinese language for "art"; the arts are such an organic part of living that there appears to be no need for such an abstraction. (1971, 13–15)

This assessment should be taken with a grain of salt. Hood was a product of his time, with his own style and agendas; the risk of misrepresentation in rhetorically essentializing entire societies is high, and much has changed in both Bali and the United States in the past half century. Yet the fundamental differences that these words underscore remain accurate. Within Bali, the arts remain central to the majority Hindu religious contexts as well as serving supporting roles in education, the tourist industry, and political discourse; artists also pursue their work as a form of pure creative expression. While arts practitioners may lament the decline of specific genres, the overall quality of the craft and artistic interests of younger generations, and the increasing need to bend to capitalist market systems in order to be able to pursue the arts as a part of one's life work, art and performance remain a palpable presence within daily life. In contrast, although the United States is home to the world's largest film and popular music industries, a substantive disconnect remains between the substance and valuation of commercially viable art and artistic production at a local level, in particular as a part of education. When their work is commercially viable, performing artists are praised for their individual artistic vision and business savvy; teachers and performers at the community level tend to have the social and cultural value of their work systematically marginalized.

Yet for the past six decades, Balinese performing arts—and Indonesian performing arts, and other global performing arts more generally—have expanded their roles in American life, albeit with significant adaptations from their native contexts. It is likely that the largely marginal status of Indonesian music in North America and the degree of perceived difference between Balinese and American culture have in fact supported this expansion. Gamelan is attractive to practitioners and pedagogues alike owing to the ways in which gamelan's form of communal practice and deep cultural heritage, real and imagined, seemingly provides a refreshing contrast for players from the individualism and identity politics of American culture. At the same time, there has been little pressure for gamelan teaching or performance to maintain a particular level of economic viability, other than on the highly localized scale necessary to support the acquisition and maintenance of instruments and the livelihood of a leader.

This does not mean that gamelan in America is disconnected from the vicissitudes of artistic and educational popularity. Indeed, because they have been successfully transplanted into such a variety of American communities over the course of so many decades, gamelan ensembles can serve as a bellwether for understanding the conditions that are necessary for academic ensemble communities to flourish, both as pedagogical enterprises and as influential parts of transnational traditional music communities. Just as some academic gamelan ensembles such as those at Hawaii, Michigan, and UCLA are nearing or have surpassed five decades of activity, others were shuttered within just a few years of their openings or, instruments present, never truly got started. Some have maintained profound connections within their university and local communities or developed international profiles, serving as a satisfying creative portion of the careers of their leaders. Others are plagued by high turnover and quick transitions between instructors and musicians, rarely achieving more than a minimal level of musical competency or acknowledgment in local culture.

This chapter examines issues of cultural sustainability as they pertain to American academic gamelan specifically and academic world music ensembles more generally. Working from Schippers and Grant's sustainability index, the chapter reinforces the connection between American interest in gamelan cultures and the creation of a healthy transnational Indonesian performing arts ecosystem. Then, turning to the programs in North America, I examine how and why ensembles fail or fade away and the impact that such a loss has on their practitioner communities. Finally, I argue that building sustainable gamelan ensembles—indeed, sustainable non-Western academic ensembles—requires breaking out of past models of musicianship, teaching, and scholarship to embrace radical, globalized collaboration that moves gamelan from a marginalized position to sharing equal footing with other types of global music that serve as prime resources for student education.

Musical Ecosystems and Sustainability in Bali

Having previously discussed how the transnational academic pedagogical phenomenon constitutes an ecosystem, one of the clear questions is: How sustainable is this ecosystem? My expansion on Brinner's model for academic gamelans points to substantial areas of potential instability within a relatively fragile system. The work of Schippers and Grant (2016) Sustainable Futures for Music Cultures Project is helpful in conceptualizing measures of health and identifying points of concern in musical systems. The project posed sets of questions that could be used to evaluate the health of any musical system, including questions about the integration of musical practice into social events, the social status of musicians, transmission of musical knowledge, and promotion or suppression by commercial or governmental entities. Although it examined the musical health of specific genres or areas of musical culture, this musical sustainability index can nonetheless be applied to this study of gamelan in America in two ways: to examine the place of American academic music within overall gamelan ecosystems and to examine gamelan (and the world music ensemble) more generally within American academic music ecosystems. As a result, I work to blend narratives from the Balinese American community and beyond with practical systematic study to highlight both the importance of Balinese gamelan in its constituent communities and potential areas of weakness or strength.

Considering musical sustainability within Indonesia as a nation is a complex proposition. Thousands of traditional artistic practices, regional popular music styles, and international performing arts compete for resources and recognition. Although they are treated somewhat interchangeably in pedagogical contexts in the United States, Balinese and Javanese performing arts reside in interlinked but objectively different realities in Indonesia, in large part related to their orientation to religious practice and the international tourism industry. This chapter draws on structural examples from both Balinese and Javanese gamelan contexts to make its points, I start with a consideration of musical sustainability in Bali specifically—in part to continue the thematic focus from the preceding chapters and in part because it is one of the initial case studies explored in the Sustainable Futures for Music Cultures Project (Dunbar-Hall 2016).

As Dunbar-Hall reports, the traditional performing arts in Bali are thriving overall. The dozens of distinctive types of gamelans and musical repertoires native to the island remain regularly practiced and performed by groups across Bali. Even as standardized versions of traditional performance genres cross-cut the island and sometimes supplant regional variants, there is true interest on the part of musicians, from the villages to the conservatories, in both preserving old musical genres and creating new genres and works. Although it is used loosely by practitioners today, the system of classification of works as wali, bebali, or bali-balihan developed in the 1970s has encouraged artists to consider what works are appropriate for performance in different venues; the employment of the principles of desa, kala, and patra encourages them to adapt pieces to non-traditional circumstances, for example, by creating short, secularized performances for tourist venues. In addition to these, regular performances by artists of all levels occur regularly at *upacara* (religious and customary ceremonies), in lomba (contests), at arts festivals, and on recordings that are readily available on cassette, CD, and increasingly on YouTube or Internet music sales sites.

In terms of teaching and learning traditional music, Dunbar-Hall reiterates what I have described above: that face-to-face methods of musical transmission have not changed much since McPhee's time and that, conservatory and grade-school curricula aside, direct and informal music-learning experiences still constitute the predominant form of musical transmission for most musicians. Musical families built from generations of practitioners maintain strong presences in local performing arts communities and beyond. The communal ownership and organization of banjar ensembles and the proliferation of private groups—especially localized opportunities for children to study for free at sanggar—make musical learning relatively accessible, if not as egalitarian as it might appear to outsiders.[1] In terms of transmission, the only systemic issue that Dunbar-Hall notes is that the death of elder musicians who have not yet passed down specialized repertoires can result in significant culture loss. Balinese and foreign researchers and musicians continue to work collaboratively to reduce such culture loss and manage such situations when they occur (Yamin 2016).

Despite the prevalence of learning and performance opportunities, however, it is financially difficult for performing artists to support themselves fully through artistic activities in Bali. The traditional ways in which lessons or performances would be compensated—by patronage gifts from royalty or the donation of communal assistance to the teacher by neighbors—devolved over the course of the twentieth century. As artists increasingly perform for those outside the traditional Balinese social structures, including other Indonesians and foreigners, monetary compensation has become increasingly normative. The prevalence of artists to fulfill requests for tourist performances, for example, has historically led to poor compensation, with performers sometimes being awarded as little as ten thousand rupiah (less than one U.S. dollar) for a multi-hour engagement (Dunbar-Hall 2006). This low compensation, coupled with the relative difficulty involved in obtaining official teaching posts—which, as discussed previously, requires a substantial bribe by those not personally connected to artistic luminaries—is particularly discouraging to the younger generation of ISI graduates, who believed that college-level training in the performing arts would come with a relatively secure expectation of a career in the performing arts.[2]

Nonetheless, the performing arts also continue to serve as a means of winning the hearts and minds of the Balinese via political and social movements. Government officials have long used the performing arts to express power or demonstrate prestige. For example, in the 1960s, President Sukarno employed hundreds of musicians and dancers at his palace adjacent to the water temple Tirta Empul in Tampaksiring to showcase his power and influence. In the 1990s, the results of musical contests were often politicized, with winners chosen on the basis of competing teams' levels of support for certain political candidates (Bakan 1999, 209–240). Traditional music genres have also found a central place within a diverse array of contemporary social movements. For example, in the Ajeg Bali social movement of the early twenty-first century, which sought to "steady" Balinese culture against Western and Islamic influences, older Balinese genres such as *wayang wong* and *gambuh* were promoted as exemplars of the pure and refined type of Balinese culture that should be promoted, while artists protesting the *ajeg* rhetoric staged works that purposefully highlighted multireligious and multicultural heritages (Allen and Palermo 2005; McGraw

2013a, 93–96). In the Tolak Reklamasi environmental movement of the second decade of the twenty-first century, which fought against the reclamation and development of land from Bali's Benoa Bay by outside stakeholders, rock and pop music became the soundtrack of the movement's protest, but visual representations of traditional dances became a central theme for posters and other visual forms of protest. Although debates continue on Bali concerning what exactly constitutes traditional cultural and religious practice and what that entails for political, economic, and social policies and practices, it is certain that the traditional performing arts remain central to that discourse.

In sum, although the popularity and prevalence of specific art forms waxes and wanes, overall, the Balinese public values the traditional performing arts as an essential element of religious and social life and as an emblem of cultural pride. The study of performing arts specifically can serve as a unifying force. As Dewa Putu Berata notes,

> Teaching gamelan is important not only for teaching how to play a particular piece, but there are many positive aspects that I've experienced, like the feeling of unity and learning how to accept different attitudes, so that different characters, different social and educational backgrounds can all come together as one. (quoted in Dunbar-Hall 2016, 153)

Berata's sentiment resonates not only with intra-Balinese performance of the past century but also with the types of multicultural education envisioned within the transnational Balinese American performing arts community (of which Berata has been an integral member owing to his teaching and performing with Gamelan Çudamani). Dunbar-Hall's brief recognition of the importance of this international branch of the Balinese performing arts as a source of innovation and repertoire preservation for Balinese and non-Balinese musicians alike positions foreign interest in Balinese arts as an important aspect of the ecosystem.

Sustainability in Academic Music: Indonesia and the United States

What would musical sustainability look like in an academic context? Schippers and Grant (2016) explicate an analytical framework for sustainability based on five domains for investigation: systems of learning music, relationships between musicians and communities, contexts and constructs (artistic aesthetics and cultural contexts), regulations and infrastructure, and media and the music industry. Alteration of any of these domains affects the overall artistic ecosystem and potentially the health of artistic practice. How do American academic gamelans fare as their own portion of the ecosystem? What manner of the vitality of the Balinese artistic scene are they able to capture, and do they form a vital and self-sustaining part of American communities? While continuing to focus on Balinese performing arts, the following section addresses the gamelan ensemble more broadly as a structural unit in order to examine issues of sustainability.

Owing to the regional diversity of Indonesian society, nationalized art forms complement art forms that are popular or sustainable in certain locations. In the Balinese context, gamelan culture is thoroughly integrated into the social and cultural lives of the island's native Hindu majority. As such, the pursuit of traditional arts is generally supported at every level, from formal and informal teaching contexts to religious and secular performance contexts to the recording industry. Even taken as one among many Indonesian and globalized musical genres popular across Bali, gamelan permeates a substantial portion of Balinese life; although one could imagine the gradual erosion of specific traditions, the disconnection of the entire artistic system would entail substantial social upheaval.

In contrast, the immigration-based nature of multicultural society in the United States means that no set of artistic practices has such a total hold on the American people, even on a regional level. While perhaps Hood's dire estimation (1960) of the American lack of musical interest and respect for musicians is overstated, there is certainly the sense that music serves as an accessory for personal expression more than a point of cultural unification. Vernacular American traditions are largely regional or affinitive in their popularity; Western classical music, which might once have rightly claimed the title of cultural unifier, has been retreating from the public eye and ear for decades. Other musics, such as those from different locations around the world, also have their select pockets of adherents and enthusiasts. If commercial musical success is any indicator, mainstream pop, country, and hip-hop are likely the most viable candidates to serve as a core musical language. The fact that the diversity of these musics has only recently begun to have substantive representation in formal systems of music education demonstrates a substantial disconnect between musical learning, social contexts for musical consumption, and musical media. While this ecosystem remains so fractured, the role of the academic world music ensemble is by its very nature going to be limited and liminal.

As we have seen in previous chapters, the transplantation of Balinese musical cultures to American academic contexts has required substantial alterations from its practice in Bali; it also has significantly altered American collegiate musical ecosystems. Although they capture basic pedagogical elements of Balinese learning systems, the hybrid approaches to teaching gamelan music required in foreign academic contexts challenge both teachers and students. The ensembles are frequently subjected to competing expectations of what constitutes pedagogical and artistic success on the part of nonspecialist academic faculty and administrators as well as community members that differ from Balinese and Western aesthetic and pedagogical norms. As a result, limitations on musical competence—frequently on the part of beginning-level students, sometimes on the part of teachers, and almost always on the part of audiences—constrain the expressive potential of ensembles. Largely unable to truly re-create the social attitudes about music found in Bali, student performances serve entirely different social roles, such as representing cultural diversity, that rely far less on the specific form of musical expression than on the presence of some sort of musical Other. Whereas some community gamelans such as Gamelan Sekar Jaya, Gamelan Tunas Mekar, and Gamelan Son of Lion release professional recordings, gamelan as a whole has a limited commercial presence outside Indonesia; it remains, truly, a niche activity and a signifier of a certain subculture.

Competition for resources and support is often fierce, even within academic environments that are in principle supportive of a gamelan ensemble. Institutions may have the initial capital and desire to acquire a gamelan, but the maintenance of the instruments, the appointment of the teachers, and the development of the program are long-term investments that are not always well considered. The position of the teacher is often precarious, especially for Indonesians who have not become bi-academic—that is, completed terminal coursework in a Western academic system that offers greater employability in a full-time capacity, with additional institutional responsibilities apart from ensemble teaching. If ensembles go through an extended period with low student enrollment, or a teacher leaves and no other suitable instructor is found, the groups may be canceled. The combination of inter- and intragroup vitality, professional dedication, and artistic importance that is palpable in any established American gamelan community is often almost equally matched by idle fascination or overall indifference from the outside. The success of a group often relies on the efforts of a small number of individuals who must continuously demonstrate that their subcultural practice is adding value to the larger system. These factors make the long-term success of even established programs quite uncertain.

Selection, Competition, Adaptation, Reciprocity

World music ensembles, still at the periphery of many collegiate music performance programs, often occupy a more precarious position than do their Western classical neighbors. If any link in their fragile ecosystem fails, the entire enterprise may fail, keeping new ensembles from starting and causing established groups to dissolve suddenly and without warning. Brinner (2016) links the pillars of viability in an academic gamelan ecosystem to four main ecological concepts. *Selection* refers to those chosen to participate—who is selected and who self-selects to participate as teachers and students—as well as what ensembles are chosen to be supported in different settings. At and after the point of selection, the individuals and groups enter *competition* for resources, which can be financial, tangible (such as rehearsal space), or intangible (such as time or attention from audiences). *Adaptation*, as we have seen, is required in nearly every aspect of cultural exchange because teachers must adapt both their repertoire and themselves in order to have a pedagogical career, students must adapt their expectations in order to learn, and entire musical ecosystems are altered on the basis of individual interactions. Finally, *reciprocity* embodies the complex give-and-take relationship that emerges from the exchange of resources.

Although each of the four parameters represents points of potential success or failure, their entanglement with each other means that often two or more factors influence a point of systemic stability or instability. For example, in order to start or maintain a Balinese gamelan program there must be a sufficient local supply of individuals who have chosen to become teachers, but those teachers are in competition with other potential teachers and with other types of ensembles for employment and resources. In the example of students traveling abroad, pedagogical styles conceivably were adapted twice—from the Balinese norm to a norm of teaching Americans in the United States, and finally to a pattern of teaching used for Americans in Balinese contexts—and the institution of such a system at all presented substantive changes to American and Balinese experiences of the performing arts and of community. In both cases, alteration of one aspect of the pedagogic system has clear ramifications for the others.

Of the four parameters, perhaps the one most directly implicated in achieving sustainability is competition for resources. In particular, finding and funding appropriate teachers for the ensembles can present a challenge. Full-time faculty represent the ultimate in potential for the longevity and security of an ensemble, but it is rare to find individuals who possess ideal performance experience, have the experience and desire to also teach academic courses, and have the formal credentials that a university administration would recognize to allow them to do so. The ensembles are therefore left to rely on any number of unstable teaching situations: a full-time faculty member whose vision and skill set might or might not be replicated after his or her leave or retirement, a part-time faculty member or guest teacher whose time and attention must be divided between multiple institutions, or a graduate student who will eventually complete his or her work and leave. The fundamental difficulty in finding and sustaining these relationships, exacerbated by the differences between Indonesian and American systems of economic and educational capital, shapes the overall potential of such programs.

In this sense, perhaps things have not changed very much since the proliferation of "curry concerts" at Wesleyan in the 1960s (Averill 2004). Although the assumption that experienced native teachers are in general more qualified to lead ensembles than their American peers gives them privilege in hiring, the inequities of a system that does not recognize foreign credentials or the value of their expertise can mean that such teachers are either vastly underpaid or not able to be hired as autonomous directors at all. Even as the ability to teach world music ensembles remains a portion of the regular jobs of academic ethnomusicologists and is an increasingly desirable qualification for other professional music educators, world music ensemble instruction continues to be primarily contracted out to contingent laborers much more often than is the case for other types of ensembles.

As we have seen, securing institutional and financial support for Lasmawan and his family has been a major challenge in maintaining the gamelan programs that he teaches. Since Lasmawan originally arrived to teach at San Diego State under a temporary, non-immigrant J-1 visa, it was crucial for Lasmawan to receive a more permanent visa type to continue teaching. This process took several years. Additional difficulties came in obtaining enough funding for him to remain in residence in the Colorado Springs area, which would not have been possible without the economic support that Levine was able to secure for Lasmawan at Colorado College. Despite his extensive and prestigious formal education by Indonesian standards, Lasmawan's lack of a terminal degree from a recognized Western institution hurt his chances for full-time employment. Levine's persistence, however, enabled her to secure him a half-time faculty position to teach gamelan and to co-teach an Indonesian music course with her. This allowed Lasmawan to continue teaching the Colorado College gamelans and gave him the financial support for his family that eventually allowed him to continue working with the other local gamelans. In Lasmawan's case, then, economics was a key factor in taking on all of these groups. Although his initial combined salaries in Colorado were more than he had been paid at San Diego State, it was still difficult to make ends meet; for the first few years he taught in Colorado, he and his family lived in the Fitts's house and Lasmawan also took odd jobs to supplement his income, such as delivering newspapers. Now, three decades later, his economic support from Colorado College has continued to expand, and a steady stream of guest teaching and performance jobs supplements the family's teaching income.

In addition to the demand for teachers, another major concern for world music ensembles is finding an appropriate space to store instruments and to rehearse. Gamelans pose a threat to departmental real estate; most gamelans can occupy a whole room, if arranged in a performance configuration, or a whole wall if stored in cabinets. Their aural presence is even more substantial than their physical one. Since gamelans are sometimes given to institutions as part of a bequest rather than being a planned acquisition, space constraints can limit the ensemble from the beginning. For example, although Appalachian State University received a gamelan gong kebyar as a bequest of alumnus Max Smith, the size of the collection of instruments and a lack of storage and rehearsal space have restricted the instruments to being played only on occasion, within the context of world music seminar courses. Problems with space can also emerge after an ensemble has been practicing for years if the ensemble's historic practice space becomes unavailable or the program is opened to new communities spread across multiple locations.

Another potential point of disruption is at the level of supply of students. Because they are positioned primarily as experience ensembles, gamelans and other types of world music ensembles rely on recruiting students during their college years rather than being able to count on attracting new students to the university who are already experienced in these musical styles. Finally, though part of the tangible diversity apparatus of many institutions, ensemble course participation rarely meets institutional cultural diversity or arts education requirements, making it a lower priority than other courses for requirement-minded students. Although, as long-time gamelan ensemble directors confirmed, ensemble enrollments fluctuate over time, it is rare for ensemble classes to be canceled outright. More problematic is the number and level of students involved. As discussed in chapter 4, having community members involved, either as a consistent presence in a student ensemble or playing in a parallel group close by, adds security and longevity to the collegiate group.

Sustainability and the Gamelan

Whereas many world music ensembles slip away silently into the night when they are threatened, others' struggles have been broadcast so publicly as to resonate in interested communities across the continent and beyond. In 2014 the Javanese gamelan at the University of Michigan, Kyai Telaga Madu (Venerable

Lake of Honey), was threatened with disbandment; the instruments' dedicated space was to be reallocated. A part of the Stearns Collection of Musical Instruments, the full Javanese gamelan, with sets of instruments in both slendro and pelog tuning, had been founded in 1966 by professor of musicology William Malm and was formed into a practicing ensemble by Judith Becker by 1968. Since that time, the university has offered consistent gamelan ensemble courses to students and public performances of the gamelan frequented by members of the Ann Arbor community. No permanent solution was initially proposed that would allow the instruments to remain in use; neither was there room to display them within the public spaces of the Stearns Collection. The move was particularly surprising given that in 2010 several substantial donations had been made to the gamelan program. It appeared that after all these years, the instruments would fall silent.

Interest in the ensemble had fluctuated over the years, but the program had maintained not only two resident faculty teachers and coordinators (Becker and Susan Walton) but also a consistent presence of Javanese instructors for decades. It was not lack of participation or interest, it seemed, that threatened the ensemble, but shifting perceptions of geopolitical relationships and their perceived connection to higher education—the very same political currents that brought gamelan in the first place. For example, in the case of the Michigan gamelan, Elizabeth McLain wrote, "Expensive programs are now being put in place to promote 'globalization' at the University, yet the gamelan program is in danger of disappearing because despite multiple searches throughout the university, a space cannot be found for it" (McLain 2014, n.p.). Dane Harwood, one of the initial members of the gamelan ensemble at the University of Michigan and an active gamelan player for forty years, elaborated further on the situation in a post to the petition:

> We must keep in mind that, unlike the era of the 1960s-1970s, when geopolitical focus was on Southeast Asia, American political and cultural attention has shifted to the Far East and India. (For now, I'll duck the issue of the Middle East, since that's more or less a constant.) That means that the urgency of academic programs to make themselves relevant to extra-university funding sources has moved away from Indonesia, Vietnam, Thailand, etc., and to China, India, Korea, and to a lesser extend Pakistan and Japan.
>
> So, the politics behind the School of Music's decision to abandon the gamelan is not merely unfortunate, nor merely an insult to the history, tradition, and still active and enthusiastic leadership provided by Susan Walton and Judith Becker. It is the direct result of 1) the increasing corporatization of universities throughout the U.S.—that is, the short-term cost/benefit analysis that entrenches itself when the branding mentality takes over, where money is now the main guiding

> mission, not education; 2) globalization—the shifting sources of foreign student enrollments, foundational sources of funding, and global business tie-ins with the university, and 3) long-term hostility to non-Western musical traditions that, despite 60 years of ethnomusicology's good-will attempts to broaden the curriculum, still resides amongst departments of music throughout academia. (Harwood, personal communication, February 12, 2014)

Harwood's comments, resonating with the historical materials presented in chapter 2, emphasize the perception that finding space—though surely a pressing issue—was not the only reason the ensemble was slated for closure. He proposed an endowment of $100,000 that would support housing and teachers for the ensemble but noted at the time, "We're nowhere near reaching that goal yet."

The outcry following the announcement that Gamelan Kyai Telaga Madu would be removed from operation was immediate and decisive. A petition, "Save the UM Gamelan," was posted on the web site Change.org (McLain 2014, n.p.). Within twenty-four hours, there were 925 signatures as gamelan enthusiasts in the United States, Canada, Japan, Australia, several European nations, and Indonesia quickly spread the news via email, Facebook, and word of mouth. By the time the petition closed ten days later, it had accrued more than 2,700 signatures and hundreds of comments in a section called "Reasons for Signing." Ranging in length from a few words to multiple paragraphs, the comments not only provide a snapshot of the legacy of this particular gamelan but also reveal that supporters were well aware of the personal and systemic importance of collegiate gamelan culture more broadly. For example, this comment signed by Joseph Dubiel from New York highlights the multifaceted educational role of the ensemble:

> For many Americans, to learn something about the gamelan was also to learn substantively for the first time about modes of musical behavior, perception, and thought different from those we had grown up with. It would be a shame (I mean the word exactly) for The University of Michigan to break faith with its genuinely historic contribution to all our education in and about music by undermining its ensemble and making its instruments inaccessible.

Teachers of gamelan, both American and Indonesian, also testified to the power of the instruments as tools of instruction. Sumarsam, one of the most revered scholars, teachers, and performers of Javanese gamelan music in the United States, wrote:

> As a regular guest musician of the UM gamelan since 1970s, I am very sad to know the uncertainty of the future of gamelan: whether it will be available to students or not. Having taught gamelan for more than 40 years in the US, I can testify

> that teaching gamelan is one of the best educational enterprises for American students to be exposed to non-Western music. I hope that UMich reconsiders its decision. Sincerely, Sumarsam, University Professor of Music [Wesleyan University].

Other pleas were more personal. The instruments and the musical opportunities that they brought to the community held deep significance for those who had experienced them. For example, Stewart Gordon of Ann Arbor wrote:

> More than forty years ago I took a girl on a date to hear this gamelan. When she loved the music I knew she was a "winner." We're still married. It would be a tragedy if others now cannot enjoy gamelan as we have.

Finally, commenters cited the instruments as an integral part of the institution's identity—and not only those who had attended or taught at the university. Minda Dettman from Tucson, Arizona, wrote:

> I am a high school senior in the middle of the college search processes. I applied to the University of Michigan and got my acceptance letter this past December. . . . One of the largest reasons I was interested in Michigan was because you have a gamelan. I have been playing gamelan in a local community group since I was in fourth grade. . . . When asked in essay questions on applications my three main reasons for picking a college were a strong, real sense of globalism, a small liberal arts college (the residential college), and equally important, a gamelan. Please don't take the gamelan away from all of us.

In the case of the University of Michigan, the immediate national outcry from a small but vocal group of supporters yielded substantial results. Ten days after the petition was launched, petition organizer Elizabeth McLain announced that the gamelan ensemble would continue to rehearse using a limited set of instruments throughout the 2014–2015 academic year. In 2017, the year marking the bicentennial of the university and the fiftieth anniversary of the gamelan ensemble, donations arrived that should financially support the gamelan in perpetuity. The University of Michigan Alumni Association of Indonesia pledged $400,000 to the existing UM Javanese Gamelan Endowment and promised a further $100,000 to establish a UM Indonesian Alumni Student Support Fund, which will back study of Indonesian culture. Yet, according to Walton in an email posted to the international gamelan listserv on August 30, 2017, the gamelan was continuing to face declining enrollment, regardless of whether Indonesian guests or Americans were teaching the ensemble. Although the university gamelan had previously supported full courses for beginning and intermediate musicians, only the participation of local community members enables the ensembles to be sustained.

A Collaborative Vision for Sustainability

Despite the degree to which gamelans have come to thrive in North America since the mid-twentieth century, there are substantial challenges to sustaining gamelan communities, academic and otherwise, outside Indonesia. Solving individual logistical problems is certainly important, but it is impossible to advance gamelan as a musical genre without additionally considering what success would entail. Perspectives from the youngest generations of Balinese and American gamelan musicians working transnationally, those born in the last quarter of the twentieth century, present an array of goals to focus on in gamelan's second half century as a part of the American educational landscape.

This generation places a heavy emphasis on further exposure to gamelan in the American mainstream, both within educational systems and in the public eye. In some senses, this is hardly revolutionary—most American gamelan programs have sponsored some form of outreach outside of their own communities—but younger generations believe that more can be done. For some individuals, this effort is about artistic development. Sudirana, for example, argues that it is important to have gamelan idioms accepted more broadly into global compositional practice even as global musical idioms are more often incorporated into Balinese composition. Doing so, he believes, would allow a new generation to not only preserve the older traditions but also add to them, increasingly making Balinese gamelan a part of a global musical heritage. Others focus on expanding the social benefits of gamelan to a broader audience. For Sonja Downing, one of the most difficult challenges is that she knows the benefits of gamelan well and considers more widespread learning of gamelan as a key way to cure societal issues. But outside progressive circles where parents fight to have the "most multicultural" child, she wonders, how do you convince someone to play when they are simply struggling to pay their rent and take care of their families? For some, exposure is an end in itself; for example, Ade Wijaya hopes that gamelan music will become so popular that it is played on the radio, that it transcends the status of being a micromusic altogether and takes a more visible place beyond academia in the multimusical auditory fabric of America.

Extending and deepening the educational exchange between Bali and America, too, is a central goal, and one that must be pursued in partnership between musicians of both nations. The value of having native Balinese involved in teaching American students is at the heart of this consideration. For teachers like

Elizabeth Macy, leading experiential study abroad programs in Bali during the summer or winter break is perhaps one of the most important ways to engage students in cross-cultural learning; the dozens of institutions that sponsor such programs in partnership with Balinese hosts is an endorsement in the value of that ideal. Although hundreds of American colleges and universities sponsor semester- or quarter-long terms of study in Europe during the academic year, few offer such programs in Indonesia. The development of such programs in and beyond the performing arts would not only promote Indonesian artistic traditions such as gamelan but also create stronger intercultural exchanges.

Overall, the types of academic and artistic exchanges that have been fostered by the spread of gamelan in the past half century have not been equally accessible. We have seen that completing graduate education in North America has profoundly enhanced the career prospects of Balinese artists and educators, but there is no widely established mechanism for Indonesian undergraduates to study abroad in North America. The fact that such travel remains an activity of the elite, even in America, means that most young Indonesian students are precluded from joining the cosmopolitan class of individuals who are expected as global citizens to become leaders in and beyond their future professions. Although pursuing such programs would remain economically, linguistically, and politically difficult, amending such inequality—potentially via further artistic exchanges—would again create a stronger, more sustainable, and more equitable global dialogue.

Even as ethnomusicology as a discipline has aimed to deconstruct the inequalities in global representation and discourse, in the case of the Indonesian performing arts, access to internationally recognized publication in this field is still largely controlled by foreign scholars writing primarily in English as well as Japanese, French, and German. The portrayals of Indonesian performing arts in English-language textbooks and other general written sources, too, remains largely out of the hands of Indonesian authors. For young faculty in the ISI educational system like Indra Sadguna, who hopes to subscribe to his father I Wayan Rai's vision of being "a complete musician" who performs, composes, and researches, it is crucial that Indonesian musicians be able participate more vocally in this scholarly tradition. According to those who teach within them, the development of ethnomusicology courses and programs in the Indonesian conservatory system in the past few decades has done little to encourage rigorous documentation of Indonesian musics by Indonesian scholars. A particularly cutting critique comes from Citra Aryandari, faculty member in ethnomusicology at ISI-Yogyakarta, who wrote the following (original in Indonesian) on her public blog:

> Ethnomusicology in Indonesia is not yet well known, even though in addition to ISI Yogyakarta, ethnomusicology is also a program of study at ISI Padang Panjang, University of North Sumatra, STSI Bandung (now ISBI Bandung), Jakarta Art Institute, ISI Surakarta, ISI Denpasar, and ISBI in Kalimantan. However, even though ethnomusicology has been spread to a handful of educational institutions, it is important to realize that this discipline has been quite slow in its course to develop—even though Indonesia contributed to its birth. [. . .]
>
> Ironically, the half-hearted development of ethnomusicology in Indonesia causes us to continue to be treated as "objects" by Western researchers, and we have not yet become "subjects" who independently research and understand Indonesian music on our own. Instead of skillfully researching various musics native to our archipelago, our academic ethnomusicologists seem to be busy becoming an extension of the government's tourism program that likes to sell jargon about "national cultural exoticism" for the sake of foreign exchange and admiration from foreign countries.
>
> Ethnomusicology in Indonesia needs to reflect on itself: is it ready to open up and welcome changes to the ethnomusicological paradigm in order to become an independent subject capable of researching, writing, and developing the music of our archipelago independently? Or will we continue to remain silent, our cultural documentation made the target of Western researchers?[3]

Some elements of the development of strong scholarly traditions in Indonesian ethnomusicology are clearly within the purview of Indonesian musicians, academics, and administrators. Yet, though the development of Indonesian ethnomusicology may seem but distantly related to the development of gamelan ensemble courses in North America, the infrastructure needed to strengthen American academic programs may also strengthen Indonesian ones. Scholars at institutions such as the University of British Columbia, UCLA, Wesleyan, and the University of Maryland, Baltimore County who have historically supported individual Indonesian musicians in teaching while they obtained advanced degrees, serve as the bedrock of such initiatives by giving Indonesian artists exposure to and within American scholarly systems; however, this system has helped only one or two musicians at a time. Creating formal partnerships with Indonesian universities, shifting toward valuing more flexible and collaborative models of artistry and scholarship within American academic systems of career development and promotion, and encouraging American scholars (including students) to develop scholarly and creative projects with (rather than on) Indonesian subjects would allow for further self-representation on the part of Indonesians. Finally, further public education about gamelan that increases knowledge about it yet defies its positioning as exotic will reinforce the value of Indonesian self-documentation not for the purpose of tourist spectacle, but because—as touted in the Indonesian governmental campaign for gamelan to be recognized in the UNESCO category of intangible cultural heritage—gamelan is truly a part of our global artistic heritage, one that is valued in a variety of circumstances within and outside Indonesia.

The importance of creating an equitable international dialogue about gamelan can be illustrated by returning to consider Bali, where traditional culture has been perceived locally and internationally as being under dire threat for generations. As Dunbar-Hall argues, religion and tourism have been considered as central pillars of the sustenance of Balinese artistic culture, even as they are supplemented by artistic developments outside these two realms. For many Balinese (as well as outsiders concerned by the encroachment of tourism into Balinese ways of life), the point at which the island's culture would be considered dead is when the Balinese Hindu religion is no longer central to people's lives. For some contemporary artists, however, that death knell would also be sounded loudly by the disappearance of the Balinese performing arts, which are both integral to and transcend religion. International reinforcement of local efforts to sustain and develop Balinese art, therefore, provides not only a healthy education for American students but also an extra impetus to provide a space for the continued practice, growth, and development of Balinese artistic culture.

Enacting Sustainable Futures for Academic Ensembles

Like the discourse surrounding artistic and cultural preservation, the rhetoric surrounding the maintenance and development of academic programs in the arts and humanities is often one of fear and negativity not only in America and now in contemporary Indonesia, but also around the world. Artistic subjects are perceived as being impractical courses of study for students seeking employment after college graduation or, almost as bad, ones that will not allow the accumulation of wealth, the ultimate sign of success to many (but not to most artists) in a modern neoliberal capitalist society. As such, artistic practices have been multiply marginalized. Ensembles in ethnomusicology and in collegiate music education have largely been deemed nice but not necessary to their core missions or to the public at large. As a result, the lifelong work of individuals like Lasmawan who have positively affected the lives of thousands of students, colleagues, and audience members remains undercompensated and recognized primarily within the teacher's immediate community alone.

Arguably, the second half of the twentieth century in the United States saw a complete disruption of the intellectual canons of the first half of the century by the introduction of non-European sources and a postmodern approach to knowledge that favored dialecticism over objective truth. If the twenty-first century seeks to reconstitute intellectual (and artistic) canons, it is likely that gamelan will be at the heart of such efforts, much as it was in the past half century. Those who teach and practice gamelan, therefore, come from a position of strength. They know the benefits of gamelan in terms of artistic development and community building; such benefits need to be better documented and allowed to spread outside the ensembles' traditional homes in ethnomusicology. One way of doing this would be to strengthen the role of gamelan in cognate areas of musical study, particularly percussion, composition, and music education.

In order to widen their reach, gamelans and similar ensembles must not be restricted to marginalized institutional structures as in the past but, rather, be available for collaboration within American communities and as the subject of cross-cultural collaboration. Their ability to play an activist role in public ethnomusicology is also integral to this endeavor. Such activism must be recognized as a desirable and credited part of the system of academic employment and compensated fairly. This activism includes not only performing and conducting workshops, but also creating print and video resources by experts (preferably Balinese in collaboration with Westerners) that are able to reach general American audiences where no gamelans are present.

A part of breaking out of these institutional structures is the necessity for new gamelans to be initiated and supported not for the traditional reason of educational exoticism, though they may still play that role, but on their own merits: because gamelan is beautiful, wonderful music. Programs and institutions must consider carefully what they hope students will take away from studying gamelan, whether it is musical competence, cultural competence, or a blend of both, and whether the program should emphasize learning about cultural diversity through music or learning about culturally diverse musical content (Dunbar-Hall 2002). In addition, careful consideration is needed to determine whether gamelan is a potentially sustainable vehicle for accomplishing these goals. Such consideration might ultimately mean the presence of fewer gamelans in North America (because establishing a new gamelan program would appear to be unsustainable), but ideally those that are established would grow to be beloved within the university, active in their regionals, and connected to ensembles across the country and across the world. Such deliberation would also open avenues for supporting other ensembles that might better speak to the "time, place, and situation" of the academic institution. The paradigm of the so-called world music ensemble, though still in place, would be more easily adaptable to address different educational situations.

It is also crucial to realize that although Americans who have committed a substantial amount of time in their lives to listening to or playing gamelan generally do truly love the music for its own sake, those who are encountering it for the first time are often at first more attracted by the novelty of the experience than anything else. New fans may come to gamelan through a love of the compositions of Debussy or rock music groups like King Crimson who included gamelan-like passages in their music, or because the frenetic energy of Balinese gamelan feels like video game music. Or perhaps they love the novelty of performing in an exotic costume. Students who aim to collect unique experiences in college may play in the gamelan once just to "check it off," like finding an item on a scavenger hunt list. Whether or not such approaches become neocolonial—whether individuals' participation in gamelans for those reasons seems like exploitation merely for their own gain—rests largely in the ability of the ensemble and its director to add complexity to this initial attraction and have gamelan music not only resonate with a person's prior musical interests but also build new ones that are more directly rooted in Indonesian artistic practice.

Finding ways to negotiate ensembles' connections to Indonesian communities remains a challenge. We have seen how educational credentials, issues of faculty fit, and negotiating complex transnational systems (such as that of visa sponsorship) can limit opportunities for collaboration. However, other social factors limit such connections, too. For all that women have sustained a notable presence in American gamelan communities since the 1960s and women's participation in Balinese performing arts has continued to expand in the past few decades, with a growing generation of female artists whose technical and artistic playing abilities are widely acknowledged, limitations on transnational artistic and educational possibilities for women remain. In addition to the general lack of independent Balinese women working in North America, it is also more common for male American musicians who have spent substantial time studying in Bali to do so independently than for female musicians, who more often travel or study as a part of an ensemble or as a part of a couple interested in gamelan. American women, as seen throughout this book, have historically played supportive or administrative roles more often than becoming independent artistic directors. Female scholars of Balinese performing arts also are much more likely to study predominantly cultural (rather than musical) phenomena, including women's or children's musical production, or to research dance or arts like gender wayang that can be pursued in private lesson settings rather than penetrating predominantly male ensembles. Although all these areas benefit from a substantive female presence, as more female gamelan enthusiasts forge ahead further into gamelan practice by pursuing mainly male areas of expertise (such as playing kendang and composing) and envisioning new forms of collaboration that are artistically and educationally rich, the ability of female ethnomusicologists to become grounding and innovative forces in their own programs will expand.

Ethnomusicologists and ethnomusicology programs have a crucial role to play in determining the future of ensembles like gamelan, and as such, should widely seek to offer well-considered support for them. It is true that contemporary research paradigms in the field have diversified substantially since the 1950s, meaning that there are many areas of ethnomusicological research for which studying music in an ensemble is perhaps no longer a necessity. Yet, equally, as the discipline moves toward greater global collaboration, skilled performers with a variety of musical backgrounds and interests seek intellectual and artistic homes in American ethnomusicology programs; collegiate ensembles support and benefit from their talents. Further, in a practical sense, as long as academic institutions seek gamelans and other world music ensembles to diversify their musical offerings, hands-on training supports the much-in-demand expertise needed to teach them. In turn, not only do general education undergraduate students benefit from the experiential possibilities of world music ensembles, but also those seeking careers in ethnomusicology, composition, education, or other areas of music. These music professionals are in a unique position to use their teaching, performance, writing, filmmaking, or other creative pursuits to cultivate intercultural and intermusical understanding for not only the specific ensemble types that they studied but also for musical and cultural diversity writ large.

Two clear ways to provide access to such training and to build stability across the entire gamelan system are to recognize the integrality of the individual in advocating for, sustaining, and motivating such communities and to train a future generation of teachers who are willing to work hard to learn and teach the musical traditions. Lasmawan, for example, feels confident that his own ensembles will survive, and in many cases, thrive after he and others of his generation have retired. In large part, this is because a select number of the younger generation of students that he has taught—including his three sons, members of the Front Range-area gamelans, and others across the country, a group numbering more than a dozen individuals ranging in age from their teens to their forties—continue to nourish and sustain the groups as far as they are able. Communication, interconnectedness, and generosity in helping others have been key to the flourishing of this extended community.

It is equally important for institutions to recognize that fully supporting a world music ensemble such as a gamelan requires substantial commitment to the instruments, the practice and performance spaces, and especially the teacher by contributing to an employment situation that is stable and provides a living wage. Although student and community involvement tend to wax and wane over the course of multiple decades, such ensembles have the potential to provide distinctive experiences in musical diversity that have the potential to last not only for one semester but for a lifetime.

CHAPTER 10

Cultivating New Flowers

Both ethnography and gamelan are nearly inescapable parts of life for those who pursue them. I was reminded of this at my husband's ten-year reunion at Swarthmore College in Pennsylvania. I had agreed to attend, fully expecting to not know anyone else who was present. But we had only made it as far as the opening reception on the quads when my husband, walking over to me with a plate of hors d'oeuvres in hand, remarked, "There's a guy over there who looks Balinese. I wonder—do you know him?"

I laughed. The chances were pretty good, considering the relatively small number of Balinese people I had met in America who were not gamelan musicians or dancers. I approached the table, stood next to the thin, tall man whom my husband had correctly identified as being Balinese, and casually filled my plate with food. At the same time, both of us looked up at each other. We hesitated for a moment, trying to identify each other in this seemingly most chance of encounters, then broke into smiles. It was Dewa Ketut Alit Adnyana, Balinese gamelan teacher, former member of Gamelan Çudamani, and husband of ethnomusicologist Sonja Downing, who approached us moments later with their daughter, Adri. I had completely forgotten that Sonja had not only attended Swarthmore but was also a founding member of the Swarthmore College gamelan ensemble. Chance upon chance, here we were in the same place.

It was almost certainly a direct result of that encounter that four months later I found myself driving a tiny neon green Ford Fiesta into Appleton, Wisconsin, to visit Sonja and Dewa where they teach at Lawrence University. I was interested in their work on children's gamelans but also more generally in their lives as members of the generation between mine and Lasmawan's and in the ways they negotiated teaching, performing, and life in general as a Balinese American couple. Luckily, both had agreed to talk to me about these things; it was in this way that I found myself sitting in a wing chair across from Adnyana in the office behind the gamelan room, watching the leaves fall and talking about his life in gamelan.

It has been my goal in this book to use the narrative of individual lives to contextualize, exemplify, and investigate certain important results of cultivating Balinese gamelans in academic contexts. I began my research for this project with Lasmawan, using his life as a framework in which to understand issues endemic to the transnational academic gamelan community. As one visit and a few interviews in Bali became years of discussions, rehearsals, concerts, and stories shared over coffee at dozens of locations in both of our native countries, however, little parts of his story became tangled in my own. Issues that had seemed clear to me in approaching that initial interview were inevitably complicated by my encounters, planned and unplanned, with the rapidly expanding group of students, teachers, colleagues, and friends who never would have entered my life except through gamelan. The act of sorting through and attempting to impose order on these events defies the essence of the overwhelming simultaneity of lived experience. Keeping them the messy jumble that they are and juxtaposing them in their multiplicity may not provide concisely delivered facts or theories, but it reveals messier and ultimately more important types of meaning.

I had begun this project to insist, by means of scholarly analysis, that creating world music ensembles was not a low-stakes nod toward evoking cultural diversity but an activity that has potential to enact real change in the way students and teachers alike view the world and lead their lives. But it is through stories, not analysis, that I believe this argument can be most convincingly conveyed, because of the inherent untidiness of using personal representations of performing arts as a form of cultural education. As a result, I have chosen to conclude this book with two narratives: an edited transcription and analysis of Adnyana's story as it was told to me, and a reflection on my own journey as a musician, student, teacher, and documenter of academic gamelans.

"This is my life": Dewa Ketut Alit Adnyana, October 27, 2018

This interview has been edited, and small bracketed insertions from other conversations have been added for clarity. The interview took place in a mix of Indonesian and English; I have italicized the portions that were spoken in Indonesian to capture the flavor of the original.[1]

My parents, my siblings, everyone in my home likes music. But it's no secret that when I was a child I rarely slept in the house; I slept in the house of Pak Dewa Berata at Sanggar Çudamani studio on the floor, with a blanket—my story is like that. I just never slept on a mattress. *The sanggar became my home because there wasn't enough money, my parents couldn't make a home for me, so I lived at the Çudamani pondok with the gamelan. Sometimes Pak Dewa, or Bu Emiko, or Bu Judy [Mitoma] would bring me a blanket from America and I was so happy. It was like this, my life.*

Later, I didn't want to continue to high school. After I finished SMP [middle school] I wanted to stop *going, I didn't want to go again, because I . . . I was stressed out about studying so many things—biology, mathematics, like that. I was so stressed, I wasn't strong . . . my memory wasn't strong . . . but I liked music school. Later, Pak Dewa and Bu Emiko, they* support me. *They said, "It's important to study music!" And so I was interested in school again.* I waited until my nephew *finished junior high*, then, *together*, together with him we went to KOKAR in Batubulan, where my teacher was Ketut Gede Asnawa.

After I studied in high school, Pak Dewa formed the group Çudamani, and later Pak Dewa and Emiko talked about making a children's group, a men's group, a women's group. There wasn't any salary yet. Dewa and Emiko asked me to teach, and I thought, "I think I am ready, I am just so happy. I have the time, I don't have a job yet, I'm finishing high school. It's good to help build a new generation."

When I was at KOKAR I had already taught children at the banjar, and Çudamani did not yet have a gamelan. When Çudamani got a gamelan, later, I returned to the sanggar, in the village of Pengosekan. They had a children's group, a men's group, a girls' group, and Bu Emiko wanted to make a mixed-gender children's group. But the children were too ashamed [malu]. I understand, right? *Maybe they were too ashamed to play with one girl and one boy . . .* one *girl on gangsa, one boy on gangsa; reyong* one-one . . . *it was not successful; the mixed group didn't last long. This is Tejur's experience joining Çudamani.*[2]

At first I joined in the village where Pak Dewa taught; Tejur played with Dewa Rai, and Super—do you know Super [I Dewa Made Suparta, who teaches at the University of Waterloo], Maisie [Sum]'s husband? I joined Çudamani, I joined the banjar gamelan, like that. It was extremely important to play at the temple ceremony. *It was why I had thought that I must study music, I must study gamelan. . . .* I had to study gamelan for the god, for the temple. This is my point. This is the most important thing for my life.

Afterwards, my friends from KOKAR taught in the villages; Tejur went here and there, taught gangsa and reyong, in Payangan, for example. Wonderful! Night after night, going out with Pak Dewa. Before that, I had only gone out a little bit because Tejur couldn't drive a motorcycle before they have the automatic motorcycle. My leg is a problem because it's not too strong. That is . . . that is my life. It's funny, I just think—like here in America, I just drive! Because I have an automatic car, it's easy with just one leg. It's amazing, right?

But anyway, then a foundation of people in Jakarta helped us. Pak Philip [Yampolsky], he was in contact with Emiko, and the Jakarta Foundation helped *with money,* they bought some costumes, *he helped us get a grant and got a Barong, instruments. The sanggar has grown. . . .* Now the musicians, it is so funny; they are my students! Pasta [I Made Pasta], the reyong players, those are my students. I take them before they are professional—and now they are professional!

When they were kids, they were just playing kites in the rice field. I just found them! I said, "Oh, hello! Come practice gamelan!" I am so happy with them now. That is my proudest thing—it's not money for me—I am proud of them now. It was my job—like I have time for you, I have time for them, to teach them, the basic pieces, like *gilak* . . . the process is the same. The same as here, with my students here. That is my experience as a teacher.

The first time I came to America was with the Çudamani tour, in 2002. I will tell you about my experience. What do you think I brought in my suitcase? I just bring *mie goreng* [fried noodles]. A lot of *mie goreng.* And then we were just cooking in the sink in the restroom because I cannot eat American food—and we cooked salad, too, and ate it with salt. We took the fire alarm down so it wouldn't go off. And Pak Dewa, he already knew [American food] before the Çudamani tour because he'd been with Sekar Jaya, right. . . . He said, "Oh it's good, it's good!" But for me, it's not good! But one time Pak Dewa told me, "This is an expensive restaurant"—the sponsor brought us to an expensive pizza place, and I'm like, "Oh, no, I cannot eat pizza, what do I do? Do they have rice? No? Oh, no!" It was so stressful about food.

But I had met Americans before, before I met Sonja, because I helped when the Sekar Jaya group came to Bali. I put the gamelan on the truck, I *helped prepare for rehearsal,* just helped every time. And then I met her. I didn't know English yet, she only knew a little Indonesian, so she just talked with me a little. She wanted to study gangsa, and Pak Dewa asked, "Oh, Tejur, do you have time to teach Sonja gangsa?" and I said okay. We just speak "cue," you know [he waved his hand around like he was holding a mallet]. That's my story about Sonja. And she came back to the USA, then came back to Bali and studied again; and then she went back to study *S3* [in a PhD program], and then she was in Bali for a long time, like six months, and she stayed in Pak Dewa's house. I was helping with housecleaning over there in the *pondok,* and I just helped Sonja every time. I went to help her [with her research] to go see different children's gamelan groups. Different cities, different teachers, different cultures like this, every night, on the motorcycle.

Later, I asked Pak Dewa and Emiko, "Can I ask Sonja to be my girlfriend?" Because Çudamani is very important for me. If they said no, I would just say no. But because they supported me, I'm just like, "Okay. *Okay.* OKAY!" [Here his smile widened with every repetition of the word.]

Pak Dewa and Emiko supported me with Sonja and we just kept going. I told Sonja, "I love you." Like this. And then Sonja asked if I had an idea about [what life would be like] if she brought me to the USA, and I said, "I just love music"—like this, I told Sonja—"I love music like this, like teaching gamelan, teaching at the campus. . . . When you get a job, I can work with you, we can work together on your campus." And she said, "Okay, I'll try."

After the Çudamani tour, I wanted to be a guest for Sekar Jaya, because it was close to Sonja's parents, because she was done in Santa Barbara but still in California. I joined Gamelan Sekar Jaya. I said, "Oh, but you have Wayne Vitale, he's a composer!" [as if to say, Why do you need me?], and [Vitale] said, "I want a Balinese guest." I stayed in Sonja's house—and we were not married yet!—but Sonja and her parents already knew me. Then Sonja got an interview here [at Lawrence University] with her boss, and he saw the video with the Çudamani group [when they asked if Dewa could be hired to teach gamelan]. Her boss said, "I already saw Çudamani in Seattle!" And Sonja clarified, "This is my boyfriend's cousin's group."

And the boss called to me [to offer me a teaching position] and asked, "Are you ready?" And I said, "Yes, I'm ready!" And to Sonja I said, "This is my life. If you're happy, I'm happy too."

We talked for several minutes about the university students, the community group, and the children's group at Lawrence and about his pedagogical style before the conversation turned again toward the personal. I had commented that it seemed as if he had adapted well to living in Wisconsin. He agreed but noted that "it's like Nyepi every day"—that with no people in the streets of Appleton and no cousins to go visit and join in making music, the town is forever fixed in the Balinese holiday nicknamed "the day of silence," when no one leaves their homes. And then there was the issue of children. He said, "My parents tell me, 'You have to make a kid!' And I tell them, 'Oh, but I don't have the money! If you sponsor me, then I can do it.'"

"Life is difficult," he continued. "You have to work, you have to find a job, and the money is not enough. If you want to have a kid . . . it's very hard."

As we continued talking, it became clear to me how important it was for Dewa to visit and to support his family, both in Bali and in the United States—and, despite his hard work, how quickly living expenses in Wisconsin alone used up his income. When I asked Dewa about going back to Bali, he said, "I don't have money. I *cannot*, yeah. Thinking about my life . . . I *cannot* go to Bali. I just want to borrow a little bit and buy a ticket . . . but I'll never have enough money by myself. But now I have a job at Java Warung [a local Indonesian restaurant]." Here, he brightened as he continued to describe how he'd been saving diligently, growing closer every month to meeting his goals. With regard to traveling to Bali, he added, "At least, now seven of my students have already gone to study in Bali. Seven! . . . It's like this, Elizabeth."

At that point, we heard someone tapping on the front door. The first participants had arrived for the children's gamelan session. Dewa unfolded himself from the chair and, with a wide smile, went to let them in.

Considering Lives in Teaching Gamelan

What conclusions can one draw from this story? Though four decades of lived experience can be outlined in less than an hour, the importance of such a tale to the listener and storyteller alike cannot be so neatly captured, ordered, and arranged. Despite the dozens of stories that I had heard in my time within the transnational gamelan community, the words of Dewa Ketut Alit Adnyana—Tejur—resonated with me, reiterating the questions that had animated much of a decade's worth of artistic, scholarly, and personal inquiry.

From one perspective, Adnyana's story is one of musical lineages. Born into one of Bali's most internationally prominent musical families (along with Dewa Berata and Dewa Alit, among others) Adnyana could hardly escape the familial focus on gamelan. He grew up with the instruments. He was trained formally as a musician and he gained employment when he was not yet out of high school by teaching gamelan, primarily to children's groups. As was the case with Asnawa, Lasmawan, and others in the generation of Balinese musicians before him, gamelan provided his first opportunities to travel abroad—something that he had not envisioned as an option before that time. It was an artistic tour rather than an academic opportunity that first brought him to the United States, but it was an opportunity in academia that allowed him to stay.

His story also highlights the inherently transnational nature of this segment of the Balinese gamelan community. Growing up in a household with Dewa Berata and Emiko Susilo, an ethnically mixed couple who taught and performed transnationally, Adnyana, too, found that the currents that shaped his professional and personal lives originated in both Bali and the United States. Although the community that he and Downing have developed in Wisconsin is more geographically limited than that of Lasmawan, Suadin, or Wenten, for example, it serves the population well, playing on unique local opportunities to provide childhood education—an area outside the historic realm of applied education in ethnomusicology. Although it has been adapted to the circumstances of his institution, with its quarter system and single concert per year, Adnyana views his pedagogical system as largely remaining the same as it was in Bali; it is the same system that produced the core members of Gamelan Çudamani, one of Bali's most elite ensembles. The legacy of his time working with children in Bali lives on in his work with American students, several of whom have followed his lineage back to the source to study with his family in Bali. Moreover, several of his former students now teach Balinese music in area public schools, as well as leading programs for summer music camps for the Lawrence Academy of Music, an extracurricular program affiliated with Lawrence University that offers lessons and ensembles for K-12 students. A member of the community gamelan has begun to build practice instruments and is providing them for a local junior high school as well. As Downing notes, "It is pretty incredible for events to come up, such as the Mile of Music—a large and growing music festival in Appleton every August—[that has] educational programs, and to be able to have Dewa's former students lead workshops instead of us." In only ten years, Appleton, too, has become home to a multigenerational, transnational Balinese arts community.

For Balinese teachers, moving to North America brings certain benefits. Although he belongs to the elite Dewa family—the name is indicative of membership in the *satria* (warrior or royal) caste, the second highest caste in Bali—the poverty of Adnyana's immediate family, his weak leg, and his lack of interest in pursuing extensive formal schooling might have limited his job prospects; even his strong musicianship, noteworthy work as a teacher of children, and guest directing of a variety of groups in South Bali potentially would have been overshadowed by the outsized legacies of his cousins. Instead, in Wisconsin, in the classroom, his accomplishments shine; the gamelan at Lawrence has been historically so popular that it has been called by students "a Lawrence cliché." Yet this way of life has brought challenges; even the popularity of the gamelan is not enough to generate enough economic support for regular trips home to be with family in Bali. Though all the teachers I met viewed their work as a calling and money as an ancillary concern, the sustainability of such ensembles is directly impacted when the structure of the academic system demands work of resident representatives of other cultures but cannot fully support their lives.

One could fit Adnyana's story and the other stories told here into the easy narratives associated with the American Dream: despite certain struggles, a hard-working individual can achieve personal success (including spouse, child, job, homeownership, and a respected niche in the community) regardless of class, caste, religion, race, or ethnicity. To embrace only this narrative would be to oversimplify the situation, however. Gamelan teachers may be selected for their jobs because of their distinctive professional skills, but they thrive because of their connection to and embodiment of family and community. A constellation of belief systems, including Hindu concepts of dharma and individual and institutional philosophies of intercultural partnership, underpin the exceptional commitments that both individuals and groups make to create Balinese gamelan communities.

Moreover, in an apparently successful program or an apparently successful life, there are always trade-offs; this is in line with the Hindu concept of *suka duka*. Meaning "joy-grief," the phrase is often translated from Indonesian as "ups and downs" or "bittersweetness." It more closely implies, however, that success and happiness cannot exist without sadness or failure; they are causally linked and even experienced at the same time, integral aspects of the inherently dual nature of the universe (in Bali, *rwa bhinneda*). Traveling far away to join a new community requires renegotiating one's relationship to home. Becoming recognized as an expert in one area requires revealing oneself as a humble learner in another. Pursuing a life devoted to performing arts education is rarely a path to accruing vast material wealth, but it is a path that can lead to richness beyond compare in friends, family, community, and experiences.

This is a life in teaching gamelan.

Reconsidering World Music Ensembles

Much has happened in the United States and in Indonesia since the establishment of the first academic gamelans at UCLA, yet, despite the two countries' vast differences, they face similar challenges at the beginning of the twenty-first century. Both struggle with securing equitable representation of their culturally diverse populations in education and in civic life. Regionalism and nationalism contribute to a rise in "us versus them" mentalities. Fundamentalist religious practices, including terrorism carried out in the name of religion, threaten to disrupt civic efforts for moderate action and peace. Concepts of family and home that were codified in the past century continue to be redefined as more women work outside the home, young people move to cities, and families have fewer children. Both countries face challenges in preserving fragile environmental ecosystems. In both countries, the performing arts and traditional cultural practices have been cast as inferior in importance to the pursuits of business and technology. Technology has supplanted older, more intimate forms of communication, allowing people to communicate faster, if not more effectively. For better and for worse, the old sociopolitical order forged in the aftermath of World War II and the Cold War is in transition—to what, no one knows.

In the shadow of such inexorable and overwhelming societal change, what of the academic gamelan? Would it be more effective to devote educational efforts to ensembles that are more closely aligned with the demographics of our communities? Is it an inherently neocolonial project to presume that it is appropriate to represent Indonesian culture by select ensembles populated by beginners? Is it selfish to play kotekan while the world burns?

As we have seen in this book, for those who teach academic gamelans, the answers to these questions would be no—with qualifications. Gamelan deserves support in American institutions of higher education because of its own pedagogical and cultural strengths in allowing students and teachers alike to build their musical skills and open their minds. The world music ensemble project could easily become neocolonial if approached casually, indiscriminately, and without concrete connections to the communities in which the ensembles originated and where they continue to thrive as a part of the social fabric. If these connections are forged, however, it is possible to build ethical and balanced academic ensemble ecosystems that provide new artistic and educational opportunities for students, artists, musicians, and teachers in a globalized context.

Though potentially difficult, such a pursuit is worthwhile not because it has an immediate or tangible effect on the greatest societal problems of the day but because of its power to animate and change the lives of individual students, teachers, and musicians. To position such ensembles as merely another course offering is to disregard their potential to foster lasting artistic connections with local communities and those situated halfway around the globe. It risks discarding the sacrifices and the triumphs of teachers and musicians who have built a life in teaching world music ensembles as cultural and artistic ambassadors. Finally, it would fail to celebrate and critique the ways in which American academic interests have transformed systems of higher education, artistic production, and the lives of individuals and communities in North America and worldwide. Understanding how and why different ensemble communities lived in the past can help current teachers and musicians recognize the social forces that shape their own artistic and educational communities and consider how to plan their actions within this broader context.

More than anyone else, Lasmawan has emphasized to me the importance of a different type of historicization, with the oft-deployed admonition to his students and community members to remember their roots. This means telling stories not only about great composers and performers but also about the individual sacrifices and triumphs of great teachers; it means staying firmly grounded in local, regional, national, and transnational communities. Rather than an insistence on maintaining abstract principles for the sake of perceived historical or cultural authenticity, however, such grounding allows for meaningful growth, exploration, and innovation as groups and as individuals. Such innovations and adaptations become imperative in new cross-cultural and cross-musical contexts so that participants can fit the time, place, and situation—and the farther the impact of that innovation can spread to students and audiences outside the traditional world music ensemble setting, the stronger and more sustainable academic ensemble communities become.

Gamelan musicians in America, students and teachers alike, all begin their participation in the ensembles for their own reasons; the benefits that they enjoy or the lessons that they take away are similarly varied. Yet those who continue to play or teach gamelan often remain interested not only because they encounter new artistic and cultural ideas but because these encounters constantly challenge their skills as musicians and their understandings of the world—reasons that also motivate scholars, teachers, and artists in the discipline of ethnomusicology. Moreover, gamelan musicians tend to face these challenges not only as individuals but also in the context of community. It is these interrelated goals and experiences of intercultural negotiation, artistic growth, and community building that gamelan and other world music ensembles uniquely offer.

With these goals in mind, it is important to recognize elements that have made such ensemble communities less sustainable and stable than they might become. Access and representation remain two persistent issues. If gamelans and other academic ensembles are marginalized in their structural positions, trapped under the load of fostering "diversity," accessible only through the collegiate course structure, and taught by contingent faculty or as a small portion of a full-time faculty member's course load, they will reach far fewer students and listeners than they might otherwise. As long as Indonesian teachers remain systematically marginalized—by not having the doctoral degrees necessary or not embodying the narrow definition of departmental "fit" to be employed full-time in American institutions, by not having economically equitable alternatives that still enable them to teach, and by being vastly underrepresented in English-language academic writings about their own musics and in discussions about Indonesian arts in American education—these educational systems will continue to be hobbled by inefficient and questionably ethical practices. Creating more sustainable futures for world music ensembles requires not only the hard work of individual teachers and their partners but also a more systematic approach to building and sustaining long-term partnerships and building programs in accordance to the needs of time, place, and situation.

Desa, Kala, Patra: A View from the South

It was February 2014, the weekend before Valentine's Day, and the sun shone hot and bright over the grass, which was already greening in anticipation of spring. As visiting instructor in ethnomusicology at Emory University for the year, I had been coaching the university gamelan ensemble in simple Central Javanese and beleganjur repertoire in preparation for a concert on the coming Tuesday. Lasmawan had flown in from Colorado to serve as the guest director, and that Sunday morning we were touring downtown Atlanta before our intensive rehearsals were to begin. "Golf weather," Pak Made said in wonderment. He is an avid golfer. "It's so warm. Maybe I should retire down here—what do you think?" There was no trace yet of the "snowpocalypse" that would immobilize the city and shut down the campus a few days later, just in time to cancel our official concert and transform the gamelan's performance with our guest into a clandestine, invitation-only affair held in secret in our basement rehearsal room.

I smiled and told him that it would be fabulous to have him in the area; no matter how one defines the southeastern United States, it is a region with few gamelans and indeed, few Indonesians. Other than the gamelan gong kebyar and gamelan beleganjur ensemble that I had joined while at Florida State University, I knew that the closest Balinese gamelan groups were hundreds of miles away in Virginia to the north and Texas to the west; few non-Balinese groups were any closer. It was nothing like the urban northeast, California, or Lasmawan's Rocky Mountain teaching circuit, where multiple gamelans, though still distant by Balinese standards, could be reached within a few hours' drive. "Well, you brought a beleganjur here," he said. "Perhaps it is your dharma to bring gamelan to the South." I laughed then, but not six months later I was in I Wayan Rindhi's gong shop in Bali negotiating the purchase of a gamelan for my new position as the first ethnomusicologist at Wake Forest University in Winston-Salem, North Carolina. Less than a year later, Gamelan Giri Murti (Gamelan of the Enchanted Forest) was born. To my delight, the Emory Gamelan—a group with a long heritage that was in a precarious time of transition when I worked with it in 2013—continues to thrive owing to a blend of students and longtime community members.

As new gamelans continue to be formed across the country and particularly in areas with historically few ensembles, it is worth considering what types of niches such programs might fill and how teachers and coordinators might rise to meet such challenges. Many Balinese teachers of gamelan have historically plied long weekly or biweekly routes to teach in different locations, and Americans who have gained expertise primarily by extensive study playing in community gamelan groups may also teach gamelan as an adjunct at a local college. These models allow for the sustenance of gamelan programs in institutions that otherwise have insufficient faculty expertise and resources to support a gamelan ensemble on their own, but the patterns of living and teaching that are associated with such models come at a cost to teachers and students, since the teacher's time and energy are divided. Short residencies in which teachers who already live in America drive or fly long distances to teach for a few days or a week are also educationally and artistically important options, and often pay artists as well as half a semester of teaching a regular class, but do not give students the same benefits as long-term work with an expert teacher.

More sustainable models can be found among educational institutions that have a gamelan specialist on the regular faculty. These faculty members, who so far have been almost exclusively American, are important in that they can support curricular and community ensembles on a semesterly basis and advocate for the Indonesian performing arts at their institutions. With fuller access to university resources, such instructors can build musically and culturally informed programs that can change and respond individually to educational and artistic trends in the global gamelan community. They also frequently have scholarly and artistic connections to counterparts in Indonesia through which they can organize collaborations and residencies ranging in length from several weeks to several years and that impact other local programs as well as their own. Such collaborations are advantageous not only to American programs, but also to Indonesian artists who may want to maintain regular lives in Indonesia while pursuing occasional work overseas.

Finally, with the growing interest in gamelan and world music in North American educational circles and growing opportunities for higher education in Indonesia, it is important to recognize that there are small but increasing numbers of Indonesians and Indonesian Americans who can teach gamelan and also have the skills and interest to become regular full-time faculty members. Though there are precedents for this model—for example, Sumarsam, who has taught at Wesleyan since 1972 and has published numerous articles and several books—the majority of Indonesian gamelan teachers (including those who hold American doctorates) have not pursued or have not been able to obtain positions in North America that acknowledge and value their work as gamelan teachers, as well as their professional scholarship, performance, compositions, or service to their institution or their craft. Similarly, if employed in Indonesia, certain aspects of their skills and potential are routinely unsupported or ignored. Working on both sides of the Pacific to support Indonesian artists as full members of transnational scholarly and artistic communities will be an important part of cultivating both stronger individual gamelan programs and stronger transnational dialogue and collaborations.

Though American and Indonesian teacher-artist-scholars generally pursue their myriad artistic and pedagogical interests as best they can regardless of specific professional rewards, relaxing the historical disciplinary boundaries within music in American higher education will only help further the development of strong ensemble teaching and fresh, innovative, and rewarding careers for ensemble directors. Some of these traditional boundaries include valuing an individual's skill in research, performance, or composition but not a combination of the above; viewing ensemble courses and academic courses as being educationally and administratively separate from each other; and artificially separating certain musical practices based on their place of origin and hierarchically valuing of certain types of art over others. Finding ways to accommodate and celebrate the cultivation of "complete musicians" will not only allow individuals to nurture the fullness of their potentials as artists, scholars, and teachers but will allow them to collaborate to create and sustain vibrant, dynamic educational and artistic transnational communities.

Gamelan as Lifelong Education

In July 2019 I visited the home of my first Balinese dance teacher, I Gusti Ayu Candra Dewi, during my first trip to Jakarta. I recognized her home on the quiet suburban street from the curling decorations of the household shrine perched on the second-floor balcony. When I entered the house, Candra embraced me and commented positively on how I'd stayed slim over the years—then proceeded to ply me with half a dozen different types of delicious *kue* (pastries) that she regularly bakes to sell at the university where her husband teaches. We spent several hours that afternoon chatting together about the lives of people we both knew before heading the next day to the Balinese temple Pura Parahyangan Agung Jagatkarta and the royal botanical gardens at Bogor, where we took enough selfies to make up for the time together that we'd missed. Her daughter, who had been in elementary school when she had first moved to the United States, was now home from college and joined us on the expedition.

It seemed in some ways that little time had passed at all since we'd met, but in fact, a decade had passed since I had first seen her dance at the beginning of our gamelan ensemble course in 2009. I was twenty-two years old. I still remember how her costume, in brilliant hues of pink and green and gold, shimmered under the rehearsal room's fluorescent lights. The precision with which she moved her arms, her hands, her head, her eyes—it had pulled me in; I was stunned, speechless. I knew that I had to study with her, that I had to learn more of this dance and this music. I began to spend four hours per week in gamelan rehearsal and four hours per week with her, trying to teach my hands to be quick, my mind to be nimble, my body to be graceful, and my heart to be full of enough courage to fail, fail more, and fail again until I began to get things right.

These studies were completely different from my prior educational experiences. I grew up learning that making music was replicating a set of notes fixed on a page, that practicing was a punishing and tedious task to be endured alone (and avoided if possible), and that the assigned location of one's chair in an ensemble was the ultimate assessment of both current musical skill and determination of future musical potential. In school, I was surrounded by friends for whom college was an expectation; scoring less than 95 percent on a test was a failure. In sum, success in music and in academics was narrowly and tangibly defined, based on individual work, and expected at all times.

Over time, playing in world music ensembles and particularly studying and teaching gamelan has completely changed my perspectives on music, learning, and community. Although technical perfection is highly valued in gamelans, I began to understand my studies as undertaking a collective journey focused on increasing the success of the group rather than an individual attempt to try to reduce failure. Working with musicians from many different backgrounds and a wide variety of skill levels and motivations has taught me to accept, work with, and encourage people based on where they are in their lives, rather than obsess about their own or others' perceptions about where they should be as students, musicians, or people. I came to view my own efforts as a teacher, artist, scholar, colleague, and friend as an offering: something that, though imperfect, must be given and is being valued, even when I cannot see immediate results or comprehend its eventual impact on others or on myself. These extramusical lessons are a gift that, given to me little by little in countless rehearsals, I hope to pass on to my students.

I continue to study gamelan because I love the music and the community, but also because it challenges the whole of my being—body, mind, and spirit—like nothing else ever has. In approaching these challenges, I have found my life to be constantly enriched by the experiences I have shared with friends, colleagues, students, and teachers from around the world, all of whom guide me to become a better artist, teacher, and person. I teach gamelan not because I believe that my students will or should follow my path but because playing for even one semester helps them discover and enjoy their own paths as learners and musicians. The complex questions that members of my gamelan pose to me about Balinese culture, art, and beliefs; their improved dexterity; the increase in their self-confidence; their openness to exploration and experimentation; and their warmth toward others in the ensemble all are small, gradual, and rewarding signals to me that encountering this music is making a real difference in their lives.

In thinking about the lives of my own teachers, who constantly encourage and humble me, it is difficult not to wonder: What brought them so far away from their homes, pursuing a career that is considered so narrow, both in Indonesia and in North America? Was it luck? Was it individual choice? Was it fate? What is the impact of the seemingly inconsequential individual actions taken in an ensemble rehearsal space? What if teachers like Lasmawan had decided to stay in Indonesia? Moreover, what if Hood had never brought gamelan to UCLA? Would there be gamelan in North America? Would the discipline of ethnomusicology have developed in the same way without this model for cross-cultural learning and exchange? For myself, I do not know if I chose the gamelan or if it chose me, only that it has transformed my life in ways that would have been unimaginable when I first picked up a mallet many years ago.

The gamelan community and global music education in North America have come a long way since the mid-twentieth century. There is still much left to be accomplished. With a firm grounding in the wisdom of our teachers and an eye toward the future, the task is one that those who care about this music and these people can accomplish together. The Balinese poem and children's song "Eda Ngaden Awak Bisa" reminds me that the best teachers are still learners and that the next steps in our work as a community will become clear as we walk the educational and artistic paths unfolding before us together. A dedicated generation of teachers planted the seeds of this community; I will stand among the other members of my generation and help new flowers continue to bloom.

"EDA NGADEN AWAK BISA" (TRADITIONAL BALINESE CHILDREN'S SONG)

Eda ngaden awak bisa	Don't think you can do it all; humble yourself.
Depang anake ngadanin	Let others name you (judge you).
Gaginane buka nyampat	Like a broom cleaning a floor (your work/karma will tell you who/what you are).
Anak sai tumbuh luu	There will always be fallen leaves.
Ilang luu obuk katah	Once the fallen leaves are gone, lots of dust remains.
Yadin ririh liu enu paplajahan.	Even though you may be clever, there are still lessons to learn.[3]

Glossary

angklung, gamelan Used primarily for cremations and processions, this gamelan comes in four-tone and (in Northern Bali) five-tone versions

angklung, bamboo A bamboo rattle; an ensemble of such instruments, today found primarily in West Java

ASTI Akademi Seni Tari Indonesia. *See* ISI.

ASKI Akademi Seni Karawitan Indonesia. *See* ISI.

banjar Village ward or its community association

baris A genre of male warrior dances

Barong A dance and associated costume set representing a mythical creature; the most common type resembles a Chinese lion

beleganjur A processional genre of gamelan with gongs, drums, and cymbals, historically used to accompany warriors into battle. In contemporary times, it is used for religious processions and in competitions.

dalang A puppeteer

desa, kala, patra A Balinese Hindu philosophical statement meaning "time, place, situation"

dharma A Hindu concept denoting a person's avocation, calling, or destiny

gamelan A general word for any number of different types of Indonesian percussion-based sets of instruments or orchestras

gambuh A type of gamelan or associated dance-drama dating to the fifteenth century; now rarely performed

gangsa A keyed metallophone of middle register used to play melodic elaboration

gender A keyed metallophone played with a two-mallet technique

gender wayang A small gamelan ensemble in slendro tuning used mainly to accompany shadow puppet performances

gong kebyar Invented at the beginning of the twentieth century, it is currently the most popular genre of gamelan used to perform modern concert repertoire

ISI Institut Seni Indonesia, state-sponsored, university-level conservatories with campuses in several locations across the country. The location in Denpasar was previously known as ASTI Denpasar (1967–1988) and STSI Denpasar (1988–2003). The location in Surakarta was previously known as ASTI Surakarta (1965–1983) and STSI Surakarta (1983–2006).

joged bumbung A flirtatious female dance, or the bamboo gamelan ensemble that accompanies it

karawitan A general word for traditional instrumental (gamelan) music

kebalian "Balinese-ness"

kecak Vocal gamelan; also called gamelan suara

kembali To return; to change or experience a renaissance

kendang The double-headed, cylindrical drum that is placed on the lap and played with two hands; it serves as lead instrument in many styles of gamelan

KOKAR Konservatori Karawitan, the name of the high school–level arts conservatory in Bali from 1960 to 1976, called SMKI from 1976 to 1997 and SMKN 3 Sukawati since 1997. *See also* SMKI.

kotekan A melodic ornamentation created by two interlocking instrumental parts

kreasi baru "New creation"; new compositions or choreography

kroncong A hybrid Indonesian popular music style originating on the coast of Java in the sixteenth century, characterized by the incorporation of Western-style string instruments within gamelan-like musical textures

maguru panggul "Mallet as teacher," a traditional teaching method

musik kontemporer A modern compositional style incorporating traditional Balinese, ethnic Indonesian, and globalized technologies and concepts

ngayah Voluntary devotional service

odalan The anniversary celebration for a temple, occurring once per 210-day calendar year

pedalangan Puppetry

pelegongan/semar pegulingan Related varieties of courtly gamelan dating to the seventeenth century

pelog One of two commonly used musical tuning systems in Bali, consisting of seven notes

pokok The core melody in Balinese gamelan music, generally performed at the pulse level

polos One of the interlocking kotekan parts, generally leading and with more on-beat accents. *See also* sangsih.

pura A temple

rame Crowded, busy; a preferred Balinese aesthetic

reyong A gamelan instrument consisting of small gongs arranged in a frame

sanggar A privately owned club or arts foundation

sangsih One of the interlocking kotekan parts, generally following and with more off-beat accents. *See also* polos.

sekaa, sekaha A club or society

semaradana A seven-tone gamelan originating in the second half of the twentieth century

semar pegulingan/pelegongan Related varieties of courtly gamelan dating to the seventeenth century

slendro One of two commonly used musical tuning systems in Bali, consisting of five tones

SMKI Sekolah Menengah Karawitan Indonesia, the name of the high school–level arts conservatory in Bali from 1976 to 1997, now called Sekolah Menengah Karawitan Negeri 3 Sukawati (since 1997). *See also* KOKAR.

STSI Sekolah Tinggi Seni Indonesia. *See* ISI.

subak A society for governing the regulation of Balinese irrigation systems

ugal The instrument or instrumental role of lead gangsa

wali, bebali, bali-balihan A Balinese conceptual division of performing arts practices designated as sacred, semi-sacred, and secular; first adopted in the 1970s

warung A family-owned snack stand or small restaurant

wayang Puppetry or a puppet

Notes

Chapter 1. Interlocking Sounds, Interlocking Communities

1. It was co-founded with Victoria Levine, professor of music (ethnomusicology) at Colorado College. The name *Made* is pronounced [mɑd′e].

2. In a practical sense, the development of academic and community gamelan ensembles within the United States and Canada is heavily intertwined, yet particularities of educational practice and political history create some points of differentiation between the two nations. In this book I specify the country when an issue is particular to a specific location and use the terms *North America* or *American* when a practice is widespread or when referring to a group that may contain members from both nations. Few gamelans are found in Mexico, the Caribbean, or Central America, so ensembles from those locations are not discussed here.

3. These melodies can be played explicitly or remain unplayed but simply conceptualized (see Perlman 2004).

4. The past few decades have seen the establishment of ensembles in the United States devoted to non-gamelan Indonesian popular musics such as *dangdut* (an Indonesian folk-popular music that incorporates instruments and musical elements from the Hindustani, Arabic, and Malay worlds, as well as Western popular genres, performed by the Pittsburgh-based Dangdut Cowboys) and *kroncong* (an Indonesian string band tradition, performed by Richmond-based Rumput), as well as Fraser's *talempong* ensemble at Oberlin College. It is interesting that other genres of Balinese performing arts such as devotional vocal music (*kidung* and *kakawin*) and dramatic dance (like *arja* and *sendratari*) are rarely studied or performed in North America.

Wayang kulit, one of the most ritually important and complex artistic genres in Bali, which requires specialized linguistic, narrative, musical, and physical knowledge, is rarely mastered by non-Indonesians for those reasons.

5. As Vitale (1990, 12–13) points out, kotekan of this type is found primarily in gamelan gong kebyar music. Other types of interlocking patterns are idiomatic in other styles of Balinese gamelan music, some (but not all) with formal rules similar to those of kotekan found in gong kebyar. The concept of the interdependency of instrumental parts, however, is found throughout Balinese gamelan styles.

Chapter 2. Early Encounters in Bimusicality

1. The organizational concept for this chapter takes inspiration from Lueck (2012, 104–133), which includes a cogent discussion of seven events from 1928 to 1985 that have shaped the growth of Balinese community gamelan—many of which, unsurprisingly, form a subset of the broader, educationally focused narrative presented here.

2. The recordings are preserved in the United States Library of Congress American Folklife Center in Washington, DC.

3. For clarity, in this chapter, I largely use the term *Indonesian* to denote historic or current practices from any grouping of islands that is currently encompassed by the geopolitical Indonesian nation-state; I will use specific terminology when referring to individual practices.

4. The prince and the king of Tabanan and the king of Kesiman (a vassal of Badung) also chose death rather than Dutch rule or exile.

5. This series was re-released in 1951 by Decca and again in 1979 by Smithsonian Folkways, and it is currently available to download from the Smithsonian Folkways website.

6. In Bali the caste system consists of the *brahman* (priestly), *satria* (warrior or royal), *wesya* (merchant), and *sudra* (commoner) castes; members of each caste are considered to perform certain necessary social duties. The first three, historically considered to be upper-caste, are referred to as the *triwangsa* and consist of less than 10 percent of the Balinese Hindu population. Enforcement of Dutch colonial systems such as corvée labor arguably caused substantive inter-caste tension and solidified caste boundaries that had previously been more fluid. See Robinson (1998, 62–63).

Chapter 3. From Bali to America: Teachers and Transitions

1. *Manik* can also mean "jewel"; another translation used by group co-founder Elizabeth Macy is "Jewel of Rice."

2. Konservatori Karawitan (Conservatory for Traditional Music), also known as KOKAR, was the name of the performing arts high school in Denpasar until 1976. It is currently known as Sekolah Menengah Kesenian Indonesia.

3. The institution was founded in 1965. It became Sekolah Tinggi Seni Indonesia Surakarta after it merged with the Akademi Seni Tari Indonesia in 1983. In 2006, with the expansion of its degree offerings, it became Institut Seni Indonesia Surakarta.

Chapter 4. Creating and Conceptualizing a Balinese American Gamelan Community

1. Gamelans outside Indonesia tend to vary substantially in organizational structure from their Indonesian counterparts, and sometimes from each other. In North America, Indonesian musicians tend to officially serve as an ensemble's artistic director while an American president, director, or other form of organizer who works in partnership with the artist handles logistical details.

2. Gamelan Anak Manik Galih is a children's gamelan program founded by Ade Wijaya and Liz Macy in 2019.

3. According to Lasmawan, world music radio host Susan Ohori, who had studied Sundanese gamelan at the Center for World Music in 1974, had donated the gamelan, but it was not being played. The name Eka Mudra, "gesture of prayer," was bestowed on it by Lasmawan.

4. It is variously spelled "Candra" or "Chandra."

Chapter 5. Teaching, Learning, Representing

1. This male-centric narrative reflects historic sociopolitical structures in Bali as well as the fact that gamelan ensembles were traditionally male-only. A female-centric evaluation of ensemble and social structure would be a fascinating subject for further study.

2. For further discussion of instruments and roles in gamelan gong kebyar, see Tenzer (2011) for an introductory-level overview and Tenzer (2000) for a more comprehensive analysis.

3. See Hayes (2011) for a thorough discussion of I Nyoman Suadin's process of transferring gong kebyar repertoire (in a five-tone pelog tuning system with a ten-tone range on gangsa) to the five-tone slendro gamelan angklung.

4. In terms of musical lineages, it is often asked whether there are regional styles of gamelan playing in North America. While Lueck's (2012) informants suggested that there were not, Hiranmayena (personal communication, January 2019) points out that long-standing community groups such as Gamelan Tunas Mekar, Gamelan Sekar Jaya, Gamelan Dharma Swara, and Gamelan Gita Asmara tend to have their own idiomatic styles, ones that are shared to at least some extent with other groups consistently taught by the same instructors. Sudirana (pers. comm., January 31, 2019) emphasized to me the variety of stylistic choices that an experienced teacher can make, ones which may be chosen based on personal preference rather than allegiance to one region. There seems to be a wide consensus that academic groups do not play sufficiently well or consistently to develop a style.

5. These three principles are also found within discourse about Yogyanese and Solonese courtly dance style; Hughes-Freeland translates them in that context as meaning "timing, pleasure, and expression" (2008, 98).

6. My information is drawn primarily from an interview with Asnawa in July 2016. See also Horton 2019.

7. Here I primarily refer to male musicians. Susilo (2003) notes that the patrilocality of Balinese traditional society has caused substantive difficulties for the foundation and maintenance of women's gamelans. Because women move to their husband's family home on marriage, sometimes moving across the island, young female musicians usually lose the opportunity to play with the gamelan in their home banjar. Because of the added obligation to have and rear children, women often find it difficult to play continuously for long periods of time and make artistic commitments as long-lasting as can men. However, as Downing (2019) notes, this situation has changed rapidly in the first two decades of the twenty-first century.

8. The portion of the myth in which Sita must undergo a trial by fire to prove her chastity—and, indeed, is eventually banished from Rama's kingdom as a result of public doubt of her faithfulness during her long captivity—are not generally portrayed in Bali.

9. Though the question above is meant to be rhetorical, one practical solution is to have ensemble members perform in gender-neutral costumes such as t-shirts and choice of pants or kain.

Chapter 6. Americans Learning Gamelan in Bali

1. The Center for World Music, formally founded in 1963, grew from the American Society for Eastern Arts. Following the current terminology used by the center in its publicity materials, I refer to all of the historical programs sponsored by this entity as being under the auspices of the center.

2. Established in 1974 as an initiative of the Association of South East Asian Nations (ASEAN), the programs at first only admitted students from ASEAN member nations. The program expanded in 1976 to include Australia, Canada, Japan, and the United States (among other countries) and again in the 1990s to include all countries with which Indonesia has diplomatic relations. The Darmasiswa program has substantive limitations on who can enroll: Students must be under thirty-five, must be currently enrolled in a degree program or between degrees, and cannot bring any family members with them. These factors significantly limit the population of potential participants.

3. There are foreigners who arrive in Bali and do nothing except study and perform gamelan music; foreign musicians who perform in the Bali Arts Festival often fall much closer to that end of the spectrum. On the other end, visitors who squeeze in a few lessons between massages and cultural tours may arrange those lessons through the same arts institutions that host elite groups.

4. In Balinese banjar, tasks that constitute performing ngayah are traditionally assigned on the basis of gender and age; for example, while women are generally responsible for constructing offerings, the male-only banjar gamelans are responsible for providing music. This does not mean that other members of the banjar cannot perform ngayah in other ways. For example, as Susilo (2003) notes, even those who were

skeptical of women's gamelans in the 1990s found it hard to argue with the women's desire to offer their music in service to the temples. But because musical performance was not the traditional task that women were expected to perform, it was viewed as being supplementary to their primary duties. See also Downing (2019).

5. Though it is used with some frequency in academia and the tourism industry, the term *kebalian* is not widely used by the Balinese. This suggests perhaps that commodification (the reification or packaging of Balinese identity) is primarily of interest to those two communities or that even the concept is an external imposition. I use it here in the sense of capturing a self-consciously projected Balinese identity, which is a central concern for tourist program providers (and for educators).

Chapter 7. *Kembali*: To Return or Change

1. Downing notes that such assumptions can cut the opposite way as well. She told me, "One time, Dewa and I went to a tourist gamelan and dance show in Ubud. I bought a ticket and sat in a seat, and Dewa sat in the back (ditching me, haha) as he didn't feel comfortable sitting in the seats for tourists. One of the show organizers slipped him a little cash as commission for bringing a tourist to the show, even though we ostensibly went together as friends!"

Chapter 8. Bimusicality and Beyond

1. In fact, some aspects of Adnyana's teaching are not common in Bali, such as numbering the keys of the instruments not by scale degree but straight through from lowest pitch to highest. Downing (pers. comm., January 9, 2019) notes that it seems like "a missed opportunity" to engage students with Balinese solfège (for the pelog instruments of their gamelan gong kebyar, *ding-dong-deng-dung-dang*) or at least corresponding pitch numbers (1–2–3–5–6) but that it has enabled the children to learn to play quickly.

Chapter 9. Sustainability and the Academic World Music Ensemble

1. The internal politics of banjar groups is often complicated; even groups with high levels of community interest may disband for months or years because of leadership disputes or have few seats available for new, young musicians who are not from musical families. More broadly, since gamelan groups are still segregated by gender, women have had limited access to learning gamelan. Though not omnipresent, female groups have maintained a strong presence across Bali since the 1990s.

2. In discussions with ISI students in their early twenties in 2012 during the continued economic recession in the United States, I found that they were surprised to learn that American performing arts graduates at the bachelor's and master's levels faced similar concerns about employment—without the option of being able to fall back to working on the family farm.

3. Acessible at http://www.citraaryandari.com/?page_id=143. Translation by the author. The original reads:

> Etnomusikologi di Indonesia belum begitu dikenal, selain di ISI Yogyakarta, etnomusikologi juga menjadi program studi di ISI Padang Panjang, Universitas Sumatera Utara, STSI Bandung (sekarang ISBI Bandung), Institut Kesenian Jakarta, ISI Surakarta, ISI Denpasar, hingga ISBI di Kalimantan. Namun, meski telah didistribusikan dalam beberapa institusi pendidikan perlu disadari bahwa dalam perjalanannya disiplin ini cukup lambat berkembang.
>
> Padahal Indonesia memberi sumbangsih terhadap kelahiran disiplin ilmu ini. [. . .]
>
> Ironis, perkembangan setengah hati etnomusikologi di Indonesia menyebabkan kita terus menerus sekadar dijadikan "objek" oleh peneliti Barat, tetapi belum mampu menjadi "Subjek" yang secara mandiri meneliti dan memahami musik Indonesia sendiri. Alih-alih secara sangkil meneliti beragam musik nusantara, akademisi etnomusikologi kita seolah justru sibuk menjadi perpanjangan tangan program pariwisata pemerintah yang gemar menjual jargon "eksotisme budaya bangsa" demi devisa dan decak kagum negara lain. [. . .]
>
> Etnomusikologi di Indonesia harusnya dapat merefleksikan diri: siapkah membuka diri menyongsong perubahan paradigma etnomusikologi ini agar mampu menjadi Subjek mandiri yang mampu meneliti, menulis, dan mengembangkan musik nusantara secara berdikari? Atau akan terus berdiam diri menjadi bulan-bulanan peneliti Barat.

Chapter 10. Cultivating New Flowers

1. The translation and any errors therein are mine.

2. "Tejur" is a nickname for Dewa Alit Adnyana used by members of the Çudamani group and others close to him. Speakers in Bali often refer to themselves in the third person in conversation to indicate politeness; in this case, it also clarifies among the many men called "Dewa" in the family.

3. My adaptation is derived from various translations.

References

Adams, Henry. 1946. *The Education of Henry Adams*. Boston: Houghton Mifflin.

Adler, Lynn, Jim Mayer, and John Rogers. 1989. *Kembali: To Return*. Berkeley: University of California Extension Center for Media and Independent Learning.

Alit, Dewa Ketut. 2018. Interview with the author, August 13.

Alit Adnyana, Dewa Ketut. 2018. Interview with the author, October 27.

Allen, Pamela, and Carmencita Palermo. 2005. "*Ajeg Bali*: Multiple Meanings, Diverse Agendas." *Indonesia and the Malay World* 33, no. 97:239–255.

Arns, Megan. 2017. Interview with the author, January 15.

Asnawa, I Ketut Gede. 2016. Interview with the author, July 20.

Averill, Gage. 2004. "Where's 'One'? Musical Encounters of the Ensemble Kind." In *Performing Ethnomusicology: Teaching and Representation in World Music Ensembles*, edited by Ted Solís, 93–111. Berkeley: University of California Press.

"Background Information: Indonesia." U.S. Department of State. http://www.state.gov/r/pa/ei/bgn/2748.htm. Accessed November 9, 2017.

Bakan, Michael. 1994. "Lessons from a World: Balinese Applied Music Instruction and the Teaching of Western 'Art' Music." *College Music Symposium* 33–34:1–22.

———. 1999. *Music of Death and New Creation: Experiences in the World of Balinese Gamelan Beleganjur*. Chicago: University of Chicago Press.

———. 2010. "Monkey Business: Performing a Simplified Version of the Balinese Kecak Dance-Drama." In *Multicultural Perspectives in Music Education*, 3rd ed., edited by William M. Anderson and Patricia Shehan Campbell, 90–97. Lanham, MD: Rowman & Littlefield.

———. 2013. "Italian Cinema and the Balinese Sound of Greek Tragedy: Kecak Contortions and Postmodern Schizophonic Mimesis in Pasolini and Fellini." In *Performing*

Arts in Postmodern Bali: Changing Interpretations, Founding Traditions, edited by Kendra Stepputat, 363–387. Grazer Beiträge zur Ethnomusikologie/Graz Studies in Ethnomusicology 24. Graz, Austria: Institute of Ethnomusicology, University of Music and Performing Arts.

"Bali 1928 I: Gamelan Gong Kebyar: Music from Belaluan, Pangkung, Busungbiu: The Oldest New Music of Bali." 2009. Compact disc. World Arbiter Records.

Bandem, I Made. 2013. *Gamelan Bali: Di Atas Panggung Sejarah*. Denpasar, Indonesia: STIKOM Bali.

Bandem, I Made, and Fredrik Eugene DeBoer. 1995. *Balinese Dance in Transition: Kaja and Kelod*. Kuala Lumpur, Malaysia: Oxford University Press.

Barz, Gregory F., and Timothy J. Cooley. 2008. *Shadows in the Field: New Perspectives for Fieldwork in Ethnomusicology*. 2nd ed. New York: Oxford University Press.

Becker, Judith. 1979. "Time and Tune in Java." In *The Imagination of Reality: Essays in Southeast Asian Coherence Systems. Papers Presented at a Conference Held at the University of Michigan, Ann Arbor, in 1974*, edited by Alton L. Becker and Aram A. Yengoyan, 197–210. Norwood, NJ: Ablex.

——. 1983. "One Perspective on Gamelan in America." *Asian Music* 15, no. 1:81–89.

Bennett, Janet M. 2008. "Transformative Training: Designing Programs for Culture Learning." In *Contemporary Leadership and Intercultural Competence: Understanding and Utilizing Cultural Diversity to Build Successful Organizations*, edited by M. A. Moodian, 95–110. Thousand Oaks, CA: SAGE.

Bourdieu, Pierre. 1977. *Outline of a Theory of Practice*. Cambridge: Cambridge University Press.

——. 1984. *Distinction: A Social Critique of the Judgement of Taste*. Cambridge, MA: Harvard University Press.

Brinner, Benjamin. 1995. *Knowing Music, Making Music: Javanese* Gamelan *and the Theory of Musical Competence and Interaction*. Chicago: University of Chicago Press.

——. 2005. *Music in Central Java: Experiencing Music, Expressing Culture.* New York: Oxford University Press.

——. 2016. "The Ecology of Musical Transmission Between Indonesia and the United States." *Ars Orientalis*. http://archive.asia.si.edu/research/performing-indonesia/article-brinner.php. Accessed November 22, 2017.

Brown, Robert E. 1992. "World Music: Past, Present, Future." *College Music Society Newsletter* 32. https://symposium.music.org/index.php/29/item/9510-world-music-past-present-and-future. Accessed January 31, 2020.

Center for World Music and Related Arts. "A Brief History." http://www.centerforworldmusic.org/history.html. Accessed August 28, 2013.

Clendinning, Elizabeth A. 2013. "Pedagogy, Performance, and Community in the Transnational Balinese Traditional Performing Arts Scene." PhD diss., Florida State University.

——. 2016. "Air Mengalir: I Madé Lasmawan, Pedagogy, and Musical Kinship in the Transnational Balinese Gamelan Community." *Ars Orientalis*. https://www.freersackler.si.edu/essays/article-clendinning/. Accessed January 30, 2020.

——. 2017. "Learning in the 'Global Village': Performing Arts Tourism in Bali, Indonesia." Music and Tourism Special Issue of *MUSICultures* 43, no. 2:89–114.

Coast, John. 1953. *Dancers of Bali*. New York: Putnam.

Cohen, Matthew Isaac. 2010. *Performing Otherness: Java and Bali on International Stages, 1905–1952*. New York: Palgrave Macmillan.

Collins, Aleanna. 2012. Interview with the author, June 19.

Comaroff, John L., and Jean Comaroff. 2009. *Ethnicity, Inc*. Chicago: University of Chicago Press.

Conner, Ron. 2011. "History of Ethnomusicology at the University of California, Los Angeles." The UCLA Herb Alpert School of Music, Department of Ethnomusicology. http://www.ethnomusic.ucla.edu/index.php?option=com_content&view=article&id=1652:history-of-ethnomusicology-at-ucla&Itemid=226. Accessed January 26, 2018.

Crane, William F. 1893. "Crane's Visit to Midway Theaters." *Chicago Daily Tribune*, October 15, 1893, 35.

DeVale, Sue Carole. 1977. "A Sundanese Gamelan: A Gestalt Approach to Organology." PhD diss., Northwestern University.

DeVale, Sue Carole, and I Wayan Dibia. 1991. "Sekar Anyar: An Exploration of Meaning in Balinese Gamelan." *World of Music: Quarterly Journal of the International Music Council (UNESCO)* 33:5–51.

Denny, Drew. 2009. "I Nyoman Wenten: I Make a Mask About You!" *LA Record*, November 7, 2009. http://larecord.com/interviews/2009/11/07/i-nyoman-wenten-interview-make-a-mask-about-you. Accessed September 21, 2017.

Deshpande, Vāmana Harī. 1973. *Indian Musical Traditions: An Aesthetic Study of the Gharanas in Hindustani Music*. Bombay: Popular Prakashan.

Dewey, John. 1938. *Experience and Education*. New York: Macmillan.

De Zoete, Beryl, and Walter Spies. 1939. *Dance and Drama in Bali*. New York: Harper and Bros.

Diamond, Beverley. 2014. "Whose Ethnomusicology?" *Newsletter for the Society for Ethnomusicology* 49, no. 2:3–12.

Diamond, Jody. 1985. "I Wayan Sinti: Combining the Old with the New." *Balungan* 1, no. 3:5–10.

——. 1990. "There Is No They There: Global Values in Cross-Cultural Research." *Musicworks* 37:12–23.

——. 1992. "Making Choices: American Gamelan in Composition and Education (From the Java Jive to Eine Kleine Gamelan Music)." In *Essays on Southeast Asian Performing Arts: Local Manifestations and Cross-Cultural Implications*, edited by Kathy Foley, 115–139. Berkeley: Centers for South and Southeast Asian Studies.

Dibia, I Wayan. 1996. *Kecak: The Vocal Chant of Bali*. Denpasar, Indonesia: Hartanto Art Books.

Dibia, I Wayan, and Rucina Ballinger. 2004. *Balinese Dance, Drama and Music: A Guide to the Performing Arts of Bali*. Singapore: Periplus.

Djajadiningrat, Madelon, and Clara Brinkgreve. 2014. "A Musical Friendship: The Correspondence Between Mangkunegoro VII and the Ethnomusicologist Jaap Kunst, 1919 to 1940." In *Recollecting Resonances: Indonesian-Dutch Musical Encounters*, edited by Bart Barendregt and Els Bogaerts, 179–202. Leiden: Brill.

Dor, George Worlasi Kwasi. 2014. *West African Drumming and Dance in North American Universities: An Ethnomusicological Perspective*. Jackson: University of Mississippi Press.

Downing, Sonja Lynn. 2010. "Agency, Leadership, and Gender Negotiation in Balinese Girls' Gamelans." *Ethnomusicology* 54, no. 1:54–80.

——. 2018. Interview with the author, October 27.

——. 2019. *Gamelan Girls: Gender, Children, and Politics in Balinese Music Ensembles*. Urbana: University of Illinois Press.

Dunbar-Hall, Peter. 2002. "The Ambiguous Nature of Multicultural Music Education: Learning Music Through Multicultural Content, or Learning Multiculturalism Through Music?" In *World Musics and Music Education: Facing the Issues*, edited by Bennett Reimer, 57–69. Reston, VA: National Association for Music Education.

——. 2006. "Culture, Tourism and Cultural Tourism: Boundaries and Frontiers in Performances of Balinese Music and Dance." In *Ethnomusicology: A Contemporary Reader*, edited by Jennifer C. Post, 55–66. New York: Routledge.

——. 2016. "Balinese Gamelan: Continual Innovation, Community Engagement, and Links to Spirituality as Drivers for Sustainability." In *Sustainable Futures for Music Cultures: An Ecological Perspective*, edited by Huib Schippers and Catherine Grant, 145–178. Oxford: Oxford University Press.

Dwyer, Mary M., and Courtney K. Peters. 2004. "The Benefits of Study Abroad." *Transitions Abroad* 37, no. 5:56–58.

Eiseman, Fred B., Jr. 1990. *Bali: Sekala and Niskala.* Vol. 1, *Essays on Religion, Ritual and Art.* Hong Kong: Periplus.

Erviani, Ni Komang. 2012a. "Conflict Taints Stature of Once Renowned School." *Jakarta Post*, March 21, 2012. http://www.thejakartapost.com/news/2012/03/21/conflict-taints-stature-once-renowned-school.html. Accessed June 21, 2018.

——. 2012b. "Bali Faces Population Boom, Now Home to 4.2 Million Residents." *Jakarta Post*, December 17, 2012. http://www.thejakartapost.com/news/2012/12/17/bali-faces-population-boom-now-home-42-million-residents.html. Accessed June 21, 2018.

Falk, John H., Roy Ballantyne, Jan Packer, and Pierre Benckendorff. 2012. "Travel and Learning: A Neglected Tourism Research Area." *Annals of Tourism Research* 39, no. 2:908–927.

Field Museum, The. "Java Village at the 1893 World's Columbian Exposition." https://www.fieldmuseum.org/java-village-1893-worlds-columbian-exposition. Accessed November 22, 2017.

Fitts, Michael. 2013. Interview with the author, April 8.

Flower Mountain. "Flower Mountain." 2014. Ensembles and Workshops. http://www.studyabroadbali.com/Ensembles_Workshops.html. Accessed January 11, 2015.

Fraser, Jennifer. 2015. *Gongs and Pop Songs: Sounding Minangkabau in Indonesia*. Athens: Ohio University Press.

———. 2016. "The Sustainability and Evolution of Talempong: Pluralism in Minangkabau Gong Practices." *Ars Orientalis*. http://archive.asia.si.edu/research/performing-indonesia/article-fraser.php. Accessed November 29, 2017.

Gamelan Çudamani. 2015. "Gamelan Çudamani." http://cudamani.org/. Accessed January 30, 2015.

Gamelan Sekar Jaya. n.d. "Profile." http://www.gsj.org/profile. Accessed September 2, 2017.

Gamelan Tunas Mekar. 2013. "About Gamelan Tunas Mekar." http://www.tunasmekar.org/about.html. Accessed August 30, 2017.

Garrett, Charles Hiroshi. 2008. *Struggling to Define a Nation: American Music and the Twentieth Century*. Berkeley: University of California Press.

Geertz, Hildred, and Clifford Geertz. 1975. *Kinship in Bali*. Chicago: University of Chicago Press.

Gilbert, Andrew. 2014. "Music of Bali Has a Home in Berkeley." *SFGATE*, June 3, 2014. http://www.sfgate.com/performance/article/Music-of-Bali-has-a-home-in-Berkeley-5532661.php. Accessed October 3, 2017.

Gilbert, Elizabeth. 2006. *Eat, Pray, Love: One Woman's Search for Everything Across Italy, India, and Indonesia*. New York: Penguin.

Gillitt, Cobina. 2017. "Rachel Cooper." *Asian Theatre Journal* 34, no. 1:169–187.

Gold, Lisa. 2005. *Music in Bali: Experiencing Music, Expressing Culture*. New York: Oxford University Press.

———. 2013. "Time and Place Conflated: *Zaman Dulu* (A Bygone Era) and an Ecological Approach to a Century of Balinese Shadow Play Music." In *Performing Arts in Postmodern Bali: Changing Interpretations, Founding Traditions*, edited by Kendra Stepputat, 13–78. Grazer Beiträge zur Ethnomusikologie/Graz Studies in Ethnomusicology 24. Graz, Austria: Institute of Ethnomusicology, University of Music and Performing Arts.

———. 2016. "Musical Knowledge, Innovation, and Transmission Within the Ecosystem of Balinese Wayang Performance." *Ars Orientalis*. http://archive.asia.si.edu/research/performing-indonesia/article-gold.php. Accessed January 28, 2018.

Goodlander, Jennifer. 2013. "I Made Bandem." *Asian Theatre Journal* 30, no. 2:323–335.

Grimshaw, Jeremy. 2016. Interview with the author, July 16.

Hadley, Peter D. 1993. "New Music for Gamelan by North American Composers." Master's thesis, Wesleyan University.

Harnish, David. 1997. "I Madé Lebah (1905?-1996)." *Ethnomusicology* 41, no. 2:261–64.

———. 2004. "'No, Not "Bali Hai"!' Challenges of Adaptation and Orientalism in Performing and Teaching Balinese Gamelan." In *Performing Ethnomusicology: Teaching and Representation in World Music Ensembles*, edited by Ted Solís, 126–137. Berkeley: University of California Press.

Harnish, David, Ted Solís, and J. Lawrence Witzleben. 2004. "'A Bridge to Java': Four Decades Teaching Gamelan in America." In *Performing Ethnomusicology: Teaching and Representation in World Music Ensembles*, edited by Ted Solís, 53–68. Berkeley: University of California Press.

Hayes, Jordan. 2011. "Balinese Angklung Kebyar: I Nyoman Suadin's Process of Transferring 'Puspanjali.'" Master's thesis, University of Rochester.

Heimarck, Brita Renée. 2003. *Balinese Discourses on Music and Modernization: Village Voices and Urban Views*. New York: Routledge.

Heins, Ernst. 1969. "Review: Music of the Venerable Dark Cloud: The Javanese Gamelan Khjai Mendung by Mantle Hood, Hardja Susila." *Ethnomusicology* 13, no. 2:393–96.

Henry Cowell papers, JPB 00–03 [Text]. New York Public Library, New York, NY.

Hiranmayena, I Putu Tankgas Adi. 2013. Interview with the author, April 8.

———. 2016. "Putting the 'Game' in Gamelan: Improvising Gamelan as Praxis in Public Charter Schools." Paper given at the 4th Symposium of the ICTM Study Group on Performing Arts of Southeast Asia, Penang, Malysia, August 3.

———. 2018. "'Fix Your Face': Performing Attitudes Between Heavy Metal and Baleganjur." Paper given at the Sounding Out the State of Indonesian Music conference, Ithaca, New York, March 31.

Hood, Mantle. 1960. "The Challenge of 'Bi-Musicality.'" *Ethnomusicology* 4, no. 2:55–59.

———. 1971. *The Ethnomusicologist*. New York: McGraw-Hill.

Horton, Christina. 2019. "Cyclical Narratives and the Power of Three: Institutional Histories and Pedagogical Practices of Gamelan Ensembles at the University of Illinois." Master's thesis, University of Illinois at Urbana-Champaign.

Hough, Brett. 1999. "Education for the Performing Arts: Contesting and Mediating Identity in Contemporary Bali." In *Staying Local in the Global Village: Bali in the Twentieth Century*, edited by Raechelle Rubinstein and Linda H. Connor, 231–263. Honolulu: University of Hawaii Press.

House, Ginevra. 2014. "Strange Flowers: Cultivating New Music for Gamelan on British Soil." PhD diss., University of York.

Howard, Keith. 2016. "Reviving Korean Identity Through Intangible Cultural Heritage." In *The Oxford Handbook of Music Revival*, edited by Caroline Bithell and Juniper Hill, 135–159. New York: Oxford University Press.

Howe, Leo. 2005. *The Changing World of Bali: Religion, Society and Tourism*. London: Routledge.

Hughes-Freeland, Felicia. 2008. *Embodied Communities: Dance Traditions and Change in Java*. New York: Berghahn Books.

Khalil, Alexander. 2016. "The Gamelan Project: Teaching, Playing with, and Learning from American Schoolchildren Playing Balinese Gamelan." *Ars Orientalis*. http://archive.asia.si.edu/research/performing-indonesia/article-khalil.php. Accessed January 21, 2018.

Kingsbury, Henry. 1988. *Music, Talent, and Performance: A Conservatory Cultural System*. Philadelphia: Temple University Press.

Koskoff, Ellen. 2016. Interview with the author, November 12.

Kunst, Jaap. 1959. *Ethnomusicology: A Study of Its Nature, Its Problems, Methods and Representative Personalities, to Which Is Added a Bibliography*. 3rd much enlarged ed. of *Musicologica*. The Hague: M. Nijhoff.

———. 1994. *Indonesian Music and Dance: Traditional Music and Its Interaction with the West; A Compilation of Articles (1934–1952)*. Originally published in Dutch. Amsterdam: Royal Tropical Institute.

Kunst, Jaap, and C. J. A. Kunst–van Wely. 1925. *De Toonkunst van Bali II: Aanvullende Beschouwingen Naar Aanleiding van Nieuwe Vondsten en van Von Hornbostels Blaaskwintentheorie*. Weltevreden, The Netherlands: Albrecht.

Lantis, Jeffery S., and Jessica DuPlaga. 2010. *The Global Classroom: An Essential Guide to Study Abroad.* Boulder, CO: Paradigm.

Lasmawan, I Made. 2012a. Interview with the author, June 19.

———. 2012b. Interview with the author, June 22.

———. 2013. Interview with the author, March 3.

Ledbetter, Robert. 2012. Interview with the author, June 9.

Levine, Victoria Lindsay, and Emily Kohut. 2017. "Finding a Balance: Music at Liberal Arts Colleges." In *College Music Curricula for a New Century*, edited by Robin D. Moore, 47–68. Oxford: Oxford University Press.

Lewiston, David. 2003. *Bali: Music from the Morning of the World*. New York: Nonesuch.

Lueck, Ellen. 2012. "'Sekaha Gong Amerika': Affinity and the Balinese Gamelan Community in the United States and Canada." Master's thesis, Wesleyan University.

Lysloff, Rene T. A. 2016. "Worlding Music in Jogjakarta: Tales of the Global Postmodern." *Ethnomusicology* 60, no. 3:484–507.

Macy, Elizabeth McLean. 2010. "Music Tourism in New Orleans and Bali: A Comparative Study of Cultural Tourism Development." PhD diss., University of California, Los Angeles.

———. 2017. "'Can I write it down?' Repetition, Imitation, and Transmission in Situ." In *Proceedings of the 4th Symposium of the ICTM Study Group on Performing Arts of Southeast Asia*, 219–222. Penang: Universiti Sains Malaysia.

———. 2018. Interview with the author, January 26.

McGraw, Andrew C. 2013a. *Radical Traditions: Reimagining Culture in Balinese Contemporary Music*. Oxford: Oxford University Press.

———. 2013b. "The Gamelan and Indonesian Music in America." Oxford University Press. http://blog.oup.com/2013/11/gamelan-indonesian-music-america/. Accessed May 1, 2015.

McLain, Elizabeth. 2014. "Save the UM Gamelan." Petition on Change.org. https://www.change.org/p/university-of-michigan-school-of-music-theatre-dance-save-the-um-gamelan?source_location=minibar. Accessed January 18, 2018.

McLean, Mervin. 2006. *Pioneers of Ethnomusicology.* Coral Springs, FL: Llumina Press.

McPhee, Colin. 1966. *Music in Bali: A Study in Form and Instrumental Organization in Balinese Orchestral Music*. New Haven: Yale University Press.

——. 2000. *A House in Bali*. North Clarendon, VT: Tuttle. First published in 1947.

Mendonça, Maria. 2002. "Javanese Gamelan in Britain: Communitas, Affinity and Other Stories." PhD diss., Wesleyan University.

——. 2011. "Gamelan Performance Outside Indonesia 'Setting Sail': Babar Layar and Notions of 'Bi-musicality.'" *Asian Music* 42, no. 2:56–87.

Merriam, Alan P. 1964. *The Anthropology of Music*. Evanston, IL: Northwestern University Press.

Miller, Christopher J. 2005. "Orchids (and Other Difficult Flowers) Revisited: A Reflection on Composing for Gamelan in North America." *World of Music* 47, no. 3:81–111.

Miller, Kiri. 2003. "Americanism Musically: Nation, Evolution, and Public Education at the Columbian Exposition, 1893." *19th Century Music* 27, no. 2:137–155.

Miller, Leta E., and Fredric Lieberman. 2006. *Lou Harrison*. Urbana: University of Illinois Press.

Moore, Robin D., ed. 2017. *College Music Curricula for a New Century*. Oxford: Oxford University Press.

Morelli, Sarah. 2019. *Tales of a Modern Guru: Pandit Chitresh Das and Indian Classical Dance in Diaspora*. Urbana: University of Illinois Press.

Morrison, Dorothy. 2013. Interview with the author, March 20.

Nettl, Bruno. 1994. "American Midwestern Schools of Music as Venues of Musical Mediation and Confrontation." In *Music-Cultures in Contact: Convergences and Collisions*, edited by Margaret J. Kartomi and Stephen Blum, 169–185. Basel, Switzerland: Gordon and Breach.

——. 1995. *Heartland Excursions: Ethnomusicological Reflections on Schools of Music*. Urbana: University of Illinois Press.

——. 2010. *Nettl's Elephant: On the History of Ethnomusicology*. Urbana: University of Illinois Press.

——. 2015. *The Study of Ethnomusicology: Thirty-Three Discussions*. Urbana: University of Illinois Press.

Northern Illinois University Study Abroad Office. 2014. "Experiencing the Arts in Bali." http://www.niu.edu/studyabroad/programs/NIU-admin/Program%20PDFs/Experiencing%20the%20Arts%20in%20Bali%20Application%20Overview.pdf. Accessed May 1, 2015.

Oja, Carol J. 1990. *Colin McPhee: Composer in Two Worlds*. Washington, DC: Smithsonian Institution Press.

Ornstein, Ruby. 2006. "Wayan Gandera Redux." *Asian Music* 37, no. 2:141–146.

——. 2010. Liner notes to *From Kuno to Kebyar: Balinese Gamelan Angklung*. Smithsonian Folkways Recordings SFW50411.

Pemberton, John. 1994. *On the Subject of "Java."* Ithaca, NY: Cornell University Press.

Perlman, Marc. 2004. *Unplayed Melodies: Javanese Gamelan and the Genesis of Music Theory*. Berkeley: University of California Press.

Pew Research Center. 2019. "Generations and Age." http://www.pewresearch.org/topics/generations-and-age/. Accessed February 22, 2019.

Picard, Michel. 1996. *Bali: Cultural Tourism and Touristic Culture*. Singapore: Archipelago.

———. 1999. "The Discourse of Kebalian: Transcultural Constructions of Balinese Identity." In *Staying Local in the Global Village: Bali in the Twentieth Century*, edited by Raechelle Rubinstein and Linda Conner, 15–50. Honolulu: University of Hawaii Press.

Piekut, Benjamin. 2014. "Actor-Networks in Music History: Clarifications and Critiques." *Twentieth-Century Music* 11, no. 2:191–215.

Ramstedt, Martin. 1993. "Indonesian Cultural Policy in Relation to the Development of the Balinese Performing Arts." In *Balinese Music in Context.* Festschrift für Hans Oesch, edited by Danker Schaareman, 59–84. Winterthur, Switzerland: Amadeus-Verlag.

Ricklefs, Merle C. 2008. *A History of Modern Indonesia Since c. 1200.* London: Palgrave Macmillan.

Robinson, Geoffrey. 1998. *The Dark Side of Paradise: Political Violence in Bali.* Ithaca, NY: Cornell University Press.

Ruckert, George. 2004. *Music in North India: Experiencing Music, Expressing Culture*. New York: Oxford University Press.

Rumbaut, Rubén. 2004. "Ages, Life Stages, and Generational Cohorts: Decomposing the Immigrant First and Second Generations in the United States." *International Migration Review* 38, no. 3:1160–1205.

Sachs, Joel. 2012. *Henry Cowell: A Man Made of Music*. New York: Oxford University Press.

Sarkissian, Margaret, and Theodore Solís. 2019. *Ethnomusicological Lives: Growing Up and Into a Profession.* Urbana: University of Illinois Press.

Schippers, Huib, and Catherine Grant. 2016. *Sustainable Futures for Music Cultures: An Ecological Perspective*. Oxford: Oxford University Press.

Slobin, Mark. 1992. "Micromusics of the West: A Comparative Approach." *Ethnomusicology* 36, no. 1:1–88.

Solís, Theodore. 2004. *Performing Ethnomusicology: Teaching and Representation in World Music Ensembles*. Berkeley: University of California Press.

Sorrell, Neil. 1990. *A Guide to the Gamelan*. Portland, OR: Amadeus Press.

———. 2007. "Authenticity in Gamelan-Inspired Composition." *Indonesia and the Malay World* 35, no. 101:31–48.

Spiller, Henry. 2008. *Focus: Gamelan Music of Indonesia*. 2d ed. New York: Routledge.

———. 2015. *Javaphilia: American Love Affairs with Javanese Music and Dance*. Honolulu: University of Hawaii Press.

Steele, Peter. 2013. "Balinese Hybridities: Balinese Music as Global Phenomena." PhD diss., Wesleyan University.

Strohschein, Heather A. 2018. "Locating Affinity and Making Meaning: Gamelan(ing) in Scotland and Hawaii." PhD diss., University of Hawaii, Manoa.

Suartaya, Kadek. 1996. "Denver Awakens Bali." *Gatra* (July 7). Republished on the Gamelan Tunas Mekar website, http://www.tunasmekar.org/gatrareview.html. Accessed May 30, 2018.

Sudirana, I Wayan. 2019. *Gamelan Gong Luang: Ritual, Time, Place, Music, and Change in a Balinese Sacred Ensemble.* Denpasar: Faculty of Performing Arts, ISI Denpasar.

———. 2018. "Meguru Panggul and Meguru Kuping: The Method of Learning and Teaching Balinese Gamelan." *Lekesan: Interdisciplinary Journal of Asia Pacific Arts* 1, no. 1. http://jurnal.isi-dps.ac.id/index.php/lekesan/article/view/341/227. Accessed January 30, 2020.

Sumarsam. 1995. *Gamelan: Cultural Interaction and Musical Development in Central Java.* Chicago: University of Chicago Press.

———. 2004. "Opportunities and Interaction: The Gamelan from Java to Wesleyan." In *Performing Ethnomusicology: Teaching and Representation in World Music Ensembles*, edited by Ted Solís, 69–92. Berkeley: University of California Press.

———. 2013. *Javanese Gamelan and the West*. Rochester, NY: University of Rochester Press.

———. 2016. "Gamelan, Etnomusikologi, dan Kurikulum Perguruan Tinggi di Amerika Serikat." In *Bunga Rampai Pemikiran Akademisi Indonesia di Amerika Serikat*, edited by Deden Rukmana and Ismunadar, 185–198. Yogyakarta, Indonesia: Andi.

Susilo, Emiko Saraswati. 2003. *Gamelan Wanita: A Study of Women's Gamelan in Bali.* Southeast Asia paper series no. 43. Manoa: Center for Southeast Asian Studies, School for Hawaiian, Asian, and Pacific Studies, University of Hawaii.

Susilo, Hardja. 2010. "Enculturation and Cross-Cultural Experiences in Teaching Indonesian Gamelan." *Balungan* 11:43–54.

Talbot, Brent Cumner. 2012. *Finding a Way: Discourse Analysis of Music Transmission in Eka Sruti Illini and Implications for Music Education.* Saarbrücken, Germany: Lambert Academic Publishing.

Tang, Patricia. 2007. *Masters of the Sabar: Wolof Griot Percussionists of Senegal*. Philadelphia: Temple University Press.

Tenzer, Michael. 2000. *Gamelan Gong Kebyar: The Art of Twentieth-Century Balinese Music*. Chicago: University of Chicago Press.

———. 2005. "Wayan Gandera and the Hidden History of Gamelan Gong Kebyar." *Asian Music* 36, no. 1:109–122.

———. 2011. *Balinese Gamelan Music*. North Clarendon, VT: Tuttle.

Tiffe, Janine. 2007. "The Arrival of Steel Pan in the United States." *Percussive Notes* 45, no. 3:10–16.

Titon, Jeff Todd. 1995. "Bi-Musicality as Metaphor." *Journal of American Folklore* 108, no. 429:287–97.

———. 2015. "Applied Ethnomusicology: A Descriptive and Historical Account." In *The Oxford Handbook of Applied Ethnomusicology*, edited by Svanibor Pettan and Jeff Todd Titon, 4–28. Oxford: Oxford University Press.

Towner, John. 1985. "The Grand Tour." *Annals of Tourism Research* 12, no. 3:297–333.

Trimillos, Ricardo D. 2004. "Subject, Object, and Ethnomusicology Ensemble: The Ethnomusicological 'We' and 'Them.'" In *Performing Ethnomusicology: Teaching and Representation in World Music Ensembles*, edited by Ted Solís, 23–52. Berkeley: University of California Press.

Umeda, Hideharu. 2007. "Cultural Policy on Balinese Performing Arts: The First Decade of LISTIBIYA." *Authenticity and Cultural Identity, Senri Ethnological Reports* 65:43–59.

Ver Berkmoes, Ryan, Lisa Steer-Guérard, and Jocelyn Harewood. 2010. *Indonesia*. Oakland: Lonely Planet Press.

Vickers, Adrian. 2012. *Bali: A Paradise Created*. Singapore: Periplus. First published in 1989.

Vitale, Wayne. 1990. "Kotekan: The Technique of Interlocking Parts in Balinese Music." *Balungan* 4, no. 2:2–15.

Volk, Terese M. 1998. *Music, Education, and Multiculturalism: Foundations and Principles*. New York: Oxford University Press.

Weintraub, Andrew N. 2004. *Power Plays: Wayang Golek Puppet Theater in West Java*. Athens: Ohio University Press.

Wenten, I Nyoman. 1996. "The Creative World of Ki Wasitodipuro: The Life and Work of a Javanese Gamelan Composer." PhD diss., University of California, Los Angeles.

Wharton Conkling, Susan. 2015. "Utopian Thinking, Compliance, and Visions of Wonderful Transformation." In *Envisioning Music Teacher Education*, edited by Susan Wharton Conkling, 181–194. Lanham, MD: Rowman & Littlefield.

Wijaya, I Made Tangkas Ade. 2016. Interview with the author, July 24.

Yamashita, Shinji. 2003. *Bali and Beyond: Explorations in the Anthropology of Tourism*. New York: Berghahn Books.

Yamin, Tyler. 2016. "Defending the Past, Present, and Future of Gamelan Semara Pegulingan Saih Pitu in Kamasan, Bali." *Ars Orientalis*. http://archive.asia.si.edu/research/performing-indonesia/article-yamin.php. Accessed November 22, 2017.

Yampolsky, Philip. 2010. "Kroncong Revisited: New Evidence from Old Sources." *Archipel* 79:7–56.

Zamani, Labib. 2018. "Gamelan Diajukan Sebagai Nominasi Warisan Budaya Takbenda ke UNESCO." *Kompas*, August 10. https://regional.kompas.com/read/2018/08/10/09000041/gamelan-diajukan-sebagai-nominasi-warisan-budaya-takbenda-ke-unesco. Accessed January 29, 2020.

Ziporyn, Evan. 1997. "Golden Rain/Gong Kebyar of Gunung Sari, Bali." *Asian Music* 28, no. 2:149–151.

Index

ELIZABETH A. CLENDINNING is an associate professor of music at Wake Forest University.

The University of Illinois Press
is a founding member of the
Association of University Presses.

University of Illinois Press
1325 South Oak Street
Champaign, IL 61820-6903
www.press.uillinois.edu